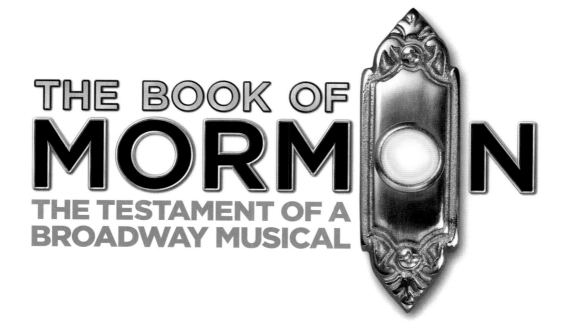

THE BOOK OF MORMON
THE TESTAMENT OF A BROADWAY MUSICAL

Book, Music and Lyrics by
Trey Parker, Robert Lopez & Matt Stone

Text, New Interviews, and Annotations by
Steven Suskin

Principal Photography by
Joan Marcus

Design by
BLT Communications

newmarket press
for itbooks

We all did this because we secretly wanted to have a
big happy Mormon family and now we do. So this is dedicated to our

big happy Mormon family...

to everyone who helped make this show what it is–

you guys are amazing.

Contents

Part 1
THE CREATION *by Steven Suskin* 1

    Latter Day Facts 10

Part 2
THE SHOW 13

Part 3
THE BOOK 93

    Reading the Script *by Mark Harris* 95

    Act 1 101

    Act 2 143

Part 4
THE EXULTATION 181

    Trey Parker and Matt Stone in Conversation with Jon Stewart 183

    Review Extracts 188

    Awards 203

HELLO.
I WOULD LIKE TO SHARE WITH YOU
THE MOST
AMAZING SHOW.

SOUTH PARK CREATORS TREY PARKER AND MATT STONE WITH (L. TO R.) BRIAN TYREE HENRY, ANDREW RANNELLS, MICHAEL POTTS, NIKKI M. JAMES, JOSH GAD, LEWIS CLEALE, RORY O'MALLEY AND REMA WEBB. PHOTO BY RAINER HOSCH.

"IT JUST BECAME RIDICULOUSLY **OBVIOUS** THAT WE SHOULD **TEAM UP** AND DO SOMETHING. SOMETHING ABOUT **MORMONS**."

TREY PARKER

PART 1
THE CREATION

The Creation

by

STEVEN SUSKIN

Our story—and this is a true story, mostly—begins on the starlit evening of September 22, 1827. We are up in western New York State, in the town of Palmyra, near Rochester. A poor treasure-hunter named Joseph Smith digs a set of golden plates out of a rocky hill. (Their existence had been revealed to him four years earlier in a vision, he says, by the Angel Moroni. Moroni returned annually to reaffirm the information until Smith finally found them.) Smith diligently translates the fourteen-hundred-year-old engraved plates, which are written in an unknown language he identifies as "reformed Egyptian." The resulting Book of Mormon—taken from those golden plates—is published in 1830 and becomes the cornerstone of a new, all-American religion.

Smith and his besieged followers flee New York for Ohio, Ohio for Missouri, Missouri for Illinois. But he is not to lead his people to a peaceful existence. On June 27, 1844, the thirty-eight-year-old prophet is being held in Carthage, Illinois, on charges of inciting a riot. A midnight mob storms the jail, and Joseph Smith is violently killed.

Brigham Young, an early follower, assumes Smith's mantle and leads the persecuted people West. Arriving in the valley of the Great Salt Lake in Utah, Young and his Mormons find salvation. They establish their Great Salt Lake City, as it is originally named, on July 24, 1847.

The next great step in the gestation of *The Book of Mormon* occurs 120 years later, when Trey Parker is born on October 19, 1969, in Conifer, Colorado (near Denver). A year and a half later, Matt Stone is born on May 26, 1971, in Houston, Texas. The family moves to North Carolina when Stone is two; three years later they head back West, settling in the Denver suburb of Littleton. The *Book of Mormon* triumvirate is completed on February 23, 1975, when Bobby Lopez is born in Greenwich Village. But it would take some years for the three creators' stars to align.

Young Parker, now in high school, appears in the chorus of the local community theater production of *The Best Little Whorehouse in Texas*—at fourteen—and goes on to star in his high school production of *Flower Drum Song*. (Yes, he plays Sammy Fong, the nightclub owner who eats litchee nuts in bed.) A piano player and musician, he starts writing comedy songs and never, ever stops.

In 1988, nineteen-year-old Parker moves to Boston, to the Berklee College of Music, after which he moves back West and enrolls at the University of Colorado at Boulder. There he meets Matt Stone of Littleton, a math and film major with a passion for heavy metal music. As heathens among cinephiles—everyone emulates Coppola and Scorsese while Parker and Stone revere Monty Python—the pair inevitably bond.

For a short film assignment in 1991, Parker shoots a pseudo "coming attractions" trailer for a nonexistent feature he calls *Alferd Packer: The Musical*. Packer—a Civil War veteran who was convicted of cannibalism—was a local celebrity, and the Littleton cemetery's most notorious resident. So intrigued are Parker and Stone that they decide to make the mythical film-within-the-trailer into a full feature. With a bunch of film school colleagues and some $120,000 they are—to their great surprise—able to raise, they spend two years making the film. They submit it to the 1993 Sundance Film Festival in Utah, where it is rejected. (It is eventually released in 1996 as *Cannibal! The Musical*.)

Trey   *Parker*

Matt   *Stone*

Robert   *Lopez*

Undaunted, they pack up the car and drive to Sundance anyway. Parker and Stone rent a hotel conference room and screen their unappreciated gem, to little avail. But they do make industry contacts. Then it's on to L.A., where they sleep on friends' couches and take meetings.

At one of these meetings a big TV executive watches one of their student films, an animated short called "The Spirit of Christmas". *Make me another one of these*, he says. Parker and Stone go off with a budget of $2,000 and do just that. Said executive sends the new "The Spirit of Christmas" to friends and colleagues as his 1995 video Christmas card. The five-minute piece—about four foul-mouthed boys in a snow-covered small town, who judiciously resolve a knock-down battle between Santa Claus and Jesus—is an immediate favorite, forwarded again and again until it becomes one of the first videos to go viral on the Internet.

This proves to be Parker and Stone's Hollywood calling card. Within months, they determine to take the video's characters (Stan, Kyle, Kenny, and Cartman) and the folksy locale (a fictional Colorado town called South Park) and transform it into a weekly animated series. Which they do. *South Park* goes on the air in August 1997 and seems likely to continue so long as Parker and Stone continue.

Through college and early animation days, Parker retains his love of music; whenever practical (or sometimes impractical), he incorporates songs into his projects. The immediate success of *South Park* results in the call for an animated feature version. *South Park: Bigger, Longer & Uncut* is, indeed, *South Park* bigger and longer; it is also stocked with fourteen sparkling—if censorable—musical comedy–type songs. One of the songs, "Blame Canada," receives an Oscar nomination. They lose, though, to Phil Collins for *Tarzan*.

ack in New York, twenty-four-year-old aspiring songwriter Bobby Lopez sits in the BMI Workshop, training ground for composers like Maury Yeston, Alan Menken, and Stephen Flaherty. Searching for and pondering ideas for a brilliant and bright and successful musical, Lopez goes to see the *South Park* movie when it opens in June 1999. He immediately smites his forehead: here's precisely the sort of combination of humor, song, and outrageousness he wants to replicate, on stage.

But how? He has been toying with the idea of a *Sesame Street*–ish puppet musical for adults. The *South Park* movie suggests how comedy and music can successfully push the boundaries of taste and hilarity. Lopez and collaborator Jeff Marx set to work on *Avenue Q*, which opens at the Golden Theatre on July 31, 2003, and enjoys a six-year run of 2,534 performances. *Avenue Q* wins Tony Awards for Best Musical, Best Score, and Best Book.

ate strikes, musical comedy–wise, one summer's night shortly after *Avenue Q* opens:

TREY PARKER: Matt and I went to see *Avenue Q*, and—we really had no idea what it was. We just heard it was this puppet thing. We were doing *Team America* at the time, and in our own puppet hell. So we were sitting there, and halfway through the first act, I was like, *Wow, this is actually really good, and Matt doesn't want to leave.* That's amazing, you know? So we started really looking through the Playbill, and in the Playbill we saw a special thank-you to us. It was very bizarre, because we thought, *Wait a minute, we don't even know these guys at all.* And so we watched the second act just going, *We love this.* And by the time the second act was over, I was thinking, *This is exactly the thing I've always dreamed about doing.* This is exactly the thing I've always aspired to do on Broadway, since I was a kid trying to write funny songs and acting in Rodgers & Hammerstein musicals in school and dreaming about Broadway. I was so excited by it. And then it happened purely by

coincidence that Bobby showed up that night, and he came down and introduced himself.

And we were like, *That was amazing.* And we asked him, *Why are we in the special thanks?* He told us that when he saw the *South Park* movie, he said, *Wow, this is exactly the kind of thing I want to do.* So it was—it was crazy, 'cause it was, like, Bobby being so influenced by us, and then us being so influenced back by him. It was so exciting. And we went out that night and obviously just hit it off so well that we started talking—and seeing that he shared a love for Mormons. It just became ridiculously obvious that we should team up and do something. Something about Mormons.

"EXACTLY
THE THING I ALWAYS
DREAMED
OF DOING."
TREY PARKER

MATT STONE: It really is one of those stories that doesn't sound true. But it really did happen in a moment, when we met Bobby Lopez the night that Trey and I saw *Avenue Q*. We were in town, meeting about *Team America*, our puppet movie, in 2003. And Scott Rudin—the film's producer— told us, *You know, there's this puppet musical on Broadway, and it's good.* So we went and saw it that night, and both of us—me and Trey—we just loved it. And we saw our names in the Playbill. Because I think Bobby had seen the *South Park* movie and took it as a big inspiration. So we're like, *Well, that's weird.*

And so somebody hooked us up that night and we went out for a drink. Bobby is about five years younger than Trey and me, so he was looking to us as, like, elder statesmen or something—totally unwarranted— like, *Hey, okay, you guys have been in the business a long time. What should I try to do next?* And so our pat, dopey answer to this is, *Well, what do you want to do?* And he said, *I want to do something about Joseph Smith and Mormons.* And we were like, *What? Wait a second. Nobody likes that stuff except for us, you know? Nobody.* Only me and Trey have ever talked about that.

BOBBY LOPEZ: Well, it first started, I guess, when the *South Park* movie came out, because a week after that, the idea came to me for *Avenue Q.* I think it just kind of got me off my ass and, you

So when I said, *Joseph Smith*, they were like, *We've wanted to do that, too.* They had done a musical called *Alferd Packer* for their college project, I guess. And they thought they might follow it up with a Joseph Smith musical, but they just never did. But they had it in their heads to do some kind of Joseph Smith musical. And basically I said, *You know, if you guys want to do that, that's fine. Because I'd really love to see what you do, more than what I would do.* And I meant it.

And they said, *No.*
Let's do it together.

know—I'd always wanted to do a musical where you laugh from beginning to end, where it's not just a—you know, I always think of a musical as—it's a concert. It's a play. And sometimes it's a dance show. And all those things have to be building, and serve a story. But I always wanted to do a show where the laughs built in the same way as the music, the story, the dancing, the costumes, and all that stuff.

And the *South Park* guys got there first. I saw that movie—I remember it was the summer of '99—and I just thought, *Oh my God, this is exactly what I want to be doing.* So I set out to do just that. And cut to four years later. *Avenue Q* was on Broadway—we had barely opened. And I came in one night, and there were Matt and Trey sitting in the audience. Their movie was so inspirational to me. And all of their work—all their comedy and all their songs had pointed the way for me in my work, that—we had actually thanked them in our bio.

And they had seen that. So when I approached them, they were like, *Hey, what's going on?* I took them across the street to the bar. I remember we just hung out and hung out and hung out. And it was sort of an epic evening. The upshot of it was, they said, *What are you working on next?* And I said, *I'd like to do something about Joseph Smith.* I wanted to do a show about religion that sort of got a huge amount of laughs on how ridiculous the stories were, you know, religious stories and miracles. But I also hoped the story could contain a lot of emotion—if not a love story, then a religious one. After all, what is a church service but live stories and music in front of an audience? The best Broadway musicals achieve that same thrilling uplift.

They talk and talk, at the now-vanished Barrymore's on West 45th Street, about life, about Joseph Smith and about musical comedy. By closing time, Parker and Stone propose that they work on this Mormon musical together. Their feature film *Team America: World Police* is just then in the throes of production, to be followed by the seventh season of *South Park.* Which means that other than intermittent *let's talk about it sometime* e-mails, nothing concrete happens. In November 2003 comes the infamous "All About Mormons" episode of *South Park*, incorporating flashbacks from the life of Joseph Smith. Lopez watches it and loves it, but figures that as far as a Broadway Mormon musical is concerned, *that was that.*

But that wasn't that.

There soon comes a call from the coast: *You want to get started on our show?* The trio meets intermittently when *South Park* allows, with Lopez flying to Hollywood for discussions. Or meeting Parker and Stone for a memorable field trip to Salt Lake City. Speaking with the cheerfully smiling locals, the idea of a musical about Joseph Smith transforms into a musical about cheerfully smiling Mormons going off on their two-year evangelizing missions. (That's part of the deal; at nineteen, young Mormon men and women fan off across the globe to find converts.) Lopez sees it as *The Music Man*, Parker and Stone as *A Bug's Life*: strangers come to town with a lie to sell, only to inadvertently save the town because the lie is true in a metaphorical way.

> **"I WANTED TO DO A SHOW ABOUT RELIGION THAT SORT OF GOT A HUGE AMOUNT OF LAUGHS ON HOW RIDICULOUS THE STORIES WERE..."**
> **— BOBBY LOPEZ**

But the months and years breeze by. As *South Park* goes on hiatus in the summer of 2006, the boys call Lopez for a work session. Lopez is heading to London to prepare the West End production of *Avenue Q*, so Parker and Stone join him there. Over the course of three weeks in a rented studio apartment, they come up with six songs, including "Hello"—which is, fittingly, the first—"Two by Two," "Hasa Diga Eebowai," and "Sal Tlay Ka Siti."

Work continues as the *South Park* schedule permits. 2007 leads into 2008, with the writers still unsure whether the piece is headed for stage, animation, or feature film. When Parker and Stone ask their in-house animators to start thinking about storyboards, Lopez counters by suggesting that they assemble some stage actors to do a reading of what they have so far. And thus it is that *The Book of Mormon* first hits the stage in March 2008 at the Vineyard Theatre off New York's Union Square, the birthplace of *Avenue Q*.

This is a so-called "twenty-nine-hour reading," under which Actors' Equity allows a total of twenty-nine hours of work. No sets, no props, no choreography, and no requirement for the actors to memorize the script. Just forty-odd minutes' worth of material interspersed with the seven completed songs.

A group of actors is casually assembled, without auditions; casting director Carrie Gardner gives Lopez names of suitable/available people, whom he researches as best he can. In an indication that this venture is perhaps blessed by the Angel Moroni on high, the initial reading includes Josh Gad as Elder Cunningham and Rory O'Malley as a then-unspecified missionary. Both—close friends since their days as college roommates at Carnegie Mellon—would three years hence receive Tony Award nominations for their roles. Astoundingly, this hastily assembled initial cast includes nine of the twenty-seven actors who eventually appear in the opening night cast on Broadway. Also on hand, at the piano, is Stephen Oremus from *Avenue Q*. He will shepherd the *Mormon* score from the first Vineyard reading onward, ultimately

Nikki M. James

Josh Gad

Rory O'Malley

serving as musical director, vocal arranger, and co-orchestrator.

Parker and Stone— unsure of what to expect—fly in with longtime producing partner Anne Garefino and huddle with Lopez for the reading. Having for so many years performed their own material over at *South Park*, it is a revelation for Parker and Stone to see other people acting what they'd written. *Why don't we just do this as a movie, because we know what to do* had been their attitude; when they see Josh Gad and the others performing the songs on a real stage, with a small but real New York audience, they fall in love with the idea of doing it as a musical comedy. For *The Book of Mormon*, it is full speed ahead—except for that yearly commitment of fourteen *South Park* episodes to Comedy Central.

The authors reconvene in December 2008 for a second reading at the Vineyard. A major element is added with the addition to the cast of Nikki M. James as Nabulungi. Lopez had worked with her a decade earlier, when he was a production assistant at Playwrights Horizons and James was just sixteen; he initially developed the role with her in mind. The authors use the readings as an opportunity to try out new ideas, working right there with the actors in the room, and hone in on what works best.

In July 2009, Parker and Stone meet Lopez in Palmyra at the annual Hill Cumorah Pageant; Cumorah is the very hill where Joseph Smith dug up those legendary golden plates. The pageant is a really big show, with a cast of more than seven hundred Mormons, a ten-level stage, and an estimated audience of 35,000 over seven performances. The field trip serves as inspiration for pageant-like prologues to the first and second acts of their own Mormon musical. They then head from Upstate New York to Lower Manhattan, for a third and final three-week stint at the Vineyard. Once again, it is a mere reading without staging, the actors reading their lines from music stands. But the show is now a full two acts, with fifteen of the actors who will ultimately continue on to Broadway.

Parker, Lopez, and Stone—six full years since that first post–*Avenue Q* drink—are now ready for the next step: an actual, full-scale workshop of the show. Unlike a reading, this will be a staged-and-memorized performance of the show, with a small orchestra even; no scenery, but a full complement of rehearsal props and costumes.

The Book of Mormon family regroups in January 2010 for this six-week workshop at New 42nd Street Studios. The fourth of the five ultimate leads joins the cast: Michael Potts, a Yale graduate more accustomed to the plays of Shakespeare and Tony Kushner than musical comedy. He undertakes the role of Mafala Hatimbi, father of Nabulungi and the guy who has to convince the audience to accept the controversial "Hasa Diga Eebowai" song.

The New 42nd workshop ends with the show in the best shape yet, inspiring the producers to forgo out-of-town tryouts and instead go directly to Broadway. But first, one final and expanded workshop is planned. The goals of the authors and producers are clear: finish developing the plot, write yet more songs, bring in investors, and line up a theater. They also make a canny decision, which proves instrumental to the show's success. Parker, whose activities have thus far been concentrated on the writing, takes on directorial chores as well. Casey Nicholaw—of *Spamalot* and *The Drowsy Chaperone*—signs on as co-director and choreographer.

The main problem still to be solved is the casting of Elder Price. There have always been two young Elders at the show's center, with the plot following them to Africa. The awkwardly, ungainly Elder Cunningham seems to have a mind of his own; this is in part due to Josh Gad, who took the role at the very first reading (without an audition). But Elder Price, the straight-as-an-arrow all-American lad, is an enigmatic mystery. Several actors were cast in the role during the early stages, but it isn't until the final workshop when a six-foot-two actor with a wide smile from Omaha, Andrew Rannells, walks in to audition that, according to Stone, Parker literally starts kicking the table in excitement.

Andrew Rannells

"ANDREW RANNELLS WALKED IN TO AUDITION AND —ACCORDING TO STONE— PARKER LITERALLY STARTED KICKING THE TABLE IN EXCITEMENT."

The final workshop begins August 2, 2010, at the Clark Studio Theater in the Rose Building at Lincoln Center. The full cast is now in place. Nicholaw quickly stages the musical numbers. The authors, meanwhile, formulate new ideas, write new material, and study their new Elder Price. In the first Vineyard reading—when only the first act existed—Price was a "doubting Thomas"; in the second reading, Price became a doubting Thomas who by the end of the second act is a true believer. Realizing that the character was simply not working, the authors next tried a new concept: Price as a straight-A student and a martinet. All the prior Prices were accomplished actors; it was the role itself that was flawed. Rannells—with his all-American looks, strong voice, and dark comedic sense—helps the authors sculpt Elder Price into an immensely likable hero (albeit one with a difficult streak). This proves to be the perfect solution to the puzzle, with Price & Cunningham becoming an instant classic comedy team along the lines of Abbott & Costello or Oscar & Felix. The workshop culminates with four run-throughs for invited audiences over Labor Day weekend. The producers quickly book the 1,066-seat Eugene O'Neill Theatre. Not too big, not too small, just right. Tickets go on sale in November, with the first preview scheduled for February 24, 2011.

The company reconvenes for the last and final rehearsal period on January 10, 2011. Parker, Lopez, Stone, and Nicholaw have continued revising and honing the show. Changes will go on through the rehearsal period and even in previews; for them, *good enough* is never good enough. Their hand-picked and loyal cast—most of whom have been through years and years of *Mormon* development—eagerly embrace each addition and each deletion, recognizing how every step improves the piece.

At the same time, the already-selected designers get to work. Scott Pask, with Tony Awards for *The Pillowman* and *The Coast of Utopia*, designs scenery that combines the Utopian paradise of Salt Lake City and its mountains, towers, and billboards with the realistic horrors of modern-day, war-torn and resource-depleted Uganda—in musical comedy style, of course. Ann Roth, the costume designer, has been working on stage and screen since 1958. Her credits range from the original *Odd Couple* on Broadway to that even odder screen couple in *Midnight Cowboy*, from musicals like *The Best Little Whorehouse in Texas* to films like *The English Patient*. Roth creates a massive wardrobe mixing simple black-and-white missionary uniforms with all the colors and textures of the African rainbow.

As the staging and the keys of the musical numbers are finalized, Oremus and co-orchestrator Larry Hochman (of *Spamalot*) translate the rehearsal room parts into full orchestrations. Lighting designer Brian MacDevitt (of *The Pillowman* and *Joe Turner's Come and Gone*) waits until the scenery is installed in the O'Neill to start his artful painting-with-light. Sound designer Brian Ronan (of *Spring Awakening* and *Next to Normal*) comes last, waiting until the cast is onstage and the orchestra in the pit to start working his magic.

As previews approach, the initial apprehensions about public reaction to the sacrilegious and scatological material return. *South Park* has ignited its share of controversy over the years, and Broadway had seen vociferous pickets earlier in the season at a far less outspoken musical. How far is too far?

And thus it is that on February 24, 2011, Trey Parker, Robert Lopez, and Matt Stone's new musical *The Book of Mormon* finally faces its first paid audience. A brand-new, wholly original, twenty-first-century Broadway musical stemming from the words on Joseph Smith's golden plates, pulled one hundred eighty-four years earlier from a sacred hill in ancient, sacred Upstate New York. ♦

LATTER DAY FACTS

SEPTEMBER 21, 1823
SMITH VISITED BY ANGEL MORONI, WHO TELLS HIM ABOUT THE GOLDEN PLATES
PALMYRA, NEW YORK

JUNE 27, 1844
SMITH KILLED BY MOB
CARTHAGE, ILLINOIS

OCTOBER 19, 1969
TREY PARKER BORN
CONIFER, COLORADO

OCTOBER 1993
PARKER AND STONE'S STUDENT FILM 'ALFERD PACKER: THE MUSICAL' (LATER KNOWN AS 'CANNIBAL! THE MUSICAL') OPENS
BOULDER, COLORADO

DECEMBER 23, 1805
JOSEPH SMITH BORN
SHARON, VERMONT

SEPTEMBER 22, 1827
SMITH DIGS UP THE GOLDEN PLATES
HILL CUMORAH, PALMYRA

JULY 24, 1847
BRIGHAM YOUNG, HAVING BROUGHT SMITH'S FOLLOWERS WEST ESTABLISHES SALT LAKE CITY

MAY 26, 1971
MATT STONE BORN
HOUSTON, TEXAS

FEBRUARY 23, 1975
BOBBY LOPEZ BORN
NEW YORK, NEW YORK

1990
TREY PARKER MEETS MATT STONE
BOULDER, COLORADO

1994
PARKER AND STONE GO TO HOLLYWOOD

AUGUST 13, 1997
FIRST EPISODE OF
'SOUTH PARK' AIRS

JULY 31, 2003
'AVENUE Q' OPENS
ON BROADWAY
JOHN GOLDEN THEATRE

OCTOBER 14, 2004
PARKER AND STONE'S
'TEAM AMERICA:
WORLD POLICE' OPENS

FEBRUARY 18, 2008
FIRST READING OF 'THE
BOOK OF MORMON' BEGINS
VINEYARD THEATRE, NEW YORK

JULY 23, 2009
THIRD READING OF 'THE
BOOK OF MORMON' BEGINS
VINEYARD THEATRE

AUGUST 2, 2010
SECOND WORKSHOP OF 'THE
BOOK OF MORMON' BEGINS
CLARK STUDIO THEATER,
LINCOLN CENTER, NEW YORK

MARCH 24, 2011
OPENING NIGHT ON BROADWAY
EUGENE O'NEILL THEATER

DECEMBER 1995
PARKER AND STONE'S
FIVE MINUTE VIDEO
'THE SPIRIT OF CHRISTMAS'
GOES VIRAL

JUNE 30, 1999
'SOUTH PARK: BIGGER,
LONGER AND UNCUT' OPENS

AUGUST 2003
PARKER AND
STONE MEET LOPEZ
NEW YORK

JUNE 2006
PARKER, LOPEZ, AND STONE
WRITE THEIR FIRST SONGS
FOR 'THE BOOK OF MORMON'
LONDON, ENGLAND

DECEMBER 8, 2008
SECOND READING OF 'THE
BOOK OF MORMON' BEGINS
VINEYARD THEATRE

JANUARY 18, 2010
FIRST WORKSHOP OF 'THE
BOOK OF MORMON' BEGINS
NEW 42ND STUDIOS, NEW YORK

FEBRUARY 24, 2011
FIRST PREVIEW
EUGENE O'NEILL THEATRE, NEW YORK

JUNE 12, 2011
'THE BOOK OF MORMON' WINS 9 TONY
AWARDS® INCLUDING BEST MUSICAL

"THIS IS SOMETHING THAT IS **THOUGHT-PROVOKING** AND REALLY HAS THE ABILITY TO **CHANGE YOUR LIFE.** AND THAT'S A PRETTY **COOL THING.**"

JOSH GAD

PART 2
THE SHOW

ACT 1

THE BOOK OF MORMON

PROLOGUE: THE HILL CUMORAH

MISSIONARY TRAINING CENTER, SALT LAKE CITY

"HELLO!"
Elder Price, Elder Cunningham & Mormon Boys

"TWO BY TWO"
Elder Price, Elder Cunningham & Mormon Boys

SALT LAKE CITY AIRPORT

"YOU AND ME (BUT MOSTLY ME)"
Elder Price & Elder Cunningham

A SMALL VILLAGE IN NORTHERN UGANDA

"HASA DIGA EEBOWAI"
Mafala, Elder Price, Elder Cunningham & Ugandans

MORMON MISSIONARIES' LIVING QUARTERS

"TURN IT OFF"
Elder McKinley & Missionaries

"I AM HERE FOR YOU"
Elder Cunningham & Elder Price

THE VILLAGE

"ALL-AMERICAN PROPHET"
Elder Price, Elder Cunningham, Joseph Smith, Moroni & Company

NABULUNGI'S HOUSE

"SAL TLAY KA SITI"
Nabulungi

MORMON MISSIONARIES' LIVING QUARTERS

THE VILLAGE

"MAN UP"
Elder Cunningham, Nabulungi, Elder Price & Company

ACT 2

THE BOOK OF MORMON

ENTR'ACTE
Orchestra

PROLOGUE: THE HILL CUMORAH

THE VILLAGE

"MAKING THINGS UP AGAIN"
Elder Cunningham & Company

THE DREAM

"SPOOKY MORMON HELL DREAM"
Elder Price & Company

THE VILLAGE / THE GENERAL'S CAMP

"I BELIEVE"
Elder Price

THE VILLAGE

"BAPTIZE ME"
Elder Cunningham & Nabulungi

DIRTY RIVER NEAR THE VILLAGE

"I AM AFRICA"
Elder McKinley, Missionaries & Ugandans

A KAFE IN KITGULI

OUTSIDE THE MORMON MISSIONARIES' LIVING QUARTERS

"JOSEPH SMITH AMERICAN MOSES"
Nabulungi & Ugandans

THE VILLAGE

"TOMORROW IS A LATTER DAY"
*Elder Price, Elder Cunningham,
Nabulungi & Company*

"HELLO"
(reprise)
Company

"FINALE"
Company

PROLOGUE

"I AM JESUS. TAKE CARE OF YOUR PLATES, MORMON, FOR SOON YOUR ENTIRE CIVILIZATION WILL BE GONE AND NO ONE WILL REMEMBER YOU."

MATT STONE: THE NAME OF THE SHOW WAS GOING TO BE *THE MUSICAL OF THE CHURCH OF JESUS CHRIST OF LATTER-DAY SAINTS.* AND THEN THE BIGGEST THING ON THE POSTER WAS GOING TO BE A BIG "OF."

LAMINITES

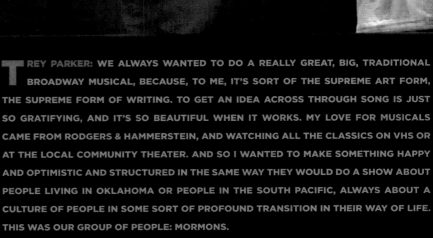

TREY PARKER: WE ALWAYS WANTED TO DO A REALLY GREAT, BIG, TRADITIONAL BROADWAY MUSICAL, BECAUSE, TO ME, IT'S SORT OF THE SUPREME ART FORM, THE SUPREME FORM OF WRITING. TO GET AN IDEA ACROSS THROUGH SONG IS JUST SO GRATIFYING, AND IT'S SO BEAUTIFUL WHEN IT WORKS. MY LOVE FOR MUSICALS CAME FROM RODGERS & HAMMERSTEIN, AND WATCHING ALL THE CLASSICS ON VHS OR AT THE LOCAL COMMUNITY THEATER. AND SO I WANTED TO MAKE SOMETHING HAPPY AND OPTIMISTIC AND STRUCTURED IN THE SAME WAY THEY WOULD DO A SHOW ABOUT PEOPLE LIVING IN OKLAHOMA OR PEOPLE IN THE SOUTH PACIFIC, ALWAYS ABOUT A CULTURE OF PEOPLE IN SOME SORT OF PROFOUND TRANSITION IN THEIR WAY OF LIFE. THIS WAS OUR GROUP OF PEOPLE: MORMONS.

BOBBY LOPEZ: EARLY ON IN OUR WRITING PROCESS WE TOOK A FIELD TRIP TO SALT LAKE CITY. MATT AND TREY TOOK ME ON ALL THE LITTLE TOURS THAT THE MISSIONARIES TAKE YOU ON, AND THEY SHOWED ME TEMPLE SQUARE. THERE'S ONE ROOM WHERE JESUS IS KIND OF STANDING THERE, AND THERE'S A STAR FIELD BEHIND HIM. THAT'S A LITTLE WEIRD, TO HAVE JESUS WITH A STAR FIELD—YOU JUST DON'T USUALLY SEE THAT. IT'S SO SCIENCE FICTIONY. BUT NOT ONLY THAT, THERE WERE THESE HUGE, BIG OL' PLANETS LIKE TATOOINE AND HOTH AND DAGOBAH. THE LIGHTS DIM, AND THE MISSIONARY PRESSES THIS VERY LAME AND OBVIOUS BUTTON, AND JESUS STARTS TALKING. HE SAYS, "I AM JESUS." THAT'S WHERE THAT CAME FROM.

MATT STONE: WE WERE INTERESTED IN MISSIONARIES BECAUSE THAT'S HOW MOST NON-MORMONS MEET THEIR FIRST MORMON. IT ACTUALLY MADE SENSE TO HAVE THEM TURN TO OUR AUDIENCE AND START SINGING ABOUT THEIR FAITH. IT'S ALMOST EXACTLY WHAT THEY DO. I REMEMBER THAT THE CHURCH OF LATTER-DAY SAINTS DID SOME TV COMMERCIALS BACK IN THE '70S AND '80S. THEY WERE THESE LITTLE SOFT-FOCUS COMMERCIALS ABOUT BEING NICE TO PEOPLE OR PICKING UP THE TRASH. WHEN AN OLD LADY FALLS DOWN, HELP HER UP. SOMEONE DROPPED SOMETHING, PICK IT UP. THEY WERE THESE LITTLE PSAs THAT JUST TOLD YOU TO BE A GOOD PERSON. AND AT THE END OF EACH COMMERCIAL, IT WOULD SAY, BROUGHT TO YOU BY 'THE CHURCH OF LATTER-DAY SAINTS.' IT'S SIMULTANEOUSLY TOTALLY GOOFY AND CHEESY AND ALSO KIND OF WEIRDLY NOBLE THAT THEY DID THESE COMMERCIALS THAT WERE JUST LIKE, HEY, YOU OUT THERE, BE NICE TO PEOPLE. THERE'S JUST SOMETHING ABOUT MORMONS.

WHEN TREY AND BOBBY AND I STARTED TALKING ABOUT MORMONS, THAT AESTHETIC, AND THAT CHOICE THE CHURCH MAKES, TO MAKE THAT THEIR PUBLIC IMAGE—IT SEEMED TO JUST FIT WITH THEM ALWAYS BEING ABOUT TO BURST INTO SONG IN A MUSICAL.

TREY PARKER: THE OTHER PART OF THE WRITING PROCESS THAT WAS NEW FOR US WAS WORKING WITH BOBBY LOPEZ, AND THAT, I HAVE TO SAY, WAS SUCH AN EASY FIT. HE'S TOTALLY BRILLIANT—CREATIVELY, HE'S A FORCE TO BE RECKONED WITH. AND HE'S WICKEDLY FUNNY. I JUST CAN'T SAY ENOUGH GOOD THINGS ABOUT HIM. BOBBY BROUGHT SUCH TREMENDOUS PERSONAL AND PROFESSIONAL EXPERIENCE TO THE WRITING—HE WAS A CHORISTER, HE HAD MOUNTED A BROADWAY MUSICAL— AND HE UNDERSTOOD THE MECHANICS OF A MUSICAL, AND HOW IT'S MEANT TO TRANSPORT YOU IN THE SAME WAY THAT RELIGION CAN. IT HELPED THAT HE HAD BASICALLY THE SAME ATTITUDE GOING IN THAT MATT AND I DID ABOUT WHAT WE WANTED TO SAY ABOUT RELIGION. HE GOT IT.

HAVE YOU HEARD?

"Have you heard of the All-American Prophet, the blond-haired, blue-eyed voice of God? He didn't come from the Middle East, like those other holy men; God's favorite prophet was All-American. I'm gonna take you back to biblical times, 1823. An American man named Joe, living on a farm in the holy land of Rochester, New York."

ORIGINS

"I'M GONNA TAKE YOU BACK TO BIBLICAL TIMES, 1823."

HELLO

"HELLO. MY NAME IS ELDER PRICE, AND I WOULD LIKE TO SHARE WITH YOU THE MOST AMAZING BOOK."

ANN ROTH: WHEN YOU GET IN A FITTING ROOM, WHAT YOU WANT TO DO IS PRESERVE THE CHARACTER INSIDE THE UNIFORM. YOU WANT TO LET THE ACTOR CREATE THE CHARACTER INSIDE A UNIFORM. ALL OF THE BOYS PLAYING THESE MORMONS ARE TOTALLY DIFFERENT. YOU CAN ALMOST TELL WHO THEIR MOTHERS AND FATHERS WERE, WHICH IS WONDERFUL. THESE BOYS WHO ARE NOT FORMED REALLY, THEY ARE CHILDREN IN A WAY, THEY'RE STILL UNDER 21. EACH ONE IS SO DIFFERENT, BUT EVERY SHIRT PROBABLY CAME FROM THE SAME CATALOG OR PENNEY'S, OR AT DILLARD'S OR WHEREVER YOU BUY WHITE SHORT-SLEEVED SHIRTS IN UTAH. THAT PARTICULAR LENGTH OF SHORT SLEEVE, I MEAN THAT SLEEVE LENGTH, IT'S NOT THE CUTE ONE UP HERE, IT'S NOT THE CHIC ONE, IT'S THAT ONE. AND THOSE BOYS ALL CREATE SPECIFIC, DETAILED, IDIOSYNCRATIC CHARACTERS WHO EACH HAVE A STORY TO TELL.

"THE MOST FUN PART ABOUT BEING IN THIS SHOW IS WATCHING MY FELLOW ACTORS. I COME DOWN EVERY SINGLE NIGHT FROM MY DRESSING ROOM, WHICH IS ON THE FIFTH FLOOR, SO IT'S A TREK DOWN TO THE DECK. I WATCH THE OPENING NUMBER, 'HELLO,' FROM THE WINGS EVERY NIGHT. I DO IT BECAUSE I THINK IT'S A REALLY BEAUTIFUL NUMBER. AND I LOVE WATCHING THE BOYS START OUR SHOW."

— NIKKI M. JAMES

"MY HOPE AND MY GOAL NIGHTLY IS TO MAKE THE AUDIENCE BELIEVE THAT *WE* BELIEVE THIS, THAT WE JUST WANT TO GO OUT AND SPREAD THE WORD OF GOD—WE WANT TO CONVERT PEOPLE TO MORMONISM BECAUSE, OF COURSE, IT'S THE GREATEST RELIGION. WE AS ACTORS HAVE THAT IN COMMON WITH OUR CHARACTERS—THE URGENCY OF COMMUNICATING OUR INVESTMENT, OUR BELIEF IN THE STORY, OUR PASSIONATE EARNESTNESS. SO I HOPE THAT THAT'S WHAT WE'RE ACCOMPLISHING."

— ANDREW RANNELLS

"MATT AND TREY LOVE MUSICAL THEATER. TREY IS LIKE A LITTLE KID ABOUT IT, YOU KNOW. HE'S SEEN ALL THE SHOWS, HE KNOWS ALL THE HISTORY. THEY ARE DEVOTED TO THE ART FORM, AND WE KNEW THAT WE COULD TRUST THE ART FORM IN THEIR HANDS BECAUSE THEY WANTED TO BE RESPECTFUL OF IT AND GET IT RIGHT."

— RORY O'MALLEY

ELDER PRICE

THE CHURCH OF
JESUS CHRIST
OF LATTER-DAY SAINTS

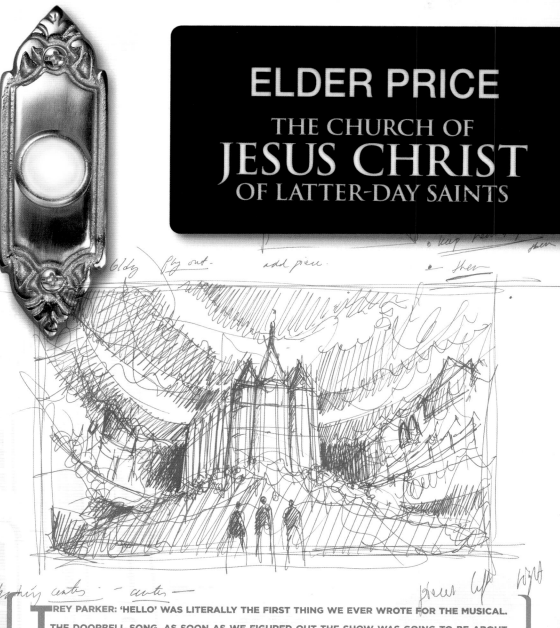

TREY PARKER: 'HELLO' WAS LITERALLY THE FIRST THING WE EVER WROTE FOR THE MUSICAL. THE DOORBELL SONG. AS SOON AS WE FIGURED OUT THE SHOW WAS GOING TO BE ABOUT MISSIONARIES, WE REALIZED THAT IT WOULD BE A GREAT INTRODUCTION TO JUST RING A MASSIVE AMOUNT OF DOORBELLS AND SOMEHOW WORK THEM INTO A MUSICAL NUMBER. IT'S THE MORMON ETHOS, AND IT SEEMED VERY OPENING NUMBER TO US—TOTALLY DISNEY IN SENSIBILITY AND TOTALLY MORMON IN ATTACK—THIS SYMPHONY OF DOORBELLS AND WHITE BOYS WITH GOOD HAIRCUTS AND WHITE SHIRTS AND BLACK TIES SAYING 'HELLO' AND OFFERING YOU A FREE BOOK.

BOBBY LOPEZ: I LOVE DOING ORIGINAL MUSICALS. ONE OF THE BEST THINGS ABOUT BUILDING SOMETHING ORIGINAL IS THAT THERE'S NO PRESSURE TO FOLLOW SOMEONE ELSE'S IDEA OF WHAT IT SHOULD BE—IT'S YOURS. YOU OWN THE PROCESS. YOU CAN EXPERIMENT, YOU CAN FAIL, YOU CAN BE AS FEARLESS AS YOU WANT, AND THE ONLY THING YOU'RE SERVING IS THE PROJECT ITSELF. IT'S SO FREEING. THERE'S NOTHING AS LIBERATING AS STARTING FROM NOTHING.

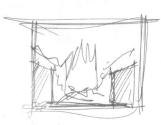

HAVE YOU HEARD?
"And God said, 'Joe, people really need to know that the Bible isn't two parts. There's a part three to the Bible, Joe! And I, God, have anointed you to dig up this part three, which is buried by a tree on the hill in your backyard.'"

TWO BY TWO

"WE'RE MARCHING DOOR TO DOOR
'CAUSE GOD LOVES MORMONS AND HE WANTS SOME MORE."

TREY PARKER: IT'S A TRADEMARK OF OURS, MAKE IT LOOK REALLY CRAPPY TO BEGIN WITH, LOWER EVERYONE'S EXPECTATIONS IN THE FIRST FEW MINUTES, PEOPLE THINK, *OH GOD, WHAT HAVE I GOTTEN MYSELF INTO?*

2 X 2

CASEY NICHOLAW: 'TWO BY TWO' IS THE FIRST NUMBER I CHOREOGRAPHED. IT CAME SO EASILY TO ME, JUST THE CHEESINESS OF THAT THEME-PARK CHOREOGRAPHY. IT CAME *TOO* EASILY TO ME, ACTUALLY—I KNOW IT MUCH TOO WELL! THE VOCABULARY WORKED SO PERFECTLY FOR THOSE MORMON BOYS THAT AS WE STARTED GOING FURTHER, WE ENDED UP PUTTING MORE OF IT IN THE SHOW BECAUSE IT JUST FIT, AND IT FELT SO RIGHT. BY THE TIME EVERYONE COMES TOGETHER AT THE END, THEY'RE ALL DOING THIS PASTICHE OF CHEESY 'UP WITH PEOPLE' THEME PARK CHOREOGRAPHY, INCLUDING THE AFRICANS. IT ENDED UP BEING A SMART, STYLISH PHYSICAL VOCABULARY FOR THE SHOW. IT'S GOOFY AND JOYOUS AND TOTALLY INFECTIOUS, AND IT WAS GREAT TO USE IT TO MAKE A VERY SOPHISTICATED POINT.

JOSH GAD: CASEY'S VISION HAS BEEN NOTHING SHORT OF GENIUS. HIS CHOREOGRAPHY HAS BEEN SO RIGHT IN PHYSICALIZING WHAT THE MORMON FAITH IS. HE GETS THAT BUBBLY, OPTIMISTIC, YOU KNOW, UTOPIAN DANCE. WHATEVER THAT EXPRESSION IS, HE KNOWS HOW TO DO IT.

TREY PARKER: WE DID A ROUGH VERSION OF THE SONG, AND I REMEMBER WE WENT BACK TO THE STUDIO AND WE WERE LIKE, LET'S MAKE IT SORT OF WHITER AND CHEESIER. AND THEN THE FIRST TIME I SANG IT, I SANG OO-WAH, SHOUT OUT WOW—'CAUSE SHOUT OUT WOW WAS A THING WE SANG IN A CHOIR SONG IN COLLEGE. AND EVEN THEN, WE WERE ACTUALLY THINKING, ARE WE REALLY GOING TO SING, SHOUT OUT WOW? AND THE CHOIR DIRECTOR GOES, YEAH—SHOUT OUT WOW. SO I SANG, SHOUT OUT WOW TO MATT AND BOBBY, AND THEN THE WHOLE REST OF THE SONG SEEMED TO FALL IN PLACE.

MATT STONE: IN 2006, TREY, BOBBY, AND I TOOK A FIELD TRIP TO SALT LAKE CITY. WE JUST WENT OUT TO LUNCH AND DINNER AT RESTAURANTS DOWNTOWN AND ASKED THE EMPLOYEES IF THEY KNEW ANYBODY WHO HAD BEEN ON A MISSION. HONESTLY, ALMOST ALL OF THEM HAD BEEN. SOME TOLD US OF GREAT AND UPLIFTING TIMES. ONE TOLD US OF GOING TO CAMBODIA AND SEEING SOME HORRIFIC SHIT. IT WAS, FOR THEM, A HUGE CAULDRON OF DISCOVERY, DOUBT, SEXUALITY, AND FEAR. IT'S LIKE AN AMPED-UP VERSION OF COLLEGE, AND IT WAS VERY TOUCHING TO HEAR ABOUT. YOU CAN ALSO CHAT ONLINE WITH A MISSIONARY. BOBBY DID THAT ONE TIME WITH A KID IN KAMPALA, UGANDA. IT'S PRETTY EASY TO FIND THEM. THEY ACTUALLY LIKE TO BE FOUND.

BOBBY LOPEZ: IT WAS SUPPOSED TO BE THIS WHOLE SONG ABOUT AN ARMY OF THESE SOLDIERS, AND THEY GO OUT ACROSS THE WORLD TO CONVERT PEOPLE. AND THEY'RE AN ARMY WITHOUT SWORDS AND GUNS. THEY'RE AN ARMY OF GUYS WITH BOOKS, BASICALLY.

YOU AND ME (BUT MOSTLY ME)

"THERE'S NO LIMIT TO WHAT WE CAN DO. ME AND YOU. BUT MOSTLY MEEEE!"

I HAD AN OPPORTUNITY TO MEET WITH SOME MISSIONARIES THIS SUMMER AND TALK TO THEM. THERE'S NO JOKE THERE. THERE'S NO IRONY. THEY ARE SINCERE. REALLY, REALLY SINCERE. KEVIN PRICE IS THE POSTER-BOY MORMON, TOP OF HIS MISSIONARY TRAINING CLASS. HE HAS THIS GIANT, PASSIONATE, EARNEST BELIEF IN WHAT HE'S TRAINING TO DO, AND EVERYTHING IN HIS LIFE HAS LED TO HIS MISSION. IT'S ALL HE'S DREAMED ABOUT SINCE HE WAS A KID AND IT'S ALL HE KNOWS HOW TO DREAM ABOUT.

— ANDREW RANNELLS

BOBBY LOPEZ: 'YOU AND ME' BECAME A HUGE SONG FOR ELDER PRICE. HE IS THIS KIND OF EGO MONSTER, BUT YOU LOVE HIM ANYWAY BECAUSE HE JUST MEANS IT SO MUCH. EVERYBODY IN THE SHOW MEANS IT AND THAT'S WHY IT'S FUNNY. WE THOUGHT IT WOULD BE GREAT TO GIVE PRICE THIS MALE VERSION OF A GIANT FEMALE EGO. SORT OF LIKE KATHIE LEE.

BRIAN MACDEVITT: THERE ARE TWO DISTINCT WORLDS THAT I TRY TO CREATE AND TRY TO ACHIEVE. THE FIRST IS THE WORLD OF THE MORMONS IN THE BEGINNING OF THE SHOW. I WANTED IT TO BE SHADOWLESS, AND THE IDEA, THE IMAGE THAT I SHARED WITH MY COLLABORATORS, WAS AS IF EVERYTHING WAS LIT WITH FLUORESCENTS, WITH A PINK GEL ON TOP OF IT, KIND OF PERFECT, CLEAN, SQUEAKY, ARTIFICIAL, BUT NOT SATURATED. LIKE A DISNEY WORLD IDEA BUT IN A FIRST-CLASS, VERY SOPHISTICATED BROADWAY PRODUCTION.

SCOTT PASK: THE FIRST IDEA I HAD WAS THE FRAME. THERE ARE SO MANY LAYERS OF STORYTELLING THAT HAPPEN IN THIS SHOW, SOMETIMES SIMULTANEOUSLY, AND THE SALT LAKE FRAME BECAME THE DEVICE THAT COULD HELP ORIENT US: IT GIVES US TONE AND TEMPERATURE, AND WHEREVER WE FIND OURSELVES, WE'RE SEEING THE WORLD THROUGH THE EYES OF THE MORMON BOYS.

ON SMILES AND CHEESINESS

BOBBY LOPEZ: There's this idea that Mormons are these very naïve, hopeful, smiling, trusting people from the Midwest. The very first moments in the show, in "Hello" and "Two by Two," it's just almost like *Up with People*. We took *Up with People* and used the energy and optimism, and the relentlessly hopeful and sunny feeling. It's a great way to start because we're going to go to the opposite in a few scenes. I think that Mormons and Disney and kitsch kind of live in the same bubble, and if you go to Salt Lake City you'll notice that the dominant architectural feature is basically this Cinderella castle right in the middle. It just looks like long ago and far away, you know, here we are. We went on a tour and our guide said, *It's not really made of actual marble, but isn't it amazing? Isn't it a miracle?* And that's the same thing they say at Disney World. *Have a magical day, dreams come true, look at that castle.*

TREY PARKER: There's a lot of Rodgers and Hammerstein references in the show, because that's what it feels like to me. When you're doing this sort of happy-go-lucky, optimistic Mormon, it just plays right into it because the Rodgers and Hammerstein/Disney/Mormon thing all really go together. If you were doing a musical about steelworkers, and they were being cheesy and doing whatever, you'd be like, *Come on.* But seeing Mormons do it, you're like, *Yeah, that's how they are.*

CASEY NICHOLAW: Cheesiness—that relentless optimism—is a good thing. It actually ended up becoming sort of our Mormon vocabulary. The cheesiness was in "Two By Two," which was the first number I choreographed. Trey loved that so much, he said, *You know what, we've got to do more of that in the show.* We ended up putting much more of that kind of choreography in the show, and that's our version of cheesiness. We would watch the Osmonds' TV show and say, *That's a good step, we have to do something like that.*

BOBBY LOPEZ: My idea had been to musicalize the actual Book of Mormon, even though I hadn't actually read the Book of

Mormon. I knew Jesus came to America in it. I knew the Hebrews sail to America. And so I got a Book of Mormon and started to read it. It was always going to be a show about how ridiculous religious stories are, and yet how important they are at the same time, the duality of that. The idea of historical, factual truth doesn't enter into it. Did Jesus live? Who cares? It doesn't matter. That's not the point. He's a work of fiction at this point that gives a lot of people direction—and a lot of people the wrong direction—but he helps a lot of people get through life in the same way that Luke Skywalker does for me and Matt and Trey.

MATT STONE: Mormons are merely our specimen for this examination of religion. Being a minority religion that most people outside of Utah don't know a lot about, it's a perfect way to get a theater crowd laughing at something. Then somewhere they start realizing that maybe they're not just laughing at this, but at some of their own beliefs.

TREY PARKER: I always had an interest in the Book of Mormon, and the stories in it and everything, since I was a kid. But now it's so weird to go in a search engine and type in "The Book of Mormon," and the first thing that comes up is us. Like, our show comes up on a Google search above the actual book! ♦

HASA DIGA EEBOWAI

"HAVING A SAYING MAKES IT ALL SEEM BETTER."

"I WAS SO NERVOUS. I REMEMBER THE VERY FIRST TIME WE DID IT, I TOOK A DEEP BREATH RIGHT BEFORE THE AFRICANS WENT INTO THAT SONG, AND I REMEMBER THINKING TO MYSELF, WELL, HERE GOES NOTHING. AND I'VE NEVER LOOKED BACK, NOT SINCE THAT MOMENT. "

—JOSH GAD

BOBBY LOPEZ: I THOUGHT, WHAT IF WE DID THIS THING WHERE THEY THINK THEY'RE GETTING DISNEY AFRICA, BUT INSTEAD THEY GET FUCK YOU, GOD? THERE'S THIS BOOK CALLED *GUNS, GERMS, AND STEEL* BY JARED DIAMOND. IT'S ALL ABOUT HOW PEOPLE OF DIFFERENT RACES ARE EXACTLY AS INTELLIGENT AS EACH OTHER. THERE'S ABSOLUTELY NO GENETIC DIFFERENCE BETWEEN AFRICANS, ASIANS, CAUCASIANS, LATINOS. NO MATTER WHAT RACE YOU ARE, THERE ARE GENIUSES IN EVERY POPULATION. WHAT IT ALL BOILS DOWN TO IS THE RESOURCES AND THE CLIMATE THAT YOUR SOCIETY EVOLVED IN. AND BECAUSE EUROPE HAD THE HORSE AND THE PIG AND THE COW AND ARABLE LAND, THAT'S WHY THEY GREW UP TO COLONIZE THE WORLD. AND THAT'S WHY, IF AFRICANS HAD HAD PIGS AND SHEEP AND COWS AND GRAIN AND STUFF LIKE THAT, THEN THEY WOULD HAVE GONE OUT AND COLONIZED US. SO ANYWAY, FUCK GOD, BASICALLY. THAT'S THE MORAL. IT IS ABSOLUTELY 100 PERCENT EARNED. IT'S TRUE. IT'S A VALID REACTION FOR ANYONE THAT GETS THE SHORT END OF THE STICK COSMICALLY.

"THERE'S THAT LINE IN 'HASA DIGA' WHERE THE ENSEMBLE FACES FRONT, AND THEY SAY, 'IF YOU DON'T LIKE WHAT WE SAY, TRY LIVING HERE A COUPLE DAYS. WATCH ALL YOUR FRIENDS AND FAMILY DIE.' I THINK THAT'S THE MOST IMPORTANT LINE IN THE SHOW BECAUSE IT'S JUST TRUE. IT SAYS, I'M SORRY, BUT THIS IS WHAT I'M DEALING WITH. SO I'M SORRY IF YOU'RE A LITTLE UNCOMFORTABLE IN YOUR VELVET SEAT THERE, BUT THIS IS MY LIFE. "

—RORY O'MALLEY

"THE MUSIC THAT STARTS THE SHOW IS VERY SQUARE, VERY 'UP WITH PEOPLE', AND THEN WE GET TO AFRICA AND ALL OF A SUDDEN WE HAVE THESE MULTI-TIERED, VERY COMPLEX AFRICAN POLYRHYTHMS WITHIN THE SONGS. AND THEN WE COMBINE THE TWO—AND WE'RE FLYING. 'HASA DIGA' WAS ONE OF THE FIRST SONGS WE DID IN A WORKSHOP ABOUT FOUR OR FIVE YEARS AGO, AND ALL OF A SUDDEN HERE WE ARE BIRTHING THIS HUGE, WONDERFUL BABY. IT WAS SO EXCITING TO BUILD THIS BEAUTIFUL MACHINE WITH TREY AND BOBBY AND MATT. "

—STEPHEN OREMUS

"I REMEMBER THE FIRST TIME WE DID 'HASA DIGA' THAT WE HAD TO HOLD FOR TWO MINUTES. AFTER I HAD JUST SAID *FUCK YOU*, YOU KNOW, AND SO THE POOR GUYS ARE BEHIND ME AND JUST VAMPING, 'CAUSE THEY HAVE TO KEEP DANCING. AND IT WAS JUST, LIKE, TWO MINUTES. I THOUGHT, IS THIS GONNA END? BECAUSE I CAN'T HEAR THE MUSIC, SO I CAN'T GO ON UNTIL YOU GUYS CALM DOWN. I NEVER EXPERIENCED ANYTHING LIKE THAT. "

—MICHAEL POTTS

"THERE'S A TEDDY BEAR STUCK IN THE RUBBLE, AND YOU CAN SEE SOMEONE'S FLIP-FLOP THAT'S SORT OF BEEN LEFT AND ABANDONED OVER THE YEARS. ALL OF THESE TINY, TINY DETAILS ARE TELLING A STORY ABOUT THE STRUGGLE OF LIFE IN THIS PLACE. "

—NIKKI M. JAMES

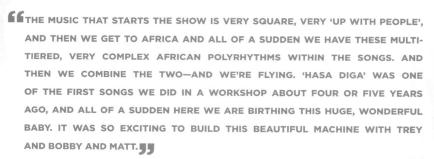

SCOTT PASK: THE DONKEY IS MY FAVORITE PIECE, I HAVE TO SAY. AND THE BEST THING ABOUT BEING IN THE AUDIENCE EVERY NIGHT WATCHING IT IS WHEN THAT IRIS OPENS AND YOU SEE UGANDA FOR THE FIRST TIME, PEOPLE ARE JUST SITTING THERE, JUST KIND OF IN SHOCK THAT THAT'S WHAT'S HAPPENING.

TREY PARKER: THERE'S THIS LINE THAT YOU CAN CROSS ALL YOU WANT AS LONG AS YOU HAVE A REASON FOR DOING IT. IF IT HAS A POINT AND IT HAS A STORY AND IT HAS GENUINE, REAL CHARACTER AND EMOTION, THEN YOU CAN PRETTY MUCH DO WHATEVER YOU WANT. THERE IS NO LINE IF YOU'RE BEING TRUTHFUL. WE LEARNED THAT LESSON A LONG TIME AGO.

{ TREADING DANGEROUSLY }

JOSH GAD: I was deeply concerned because it's a crazy world out there. Up until this point, nobody had ever done anything remotely like this. Yes, *Avenue Q* pushed boundaries, but they had puppets. Yes, *The Producers* was hysterical and rebellious, but was it really pushing boundaries? Trey and Matt decided that we were going to take on something that is probably the most sensitive source of friction in the world: religion. That's a scary thing, but if you do it right it could be a game changer. I think that we all knew that if anybody could do it right, it was going to be Trey and Matt. Along the way a lot of us had questions about whether we were going too far, if the material was pushing too hard. They insisted it wasn't, and anything that took it one beat too far was immediately excised from the script. They know when they're crossing the line just a little too much.

MICHAEL POTTS: Before previews we had security briefings. Because we just thought, people are going to pelt us with rocks and tomatoes when we come out of the stage door for saying this in this very Christian country. The surprise has been that people haven't. They hold their breath, even those who disagree, and they go, *Okay, okay, what's next?* They hang on. The few who can't, leave, but it's very few—very, very few. I haven't heard anyone say that they met someone who didn't want to see the show. Now, everyone wants to come and see it.

CASEY NICHOLAW: We were sort of warned at the beginning, Oh, my gosh, people are going to react so strongly to this, there might be picketing and this and that, and I got scared by it because I don't want to offend. But you know, that's *South Park*, and that's Matt and Trey. I think the difference is if you just looked at the lyrics, you might be offended. If you looked at the pageant on its own, you might be offended. But the package of the show is so traditional—it's so Rodgers and Hammerstein—that I think people feel comforted by that.

MICHAEL JAMES SCOTT: The very first time I heard "Hasa Diga" I was taken aback. It helped that I had done *Jerry Springer, The Opera* right before, because that was singing the word "cunt" on the

HASA DIGA EEBOWAI!

Carnegie Hall stage. I thought, I will never do anything else like *this*. And then came *The Book of Mormon*. We definitely did pray before the first presentation at the Vineyard—all the Ugandans who sang the song, we got in a little circle and were like, *Lord, this is not how we feel, we are just acting.*

LAWRENCE STALLINGS: My first day they took us to work on "Hasa Diga," and I had no idea what the show was about, none. We're singing this made-up language, and I'm learning it. When the language gets translated, I kind of just stopped, like *what did they just say?* I'm not able to make my mouth say these words. The musical director stopped rehearsal because he saw me just dumbfounded. *Oh, no one told you about this song?* And I was like, no. I am a man of faith, and I've always been, and I remember walking out on our break and thinking, *I don't know if I can do this.*

Then I had a great conversation with Bobby Lopez about why he wrote the song, and what it really means. Once I got the entire story it was a little bit easier to digest.

JOSH GAD: Nobody ever questioned that the show was extraordinarily brilliant and smart, really an amazing musical. What they questioned was whether or not America was ready for it. And I questioned it, a lot of us bought into that hype that God, people are going to storm out of the theater. We prepared ourselves mentally for that. When the first performance passed and nobody walked out we were, like, Okay, that was a very nice crowd. Then the second show passed and nobody walked out. Well, right now we've just got the real *South Park* fans. But then week after week passed and nobody walked out. And it became clear to us that they were wrong. America was ready for *The Book of Mormon.* Not only was America ready for it, but America was ready to pay thousands and thousands of dollars to be a part of it because it was so special. It goes back to Matt, Trey, and Bobby. They've always said, *We have faith in what people can handle, even if they don't necessarily know that they can handle it.* ♦

"UP UNTIL THIS POINT NOBODY HAD EVER DONE ANYTHING REMOTELY LIKE THIS."

JOSH GAD

TURN IT OFF
"LIKE A LIGHT SWITCH"

TREY PARKER: IN A FEW EARLY DRAFTS OF THE SCRIPT, THE TWO BOYS ACTUALLY ENDED UP GETTING LOST. THEY WERE LOST IN SOME VILLAGE IN AFRICA, AND WE DIDN'T HAVE ANYONE THERE WHO WAS MORMON. BUT WE REALIZED IN THE WORKSHOPS, LIKE, OH, YOU'VE GOT ALL THESE GREAT, WHITE, CHEESY MORMON BOYS DOING THIS FANTASTIC STUFF IN THE OPENING, AND THEN THEY JUST COMPLETELY DISAPPEAR. THAT'S WHEN WE DECIDED, NO, LET'S HAVE A MISSION THERE, AND HAVE OTHER MISSIONARIES THERE, TOO.

BOBBY LOPEZ: THE CLOSETED MORMON, MCKINLEY, CAME OUT OF OUR TRIP TO SALT LAKE CITY. WE WENT TO RESTAURANTS AND WE'D GRAB ONE OF THE WAITSTAFF AND SAY, DO YOU KNOW ANY MORMONS WHO WENT ON MISSIONS? THEY'D SAY, YEAH, ME AND ALL OF OUR WAITSTAFF. AND THEN WE'D SAY, DO YOU KNOW ANYONE WHO WAS GAY, ANY GAY MORMONS? AND THEY WERE LIKE, YEAH, ME AND ALL OF OUR WAITSTAFF.

MATT STONE: THE REASON 'TURN IT OFF' IS SO FUNNY IS BECAUSE IT'S SO TRAGIC AT THE SAME TIME. BESIDES ALL THE META LEVELS THE NUMBER IS WORKING ON, IT'S ALSO THIS STRAIGHT-AHEAD SONG ABOUT A GROUP OF VERY INNOCENT, VERY INEXPERIENCED BOYS, AT THE CENTER OF WHICH IS A GAY MORMON KID WHO WANTS TO SING AND DANCE BUT IS STUCK LIVING A LIFE OF TOTAL SUPPRESSED FEELING. HE'S FIGURED OUT A WAY TO LIVE WITH THE TRAGEDY THAT THE RELIGION HAS PUT UPON HIM BY MAKING THE BEST OF IT—IN A WAY, BY SINGING THIS SONG—BUT REALLY THE SONG IS AN ABSOLUTELY TRAGIC SONG. IT'S THE SADDEST SONG IN THE MUSICAL. AND IN SOME WAYS, PROBABLY BECAUSE IT'S SO SAD, IT'S ALSO ONE OF THE FUNNIEST. IN THE END HE GETS THIS HUGE TRIUMPHANT FINISH IN 'LATTER DAY.' HE GETS TO 'SCREAM AND SHOUT AND LET ALL HIS FEELINGS OUT.' WE WROTE THAT ARC FOR RORY OVER THE COURSE OF THE WORKSHOPS BECAUSE HE JUST INHABITED THE EXACT SPACE WHERE RELIGION AND THE BROADWAY MUSICAL MEET.

HAVE YOU HEARD?
"Joseph Smith went up on that hill and dug where he was told. Deep in the ground Joseph found shining plates of gold. Then appeared an angel. His name was Moroni."

"CASEY HAS SUCH A BIG HEART, IT'S ALWAYS MY FAVORITE THING TO WATCH HIM WATCH THE SHOW AND GO, OH, HE'S ABOUT TO CRY, HE'S GOING TO CRY. BECAUSE HE STILL HAS THAT CHILDLIKE WONDER. YOU CAN ALWAYS SEE THAT MOMENT WHEN HE FIRST SAT DOWN IN A THEATER AND GOT THE BUG. HE STILL HAS THAT WITHIN HIM."

—MICHAEL POTTS

> "THE FIRST READING DIDN'T HAVE MY CHARACTER. ELDER MCKINLEY WASN'T A PART OF IT. SO THEY SAID, WELL, WE'VE GOT THIS SONG 'TURN IT OFF' THAT WE WROTE. SO, RORY, WHY DON'T YOU TAKE THIS VERSE ABOUT STEVE BLADE—THIS CLOSETED MORMON VERSE? AND FROM THERE THIS CHARACTER JUST STARTED DEVELOPING, AND IT WAS AWESOME. TO BE ABLE TO MAKE THIS CHARACTER WITH THE GUYS AND TO SEE HIS JOURNEY AS WELL, IT'S VERY SPECIAL. IT'S LIKE A ONCE-IN-A-LIFETIME OPPORTUNITY THAT I'M JUST—I FEEL REALLY BLESSED."

—RORY O'MALLEY

THE BOOK OF MORMON'S
REAL (FORMER) MORMON MISSIONARY

CLARK JOHNSEN: My first exposure to the show was at New 42 Studios. During the first workshop of *The Book of Mormon*, I was doing the workshop of *The Addams Family. The Book of Mormon* was on the fifth floor, and we were rehearsing on the sixth floor, and it was this sort of untitled "secret" musical that no one could know anything about, but people in the building were like, *Oh, it's about Joseph Smith and Mormonism.* And I was like, *What?* I was like, *No, that can't be true.*

I'd never heard a thing about it, they'd been really careful not to have any sort of leakage of any kind and they'd been working on it for years. I just instantly felt, I have to be part of this.

But I couldn't; I was already in another show that was concurrently happening. The other thing I heard was, *Oh, it's very offensive.*

By this time, I'd already made my way out of the Church so I was not concerned about the Church's reputation being dragged through the mud or anything like that.

So I think, maybe I should go down to the fifth floor and offer my services as some sort of dramaturge or something. But they were being so secretive that I felt it was better to leave them to their creative process and not butt my head in, just because I had a pass into the building.

Over the summer of 2010, they were doing another workshop and they were looking for a new Elder Price. But I had this internal struggle whether I should push to be seen and say, *This is my life story!* Elder Price's two-hour journey is kind of a microcosm of my journey out of the Church. You feel sort of disillusioned, but then you come back around and see the value of what you've been taught; you take the good that you've been given and just decide to forget all the other stuff, because you've healed from it.

But I thought, I shouldn't try to audition for this. If they don't call me, maybe I should just accept that this is not meant to be. If it wasn't coming to me, then it wasn't meant to be. And I was very happy in *The Addams Family*. My other thought was, I don't want to do something that will make my family feel like I'm giving them the middle finger about their faith, because most of my family are still believers in the LDS doctrine, and my parents are actually currently serving an eighteen-month mission in Palau, near Guam in Micronesia. So I just didn't want to have anyone feel like I was being part of this musical to be the anti-Mormon, the ex-Mormon who was saying, *F you.*

So I just decided I was going to let this one go. Then in December, the casting director said a friend of mine had recommended me, and I just felt, I don't want to go in and audition unless I think I would do the show if I get it. Even though the chances were pretty slim; they had one missionary role they were looking for, replacing someone who decided he didn't want to be part of the Broadway production.

So I called my best friend who's also ex-Mormon, who was also a returned missionary; we had sort of seen each other through this whole thing. He was like, *I just think it's going to be really hard on your parents, this is something that maybe you just don't want to do.* And I was like, *Okay, maybe I won't do it.* And then I called one of my brothers, who is also a returned missionary and who is still in the Mormon Church. He was like, *Isn't this the* South Park *guys?* He was like, *You're so stupid, this is the dumbest question ever. Of course you have to audition. Of course, if you get it, you have to do it.* And I said, *Don't you think it will be offensive?* He was like, *No, the* South Park *guys never go for anybody. They just point it out, they say what it is, they wink, they nudge, they poke, and that's it. They're not going to obliterate the Church. And even if they did, the Church can stand it. And we want you to be successful, and we want you to do things that challenge you.* And I was like, *Okay.*

So I went and auditioned, and there were eight other guys that I was auditioning against, and after two short auditions they said, *Okay, you're in the show.* It was three weeks until rehearsals started, so I gave my notice to *Addams Family.*

I walked into rehearsal the first day, when pretty much the whole script and score were already on their feet. I had not heard a song, seen a lyric, nothing, and I was just blown away by what they had done. Their level of understanding what they were dealing with, and the delicate balance that they walked to create this show in a way that was both poignant but smart, funny but moving. I was sitting there listening to Andrew sing "I Believe" and I was listening to all these facts about the religion—there wasn't anyone in the room that could understand the context of those things as well as me. I mean, when they say the Garden of Eden is in Jackson County, Missouri, my family *went* to Jackson County every couple of years. It's called Adam-ondi-Ahman, you go and you see this giant field that the Church has bought, that supposedly was where the

Garden of Eden was. All of this is in my body, the very cells of my body are like containers of this information, these emotions, and then to hear them sort of exploding in song was just incredible. It's such a unique opportunity to be part of something that's so widely embraced—I mean, even members of the Church are pretty happy with it, from my exposure to it. I've met a lot of people at the stage door after the show. We're from Utah, and I always sort of cock my head a little bit, like, *Are you currently active in the Church?* They usually say, *Oh, well, no, not really.*

But I have met some who are currently active. My brother—who encouraged me to audition—came and saw the show on opening night. He just had a very peculiar sort of experience with it, because he loved it, but he sort of felt, *Should I be offended by what's happening? Should I be offended that people are kind of laughing at this story of Joseph Smith and the Angel Moroni and the plates?* He was just a little like, *I don't know how I should feel.*

> **"THE CROSSOVER FROM MY LIFE TO THE SHOW IS JUST SO BIZARRE, I CAN'T WRAP MY HEAD AROUND THE WAY THAT IT ALL SORT OF JUST CAME TOGETHER."**

But he was very happy that he saw it. My mom, on the other hand, was planning to but then decided not to. She came to visit, but she was like, *I just don't really feel great about seeing the show, and I hope you can understand.* And of course I did, because only years before I had been of a similar mindset. If I were still a mainstream Mormon, I would probably be very nervous to see the show, and yet very curious about it. If I did see it, I would feel that I had to be a little bit in a defensive stance about what was happening.

The crossover from my life to the show is just so bizarre, I can't wrap my head around the way that it all sort of just came together. And I just can't wrap my head around the fact that I'm on a Broadway stage depicting the religion that I was born into, that I fully espoused the beliefs of, that I taught to people in Mexico on a two-year full-time mission, and that I baptized people into. Then I transitioned out of the religion, only to come back around and be part of this musical. I mean, it's crazy. It's just crazy. ◆

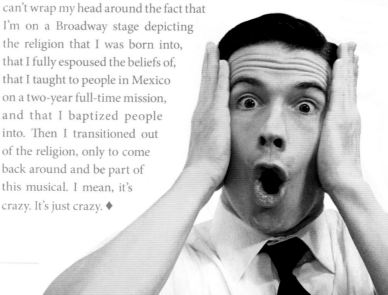

I AM HERE FOR YOU
"GOOD NIGHT, BEST FRIEND."

> "SLEEP NOW LITTLE BUDDY
> PUT YOUR CARES AWAY
> NAPPY WITH A HAPPY FACE
> TOMORROW'S A LATTER DAY."
> —ELDER CUNNINGHAM

I'D DO ANYTHING FOR YOU

BOBBY LOPEZ: I REMEMBER, I LOVED HARMONIZING THE LULLABY. IT WAS JUST—IT WAS A FUN, FUN DAY WHEN WE WROTE THAT.

TREY PARKER: WHEN WE FIRST SAW THE SHOW ON ITS FEET, THERE WAS SO MUCH ENERGY IN THE FIRST 30 OR 40 MINUTES—IT WAS HUGE NUMBER AFTER HUGE NUMBER AFTER HUGE NUMBER, AND WE REALIZED WE NEEDED TO CATCH OUR BREATH AND SIT FOR A MOMENT AND ENJOY PRICE AND CUNNINGHAM JUST BEHAVING WITH EACH OTHER, JUST BEING TOGETHER. AND WE ALSO REALIZED WE REALLY NEEDED TO SET UP THE STORY OF THE FRIENDSHIP. THAT'S OUR LOVE STORY. THE LOVE STORY IS BETWEEN THE TWO GUYS. SO WE WROTE THIS LITTLE SONG-LET, THIS LULLABY, THAT WRAPS ITSELF AROUND THE SCENE. IT'S ALMOST MY FAVORITE NUMBER BECAUSE IT HAS THE CONFIDENCE TO SIMPLY BE STILL AND GENTLE.

TREY PARKER: AS SOON AS WE SAW THAT FIRST WORKSHOP, WE KINDA GOT IT. WE SAW HOW TO WRITE THE SHOW. WE STARTED WITH JUST 45 MINUTES OF MATERIAL, LESS THAN ONE ACT. WE HAD FIVE OR SIX SONGS, SOMETHING LIKE THAT, AND IT WAS SO GALVANIZING. AND THEN EVERY SIX MONTHS WE DID ANOTHER WORKSHOP AND PROGRESSIVELY CREATED THE CHARACTERS AND THE SHAPE OF THE SHOW. WE KNEW, FROM THE FIRST READING, THAT THE SHOW LIVED AT THE INTERSECTION BETWEEN A BROADWAY MUSICAL AND A RELIGIOUS EXPERIENCE. THAT'S WHERE WE WANTED IT TO LIVE. WE JUST FOUND THAT; IT WAS SUCH A LUCKY THING TO FIND SO EARLY.

MATT STONE: BOBBY SAID, WE GOTTA DO A WORKSHOP, YOU KNOW? I THINK TREY AND I WERE LIKE, WHAT? WE DON'T EVEN KNOW WHAT A WORKSHOP IS, BECAUSE NORMALLY WHEN WE'RE WRITING, WE MAY DO AN ANIMATIC WHERE WE DRAW THINGS OUT, OR WE MIGHT SHOOT A LITTLE SHORT AND LOOK AT IT. WE SIT IN A ROOM, JUST TREY AND ME, AND DO IT. SO THIS WAS A WHOLE NEW WAY OF WORKING FOR US. EVERY ONE OF THOSE WORKSHOPS ALWAYS PROPELLED US FORWARD A LITTLE BIT. IT ALWAYS GAVE US A NEW IDEA. IT ALWAYS KINDA KICKED US TO THE NEXT PLACE. LET'S DO A FEW MORE SONGS. LET'S WRITE A FEW MORE SCENES.

BOBBY LOPEZ: I'D NEVER SEEN SOMETHING IN SUCH GOOD SHAPE THAT WE WORKED ON—THAT I WORKED ON SO HARD. AND I THINK A LOT OF THAT IS A RESULT OF MATT AND TREY'S PERFECTIONISM. I LEARNED SOMETHING ABOUT HOW GENUINELY FAR YOU CAN GO WITH PERFECTIONISM. TO JUST KEEP WORKING AND WORKING AND MAKING THINGS BETTER, CHANGING THINGS THAT ARE ALREADY GREAT AND MAKING THEM A LITTLE BIT BETTER EVERY DAY. THAT WAS THE MOST REWARDING PART OF THE WHOLE EXPERIENCE.

MY (REAL) BEST FRIEND

RORY O'MALLEY: I MET JOSH MY FIRST DAY AT CARNEGIE MELLON UNIVERSITY. I MOVED IN WITH HIM OUR SECOND SEMESTER, AND WE LIVED TOGETHER OFF CAMPUS FOR THE NEXT THREE YEARS. I WAS A SWING/UNDERSTUDY IN *SPELLING BEE*, AND MY BROADWAY DEBUT WAS GOING ON FOR JOSH WHEN HE WAS AUDITIONING FOR HIS FIRST FILM ROLE, AND I WAS IN HIS WEDDING. WE HAVE A LONG, LONG HISTORY, AND THEN TO GO THROUGH THIS TOGETHER HAS BEEN AMAZING. HAVING A BEST FRIEND BE A PART OF THE GREATEST CAREER EXPERIENCE OF YOUR LIFE IS PRETTY ASTOUNDING, BECAUSE YOU CAN'T REALLY RELATE TO YOUR LOVED ONES WHAT IT FEELS LIKE TO GO THROUGH AN EXPERIENCE LIKE THIS. TO HAVE SOMEBODY THAT YOU LOVE SO MUCH KNOW EXACTLY WHAT IT'S LIKE, TO HAVE SOMEBODY WHO YOU LOVE ALSO BE NOMINATED FOR A TONY*, TO HAVE SOMEONE YOU LOVE ALSO LOSE THE TONY—RIGHT BEHIND YOU—FOR THE REST OF OUR LIVES WE'LL HAVE THAT.

JOSH GAD: RORY AND I SEEM DESTINED COSMICALLY TO BE IN EACH OTHER'S LIVES TILL THE END OF DAYS. I'VE KNOWN RORY SINCE I WAS SEVENTEEN YEARS OLD. THE TWO OF US WENT TO CARNEGIE MELLON TOGETHER, WE WERE ROOMMATES IN COLLEGE. AND THEN WE BOTH GOT OUR FIRST BREAKS ON BROADWAY IN A SHOW CALLED *SPELLING BEE*. AND THEN ABOUT THREE YEARS LATER I GET THIS E-MAIL ABOUT WHO'S GOING TO BE IN THIS FIRST READING OF *THE BOOK OF MORMON*. AND LO AND BEHOLD I SEE THE NAME RORY O'MALLEY. AND IT WAS AMAZING BECAUSE WHEN WE STARTED, RORY WAS IN EVERY SENSE OF THE TERM AN ENSEMBLE MEMBER. HE WAS NO DIFFERENT THAN ANY OF THE OTHER MORMON BOYS IN THAT FIRST READING. BUT THERE WAS SOMETHING THAT IMMEDIATELY CAPTURED EVERYBODY'S ATTENTION. WHEN THEY LOOKED AT HIM THEY WERE LIKE, *THIS IS THE WHITEST MAN ON BROADWAY!* AND THEY IMMEDIATELY STARTED WRITING FOR THAT. IN EACH READING HE GOT MORE AND MORE LINES, THEN HE GOT HIS OWN SONG AND IT BECAME BIGGER AND BIGGER UNTIL HE TRULY IS ONE OF THE LEADS OF THE SHOW. IT WAS A REMARKABLE THING TO WATCH BECAUSE I'VE ALWAYS KNOWN WHAT RORY IS CAPABLE OF, BUT TO SEE PEOPLE LIKE TREY, MATT, AND BOBBY RECOGNIZE IT AND WRITE FOR IT WAS ONE OF THE GREAT GIFTS FOR ME, BECAUSE WE'RE BEST FRIENDS.

BFF

...DESTINED COSMICALLY
TO BE IN EACH OTHER'S LIVES TILL THE
END OF DAYS.

— JOSH GAD

THE WORKSHOPS

"AS SOON AS WE SAW THAT FIRST WORKSHOP, WE KINDA GOT IT. WE SAW HOW TO WRITE THE SHOW."

SO LET IT BE WRITTEN,

MADE IN UTAH

MORMONS AND WANTS SOME MORE, TWO B... OR, GOD LOVES MORMONS AND WANTS SOME...

DATE	EVENT/ LOCATION	SONGS ADDED		CAST/CREW ADDED
FEB 18-23, 2008	READING #1, THE VINEYARD THEATRE	"Hello", "Two By Two", "The Bible is a Trilogy" "Family Home Evening" (For Price's father, mother, & sister) "Hasa Diga Eebowai", "Sal Tlay Ka Siti", "Man Up" (Solo Version)		Josh Gad (Elder Cunningham) Benjamin Walker (Elder Price), Kevin Duda, Rory O'Malley, John Eric Parker, Rema Webb Maia Nkenge Wilson, Michael James Scott Benjamin Schräeder, Brian Sears
DEC 8-18, 2008	READING #2, THE VINEYARD THEATRE	"Baptize Me", "Man Up" "The Bible Is a Trilogy" "Tomorrow Is a Latter Day" "H-E Double Hockey Sticks" "Making Things Up Again" "Turn It Off" "Joseph Smith American Moses"	(Expanded ACT 1 Finale Version) (Expanded to include Joseph Smith story) (early version of "Spooky Mormon Hell Dream") (Without lines for fictional characters) (Preliminary version)	Cheyenne Jackson (Elder Price) Nikki M. James (Nabulungi) Rory O'Malley (Elder McKinley)
JUL 23- AUG 10, 2009	READING #3, THE VINEYARD THEATRE	"Something Incredible", "I Am Here For You" (Precursor to "You and Me (But Mostly Me)") "Nothing" (Brief second act solo for Price) "I Believe" "I Am Africa" (A brief snippet)		Daniel Reichard (Elder Price) Asmeret Ghebremichael Jason Michael Snow
JAN 18-FEB 28, 20[?] WORKSHOP #1, New 42nd Street Studios		"Hill Cumorah Pageant" (Openings of ACT 1 & ACT 2) "Zero Baptisms" (Elder McKinley Solo) "They Lie" (a nervous Breakdown Song for Price in ACT 2) "Family Home Evening" CUT!		Michael Potts (Mafala Hatimbi) Brian Tyree Henry (General)
AUG 2-SEP 1, 2010 WORKSHOP #2, Clark Studio Theater Lincoln Center		"You And Me (But Mostly Me)", "Man Up" (Expanded Version) "Making Things Up Again" (Added Hobbits & Other characters) "Spooky Mormon Hell Dream" "The Bible Is A Trilogy" (Reused early version of "All-American Prophet") "Joseph Smith American Moses" (Expanded Version) "Orlando", "Nothing", "They Lie" CUT!		✓ Andrew Rannells (Elder Price) Scott Barnhardt Lawrence Stallings Casey Nicholaw (co-director & choreographer) Glen Kelly (Dance Music Arranger)
FEB 24, 2011 FIRST PREVIEW	BROADWAY PRODUCTION, EUGENE O'NEILL THEATRE	"All-American Prophet" (Final Version)		Lewis Cleale (Joseph Smith / Mission President) Clark Johnsen, Tommar Wilson

"THE PIECE IS VERY MUCH AN ENSEMBLE PIECE, BUT IT HAS BEEN AN INTERESTING PROCESS BECAUSE THE MORMONS TENDED TO REHEARSE BY THEMSELVES AND SO DID THE AFRICANS. DURING THE PROCESS, IT WAS—IT WAS ALWAYS, OKAY, AFRICANS ARE RELEASED FOR THE DAY, WHILE THE MORMONS WORKED ON THE CHOREOGRAPHY. OR WE'D BE IN ONE ROOM WORKING ON CHOREOGRAPHY, THEY'D BE IN ANOTHER ROOM WORKING ON MUSIC, AND THEN IT WOULD FLIP LIKE THAT. IT DIDN'T HAPPEN UNTIL THE LATTER PART OF THE WORKSHOPS, AND THEN REHEARSALS UPTOWN, THAT WE STARTED BEING IN THE SAME ROOM TOGETHER. AND SO THAT WAS ALWAYS EXCITING, BECAUSE YOU WERE ALWAYS ANXIOUS TO SEE WHAT THOSE GUYS WERE WORKING ON."

—MICHAEL POTTS

"I REMEMBER WE HAD A SONG CALLED 'FAMILY HOME EVENING' THAT USED TO BE IN THE SHOW. THE FAMILY GATHERED AROUND, AND THEY SANG THIS SONG ABOUT WHAT IT'S LIKE TO BE A MORMON FAMILY. AND IT WAS THIS BEAUTIFUL, MELODIC SONG. AND PEOPLE LOVED IT. THE RESPONSE WAS HUGE. AND I REMEMBER THEY CAME IN AND CUT IT ONE DAY, AND THEY WERE LIKE, *YOU KNOW WHAT? WE DON'T NEED IT.* I WAS LIKE, *NOOOOOOOO. YOU CAN'T CUT A SONG PEOPLE LAUGH AT.* BUT THEY CUT IT, AND WE LOST NOTHING. THEY CAN AFFORD TO CUT THINGS THAT WORK BECAUSE EVERYTHING IS OPERATING AT SUCH A HIGH LEVEL."

—JOSH GAD

SO IT SHALL BE DONE

ALL-AMERICAN PROPHET

"HE DIDN'T COME FROM THE MIDDLE EAST LIKE THOSE OTHER HOLY MEN."

TREY PARKER: WHEN WE FIRST STARTED TALKING ABOUT DOING A MORMON MUSICAL, THE ORIGINAL IDEA WAS TO TELL THE WHOLE JOSEPH SMITH STORY. BUT WE REALIZED EARLY ON THAT WE WERE ALSO INTERESTED IN THE PARALLEL STORY OF THESE TWO MISSIONARY BOYS. AND YET WE ALWAYS LOVED JOSEPH SMITH AND KNEW WE WANTED TO LAND THE WHOLE ENTIRE HISTORY OF MORMONISM SOMEWHERE IN THE SHOW. THAT'S WHEN 'ALL-AMERICAN PROPHET' BECAME THIS HAROLD HILL 'MUSIC MAN' MOMENT, BUT INSTEAD OF SOMEBODY ROLLING INTO TOWN AND SAYING THE CITY NEEDS A BOYS' BAND, THIS BOY SHOWS UP TO SELL THEM A RELIGION.

MATT STONE: WITHIN AN HOUR OF MEETING CASEY, IT WAS JUST SO OBVIOUS THAT HE WAS A BIG BRAIN. HE BROUGHT SO MUCH TO THE TABLE. HE'S INCREDIBLY FOCUSED, BUT COMPLETELY SPONTANEOUS; HE COMES UP SO QUICKLY WITH THESE BEAUTIFUL PATTERNS OF MOVEMENT, AND HE'S SO IN COMMAND OF THE STAGE. 'OKAY, YOU GO OVER THERE. YOU GO HERE. LET'S SEE—NOPE, THAT DOESN'T WORK'—AND HE'S ON TO A BETTER, STRONGER IDEA. HE TAKES SUCH PLEASURE IN THE COMEDY, LIKE THOSE GREAT AGNES DE MILLE AND MARTHA GRAHAM JOKES IN 'ALL-AMERICAN PROPHET.' HE'S GOT GREAT IDEAS. HE'S 100 PERCENT ENERGY. WATCHING CASEY WORK IS LIKE WATCHING 15 PEOPLE WORK.

BOBBY LOPEZ: WE REALLY LOVED THE MELODY OF MORONI'S 'DON'T LET ANYBODY SEE THESE PLATES EXCEPT FOR YOU' LINE, AND IT BECAME SORT OF THIS LEITMOTIF THROUGHOUT THE SHOW AS A SIGNIFIER OF THE LEAP OF FAITH IT TAKES TO BELIEVE IN SCRIPTURE. WE USE IT TWICE IN 'ALL-AMERICAN PROPHET,' AND WE USE IT AT THE TOP OF 'I BELIEVE.' WE ALSO PLAY IT HUGE, ALMOST LIKE JOHN WILLIAMS, IN THE INTRODUCTIONS TO EACH ACT. IT'S ONE OF THOSE SMALL MELODIC FIGURES THAT ENDS UP CARRYING ONE OF THE BIGGEST IDEAS IN THE SHOW. WE WERE ECSTATIC TO FIND IT.

TREY PARKER: LARRY HOCHMAN AND STEPHEN OREMUS SOMEHOW GOT NINE PLAYERS TO SOUND LIKE 30. I THINK IT'S AMAZING. IT BLEW ME AWAY. AND A LOT OF THAT IS ALSO DUE TO BRIAN RONAN, THE SOUND DESIGNER, WHO DID A LOT OF GREAT WORK PUTTING IT ALL ACROSS TO EVERY SEAT.

ANN ROTH: CASEY KNOWS HOW TO BUILD GIANT COMEDIC DANCES THAT ARE BEAUTIFUL AND FUNNY. ONLY A FEW ARTISTS HAVE EVER BEEN ABLE TO DO IT THIS WELL. JERRY ROBBINS OR MICHAEL KIDD, THAT'S ABOUT IT.

THERE'S A PART 3! HAVE YOU HEARD

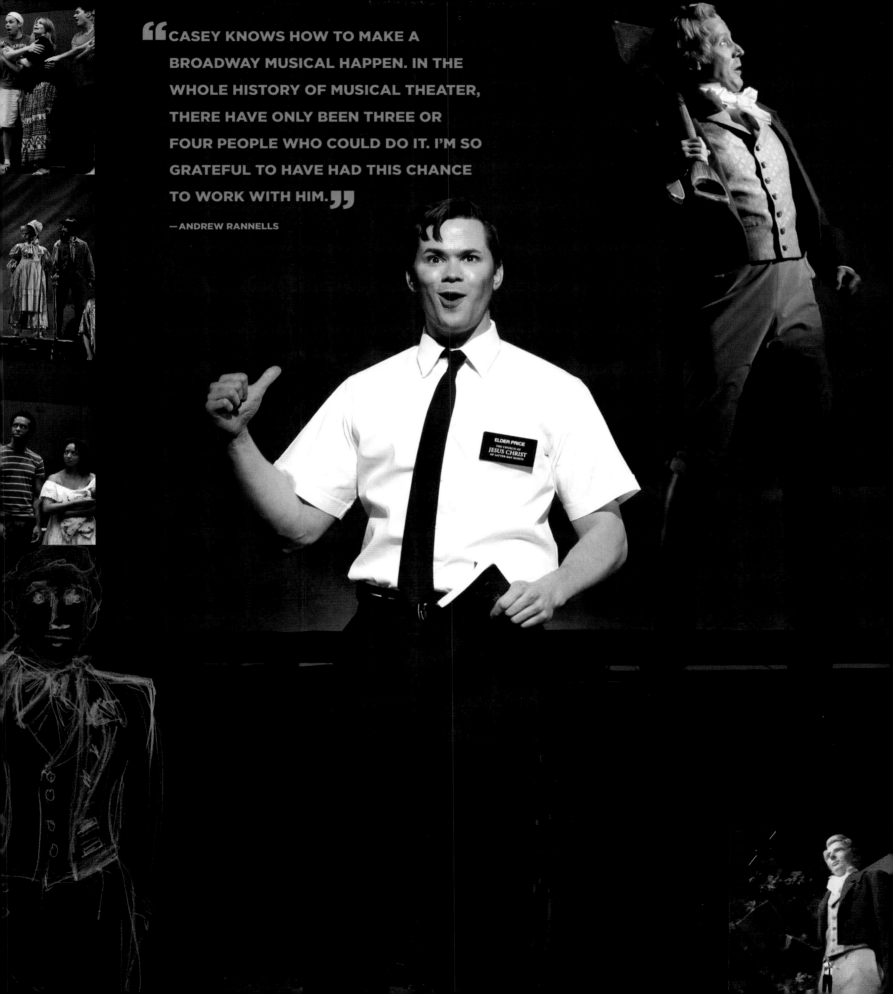

"CASEY KNOWS HOW TO MAKE A BROADWAY MUSICAL HAPPEN. IN THE WHOLE HISTORY OF MUSICAL THEATER, THERE HAVE ONLY BEEN THREE OR FOUR PEOPLE WHO COULD DO IT. I'M SO GRATEFUL TO HAVE HAD THIS CHANCE TO WORK WITH HIM."

—ANDREW RANNELLS

SAL TLAY KA SITI

"MY MOTHER ONCE TOLD ME OF A PLACE WITH WATERFALLS AND UNICORNS FLYING."

BRIAN MACDEVITT: THE PIECE IS SO DYNAMIC, IT'S GREAT THAT WE CAN GO FROM THESE REALLY BRIGHT NUMBERS—LIKE SUPER-BRIGHT, ECSTATIC TAP-DANCING MORMON BOYS—TO A REALLY INTIMATE MOMENT WITH NABULUNGI ALONE AT NIGHT, SINGING ABOUT THIS PLACE ACROSS THE WORLD THAT SHE'S BEEN DREAMING OF. YOU REALLY GET A CHANCE TO DEMONSTRATE RANGE, TO VARY THE INTENSITY AND AMOUNT OF LIGHT ON STAGE. YOU KEEP EXPANDING AND CONTRACTING THE LIGHTING BECAUSE THE STORY DEMANDS IT. WHEN THE NARRATIVE ALLOWS ME TO DO THAT KIND OF STRETCHING, THAT'S WHERE IDEAS LIKE THE SHOOTING STAR AGAINST THE NIGHTSCAPE COME FROM.

MATT STONE: IF YOU LIVED IN A OPPRESSED PLACE, YOU WOULD LOVE TO GO TO SALT LAKE CITY TOO, YOU KNOW. WOULDN'T YOU? THAT'S THE WHOLE PLEASURE IN THE IDEA— THE COMEDY LIVES IN THE CHASM BETWEEN HER CONCEPTION OF SALT LAKE CITY AND WHAT WE KNOW TO BE TRUE OF THE REAL PLACE.

BOBBY LOPEZ: FOR ME, THE EMOTIONAL ARC OF THE STORY IS THE MOST IMPORTANT THING IN A MUSICAL. IT'S THE ONLY IMPORTANT THING. I THINK IF YOU HAVE THAT, YOU HAVE A SHOW. THE THING THAT PEOPLE ARE COMING TO SEE IS THAT EMOTIONAL STORY—EVEN IF THEY DON'T KNOW THEY ARE. IT'S JUST SOMETHING INHERENT IN STORYTELLING. THAT'S WHY WE NEED STORIES. WHEN WE SET OUT TO WRITE 'SAL TLAY KA SITI,' WE REALLY WANTED TO WRITE A SONG FOR A PRINCESS IN A DISNEY MOVIE— ONE OF THOSE CLASSIC THEMES WHERE THE GIRL IS INNOCENT AND THE DREAM IS SO PURE THAT YOU CAN LATCH ON TO HER AND WANT WHAT SHE WANTS. MUSICALLY, THAT'S WHERE WE WENT. LYRICALLY, TREY AND MATT AND I HAVE EACH DONE SONGS THAT ARE JOKES ON PATOIS. I DID 'THE MORE YOU RUV SOMEONE' IN *AVENUE Q*, AND THEY DID 'I'M SO RONERY' WITH KIM JONG IL IN *TEAM AMERICA*.

MATT STONE: YOU ALWAYS IMAGINE THAT IN THIS WAR-TORN VILLAGE THAT IS OUR REAL VERSION OF AFRICA, THERE'S THIS—BASICALLY A DISNEY PRINCESS WHO NEEDS TO BE LIBERATED, WHO NEEDS TO FIND HER WAY. SHE SEES A BETTER LIFE BUT NOT A WAY TO GET TO IT. THIS GIRL REPRESENTS THE INNOCENT, NAÏVE DREAM THAT'S GETTING ERODED ON A DAILY BASIS BY THE CIRCUMSTANCE SHE'S IN.

TREY PARKER: YEARS AGO, RIGHT AROUND THE TIME WE STARTED, MATT AND I WERE WITH BOBBY IN LONDON, AND WE HAD AN APARTMENT WITH JUST A PIANO AND A MICROPHONE ON A STAND. WE WERE STARTING TO WRITE ALL THE SONGS AND RECORDING THESE SCRATCH DEMO TRACKS. WE WERE REALLY STARTING TO THINK SERIOUSLY ABOUT THE STORY WHEN WE CAME UP WITH THE NOTION THAT SOMEONE FROM UGANDA COULD SO EASILY MISUNDERSTAND THE IDEA OF SALT LAKE CITY. WE HAD THE WEEKENDS OFF, SO I TOOK A TRIP FROM LONDON TO BATH, BECAUSE I HAD NEVER BEEN TO BATH. I WAS SITTING BY MYSELF ON THIS TRAIN, SO EXCITED TO BE GOING SOMEWHERE NEW, AND I JUST STARTED WRITING THE LYRIC TO 'SAL TLAY KA SITI,' WHICH EXPRESSES EXACTLY WHAT I WAS FEELING ABOUT WHERE I WAS HEADED. THAT WAS ONE OF THE ONLY SONGS THAT WAS WRITTEN COMPLETELY AS A LYRIC, WITHOUT MUSIC FIRST. THEN I STARTED PLAYING WITH THE MELODY OF IT, AND I BROUGHT IT BACK TO THE GUYS ON MONDAY. IT WAS SO NATURAL AND SIMPLE AND THE IDEA JUST SANG TO ME—HER FANTASY OF AN EASIER LIFE AND THE POSSIBILITY THAT THESE MORMON BOYS COULD MAKE HER MOTHER'S DREAM FOR HER COME TRUE. MAYBE TWO OF THE LINES HAVE CHANGED SINCE THEN.

"I GOT A PHONE CALL ASKING IF I WOULD BE A PART OF A SMALL WORKSHOP, AND THEY TOLD ME AT THE TIME, THESE ARE THE PEOPLE INVOLVED—TREY PARKER, MATT STONE, AND BOBBY LOPEZ—AND IT IS ABOUT MORMONS. IT DOESN'T HAVE A TITLE, OR AT LEAST NOT ONE THAT WE CAN TELL YOU, AND WE CAN'T SEND YOU A SCRIPT. AND WE CAN'T PLAY YOU ANY OF THE MUSIC. DO YOU WANT TO DO IT?

THE MUSICAL IS A FANTASTICAL, BEAUTIFUL WORLD THAT CAN ONLY HAPPEN IN THE THEATER WHERE PEOPLE CAN SING AND DANCE AND AND ALL THESE AMAZING THINGS AND IT DOESN'T EVEN SEEM STRANGE. I THINK WE'VE DONE THAT HERE. I FEEL LUCKY. I GET BUTTERFLIES THINKING ABOUT, YOU KNOW, BEING A LITTLE GIRL, SEEING SHOWS LIKE THIS AND WANTING TO BE UP THERE, DOING IT."

— NIKKI M. JAMES

'SAL TLAY KA SITI,' THE MOST PERFECT PLACE ON EARTH. WHERE FLIES DON'T BITE YOUR EYEBALLS AND HUMAN LIFE HAS WORTH.

IT ISN'T A PLACE OF FAIRY TALES.

SET DESIGN

SCOTT PASK: MY COLLABORATION WITH CASEY AND TREY WAS CRUCIAL AND INSPIRING, AND IT BEGAN WITH THE WORKSHOPS. WE ALWAYS START FROM A PLACE OF, HOW DO WE WANT TO PRESENT THIS? THE HISTORY OF AMERICAN MUSICALS WAS AN IMPORTANT STARTING POINT, AND LOOKING AT HOW THOSE ARE STRUCTURED. BUT THEN DECONSTRUCTING THAT AND ALSO SUBVERTING EXPECTATIONS, LIKE BEING PRESENTED WITH A SCENIC ENVIRONMENT IN SALT LAKE CITY THAT'S INCREDIBLY ARTICULATED AND SHINY AND SPARKLY AND INSPIRATIONAL. AND THEN IT BREAKS AWAY, TO THIS PLACE WHERE THEY'RE FORCED TO HAVE THEIR MISSION. FOR THE REALITY OF THAT, I WOULD BRING RESEARCH TO TREY AND CASEY AND SHOW THEM STRUCTURES AND IMAGES THAT I'VE BEEN INSPIRED BY, AND THE WHOLE IDEA OF TAKING SOMETHING THAT SEEMED ALMOST CURATED, HAND-PAINTED AND BEAUTIFULLY APPLIED AND CAREFULLY THOUGHT OUT AND SPARKLING—AND JUST DESTROYING IT. OBLITERATING IT.

I THINK IT WAS IMPORTANT FOR ME TO USE A VIEWFINDER FOR THE SHOW, TO USE A FRAMING DEVICE. IT HARKENS BACK TO THE IDEA OF THE DESIGN BEING A KIND OF PAGEANT, AT LEAST IN ITS SORT OF THREE-DIMENSIONAL EXPERIENCE AND THE VISUAL VOCABULARY.

BECAUSE OF THE CONTRAST OF THOSE TWO SPACES—SALT LAKE CITY AND UGANDA—A LENS IMMEDIATELY INFORMED THE PALETTE OF THE SHOW. THE COOL BLUES, THE SNOW, THE BLUE SKIES, THE CRISP, WHITE SHIRTS. AND THEN THE UGANDAN COLORS OF THE RED CLAY, THE OCHRES OF THE HUTS, THE WOODS, THE WEATHER-BEATEN, SUN-BLEACHED BONES, ALL OF THOSE. AND THE VERY CONTRASTS OF THOSE COLORS AND THOSE WORLDS WAS A GREAT STARTING POINT FOR THE PALETTE OF THE SHOW.

CASEY NICHOLAW: AFRICA FEELS LIKE A PLAY SET, YOU KNOW, AND SALT LAKE CITY FEELS LIKE A MUSICAL SET, AND THAT'S WHAT IT SHOULD FEEL LIKE. FANTASY GIVES WAY TO REALITY, AND THEN WE TURN THE GRIM REALITY INTO OUR BEAUTIFUL FANTASY VERSION OF IT.

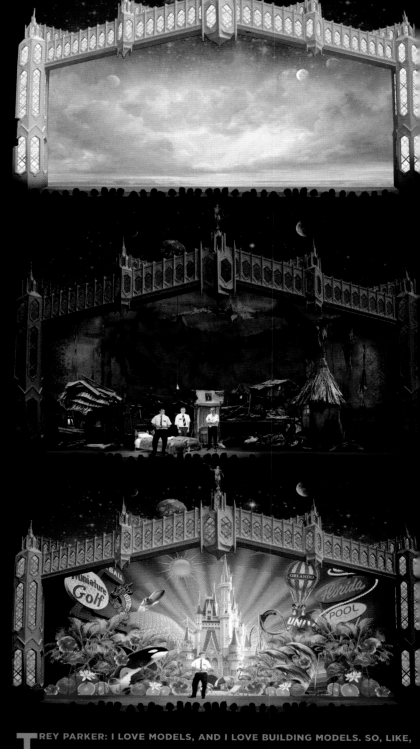

TREY PARKER: I LOVE MODELS, AND I LOVE BUILDING MODELS. SO, LIKE, WE GOT TO DO LITTLE MODELS OF THE SET AND EVERYTHING, AND I LOVED THAT PART. SCOTT WAS SO BRILLIANT AT WALKING US THROUGH IT ALL.

MICHAEL POTTS: SUDDENLY, YOU'RE IN ATHOL FUGARD TERRITORY, YOU KNOW, WHICH IS REALLY, REALLY, REALLY ROUGH. I REMEMBER FIRST SEEING THE SET AND JUST BEING BLOWN AWAY, GOING, WOW, THAT'S A REALLY GREAT SET. AND WE ARE REALLY POOR.

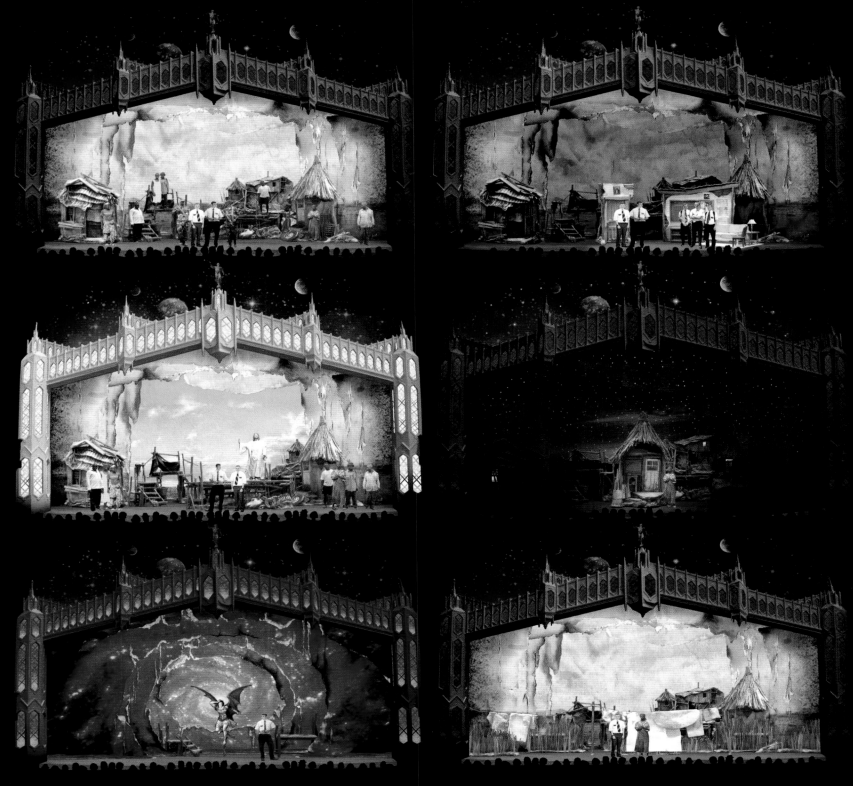

MATT STONE: ALL OF THE MORE EXPERIENCED BROADWAY PEOPLE, BEFORE WE STARTED THE PRODUCTION, WERE SAYING, SCOTT PASK WILL MAKE THIS BEAUTIFUL. AND I REALLY DIDN'T UNDERSTAND THAT. I WAS LIKE, OH, OKAY. WELL, OF COURSE IT WILL BE PRETTY, YOU KNOW? IT'S GONNA BE LIKE, YOU KNOW—PROFESSIONAL PEOPLE ARE DOING THIS, AND IT'LL BE PRETTY, RIGHT? BUT I DIDN'T REALIZE WHAT PEOPLE WERE TALKING ABOUT, THAT SUBLIME BEAUTY THAT HE COULD BRING TO A PLACE THAT WAS JUST—IS SUPPOSED TO BE OUR GOD-FORSAKEN LAND, YOU KNOW, AND HOW MANY DIFFERENT LOOKS AND DIFFERENT KINDS OF ENVIRONMENTS AND MOODS WE CAN GET OUT OF THAT AFRICA SET. AND NOW I GET WHAT THEY WERE TALKING ABOUT, THAT YOU COULD—THAT THE CONCEIT OF THE MUSICAL IS THAT THESE GUYS GO TO A TERRIBLE PLACE THAT ISN'T BEAUTIFUL AND IS JUST HORRIFIC. AND IT HAS THAT, BUT IT ALSO HOLDS THIS STRANGE, LATENT BEAUTY. AND THEN THE FEEL OF IT CHANGES, AND WE START TO APPRECIATE THE BEAUTY OF THE LOCATION, COMPARED TO WHEN YOU FIRST WERE INTRODUCED TO IT. AND IT STARTS TO TRANSFORM AND BECOME SOMEHOW ALMOST A HOLY PLACE.

MAN UP

"JESUS DUG DOWN DEEP, KNOWING WHAT HE HAD TO DO."

TREY PARKER: THE ORIGINAL CONCEPTION OF PRICE AND CUNNINGHAM WAS THAT WE WOULD START WITH YOUR PROTOTYPICAL CHISELED CAPTAIN OF THE FOOTBALL TEAM, THE PERFECT MORMON LEADING MAN, AND HE'D HAVE THIS OBVIOUS, SCHLUBBY SIDEKICK TYPE. EARLY ON, IT WASN'T GOING TO BE A RANDOM AFRICAN WHO GOT SHOT IN THE FACE, IT WAS GOING TO BE PRICE, AND HE WAS JUST GOING TO DIE AND DISAPPEAR—AND THEN THE SIDEKICK WOULD BE LEFT ALL ALONE AND HAVE TO STEP UP AND BECOME THE HERO. I THINK IT WAS ACTUALLY STRONGER TO NOT HAVE THE LEADING MAN DISAPPEAR, AND TO INSTEAD LET HIM BE FORCED BY HIS OWN FAILURE TO ASSUME THE ROLE OF SIDEKICK WHILE THE SIDEKICK IS FORCED TO STEP UP AND BE THE LEADING MAN, IN HIS OWN WAY. THE STRUCTURE HAS THIS PLEASURABLE SURPRISE UP ITS SLEEVE IN DRAWING THIS LINE IN WHICH YOU ARE LED TO BELIEVE THAT PRICE IS GOING TO BE JOSEPH SMITH AND CUNNINGHAM IS GOING TO BE BRIGHAM YOUNG, BUT REALLY IT ENDS UP BEING THE OTHER WAY AROUND.

HAVE YOU HEARD?
"Have you heard of the All-American prophet? He found a brand-new book about Jesus Christ. We're following him to Paradise, we call ourselves Mormen, and our new religion is all American."

MATT STONE: 'MAN UP' WAS DESIGNED TO BE THE SHOW-STOPPING FIRST-ACT CURTAIN THAT WOULD FOCUS THAT CUNNINGHAM STORY. WE LOVED WRITING IT FOR CUNNINGHAM BECAUSE THAT'S ESSENTIALLY WHAT JOSEPH SMITH HAD TO DO. HE HAD TO MAN UP. THERE'S SOMETHING CRAZY AND AMAZING ABOUT SOMEBODY WHO MAKES HIMSELF THE HERO OF HIS OWN LIFE, AND THERE'S SOMETHING INSPIRING IN IT, TOO. THAT'S WHAT ALL THESE STORIES ARE SUPPOSED TO POINT TOWARDS—DON'T KICK BACK, BECOME THE HERO OF YOUR OWN LIFE. IN A REALLY DOPEY WAY, THAT'S WHAT JOSEPH SMITH DID AND THAT'S WHAT JESUS DID. THEY PUT THEMSELVES AT THE CENTER OF THE NARRATIVE, AND IT'S ENDEARING WHEN CUNNINGHAM REALIZES HE HAS TO DO THE SAME THING. HE SAYS, JESUS AND JOSEPH SMITH WERE FAT SCHLUBS LIKE ME! I'M GOING TO TAKE OVER AND BE THE HERO! MUSICALLY, WE WERE IMMEDIATELY THINKING 'EYE OF THE TIGER' OR PAT BENATAR OR THAT EMINEM SONG, 'LOSE YOURSELF.' IT'S SUPPOSED TO BE THAT KIND OF SONG, THE THIS-IS-MY-MOMENT SONG. THAT KIND OF SONG WITHIN THE SCOPE OF OUR STORY SEEMED LIKE A FUNNY IDEA—LIKE, I'M GONNA BE LIKE JESUS AND JUST FUCKING DO IT. IT'S TIME TO GO AND BE NUMBER ONE LIKE JESUS WAS. 'MAN UP' WAS MEANT TO BE 'EYE OF THE TIGER', BUT ABOUT JESUS.

BOBBY LOPEZ: ONE INTERESTING THING IS THAT WE DIDN'T REALLY GET IT RIGHT UNTIL THE VERY END OF PREVIEWS. CASEY WANTED MORE TIME TO BUILD THE NUMBER, SO WE DOUBLED THE ENDING FROM FOUR BARS TO EIGHT, WHICH WAS A GREAT IDEA FOR THE SHOW—BUT MUSICALLY I DIDN'T LIKE THE SECTION JUST REPEATING. SO I TOOK IT AND CHANGED THE CHORDS AND WE CHANGED WHAT EACH OF THE THREE PRINCIPALS WAS SINGING. WE TWEAKED THE LIGHTS AND THE SOUND, AND IT WAS JUST LIKE: *YEAH!* IT WAS GREAT, THE WHOLE THING COMING TOGETHER LIKE THAT. WE WORKED IT AND WORKED IT.

> **I THINK THE GREATEST CHALLENGE IS PHYSICALLY WHAT I HAVE TO DO IN IT. IT CAN BE VERY, VERY, VERY DIFFICULT BECAUSE I'M NOT A DANCER. I'M ALWAYS LIKE, OH, MY GOD, HOW AM I GONNA PICK UP THESE STEPS? IT JUST TAKES A LOT OF WORK. IT TAKES EXTRA WORK FOR ME. THERE ARE STILL MOMENTS IN THE SHOW WHERE I'M LIKE, OH, AM I DOING THIS RIGHT? AM I GONNA GET THIS RIGHT? AM I GONNA LAND THAT PIROUETTE, WHATEVER A PIROUETTE MAY BE? BUT CASEY GOT ME TO DO IT ALL.**
>
> —JOSH GAD

JUST LIKE JESUS, I'M GROWING A PAIR!

"'MAN UP' WAS MEANT TO BE 'EYE OF THE TIGER', BUT ABOUT JESUS."

— JOSH GAD

IT'S TIME TA...

MAN UP
BOOK OF MORMON
BROADWAY.COM

CASEY NICHOLAW: TREY AND I WILL SIT THERE AND WE'LL GO OVER OUR NOTES, AND HE'LL SAY, THIS, THIS, THIS, THIS, THIS, AND THIS—AND THEY'RE ALL THINGS I'VE HAD ON MY LIST TOO. SO WE—I REALLY LUCKED OUT. I THINK WE BOTH REALLY LUCKED OUT IN THIS WAY THAT JUST ENDED UP BEING A BLESSING.

I HAVEN'T REALLY THOUGHT ABOUT IT BEFORE, BUT THE FACT THAT WE BOTH HAD TWO JOBS IN THAT WAY—HE WAS WRITING AND DIRECTING, AND I WAS CHOREO-GRAPHING AND DIRECTING—AND THE DIRECTOR PART IS WHERE WE CAME TOGETHER. I REALLY WAS ABLE TO HELP THE PHYSICALITY, AND I THOUGHT A LOT OF HIS DIRECTION REALLY CAME FROM THE WRITING—HE WAS AN AUTHOR, SO HE UNDERSTOOD THE INTENT OF WHAT WE WANTED TO HAPPEN ONSTAGE EVERY NIGHT BETTER THAN ANYONE.

THE FIRST PREVIEW

RORY O'MALLEY: A few hours before our gypsy run-through, we all had dinner together at this Italian restaurant right next to the theater. We had been working for three years, and we had signed confidentiality agreements to never speak about it to even our mothers. It was something that we loved so much, and had to work so hard to shroud in secrecy, and I just remember thinking, *I can't wait to unleash this.* And I remember sitting at that dinner, feeling sad, feeling really, really, sad, and I was like, *Why am I so sad? This is what I've been waiting for.* But I realized this thing that we had worked on, and had become so close to all these people on, was about to not be ours anymore. It wasn't going to be this fun play we were putting on with friends; I knew the audience would come and it was going to be theirs. This moment of knowing everything was going to change, it was definitely scary. My mom called from Cleveland after that first preview, just so nervous that we were going to have things thrown at us. But it was absolutely the opposite. It was screaming and laughter like I had never heard before.

After the finale of Act One, when the lights went out, there was this wave from the audience of cheers like I had never heard on a stage before. It physically hit me, and I was standing between two other actors from the first reading and we had our arms out, up in the air, next to each other. We just instinctively grabbed each other's arms and started sobbing. It was a great night, because we knew that we had unleashed it.

JASON MICHAEL SNOW: Once you start laughing every day in rehearsal then you kind of think, *Oh, this could really go somewhere big.* And then we come to Broadway, and that first night you're like: *Okay, they're either going to get it and they're going to love it, or we're just going to have complete and utter silence.* And they went nuts after that opening number.

BRIAN SEARS: You could just feel it, right after the beginning of "Hello." From the start, we felt this sense of overwhelming awe of the show, like people were just transformed by the genius in the writing. When they did "Hasa Diga" we could hear how crazy the audience went. And then "All-American Prophet," one of the songs that I never thought was going to sell. When we finished that number the first time, it was the craziest applause I've ever heard in my entire life. It was so loud and so vibrant, and I think I started getting choked up, because I've never been a part of something like this.

TOMMAR WILSON: They went crazy and leapt to their feet! I mean, I've done some successful shows before but I've never seen a reaction like that or heard that kind of laughter—people laughing for two and a half hours straight. I knew from rehearsals that I loved it but I wasn't sure it would translate to a theater audience that likes the classics, *Oklahoma!* and *Carousel*. This is not that kind of theater so I wasn't sure if it would translate, but it did.

NIKKI M. JAMES: I always knew that if we could find producers who were smart enough to position the show the way it needed to be positioned, it was going to make a huge splash no matter what. I knew that people were going to be paying attention to this and feel something about it, one way or the other. And I had a feeling; you always know when you're in a flop, you're not always sure you're in a hit. But I knew that what we were doing was good.

Then came the first preview. During "Hasa Diga"—when Mafala first says, It means "fuck you, God"—the Ugandan ensemble is upstage with our backs to the audience, so that the audience focuses on him saying the line and the boys' reaction. During that first preview, I was standing upstage with the others.

In rehearsal, we would vamp for a moment. But that night, we're vamping and vamping and vamping, 'cause the audience had this outrageous, visceral reaction. They were laughing, they were shocked, they were talking to their friends audibly. We had to just hold and wait; we ended up building a vamp into the show because it still gets a huge, huge laugh. I'd never heard a laugh like that in all my years in musical comedy. It literally stops the show cold while the audience sort of collects itself, and then we can move on. And that for me was the moment when I knew, *This is going to be something special!*

At the end of that performance, everyone in the audience was on their feet. This wasn't like a few people stood so the people behind them had to stand so they could see. This was like the entire audience lifted up. They were moved. They were shocked. They cried, they laughed, it was really awesome. And that's when I started telling people, *You should buy tickets now if you want to see the show, 'cause I have a feeling.* ◆

> **THEY WERE MOVED. THEY WERE SHOCKED. THEY CRIED, THEY LAUGHED, IT WAS REALLY AWESOME. AND THAT'S WHEN I STARTED TELLING PEOPLE, YOU SHOULD BUY TICKETS NOW IF YOU WANT TO SEE THE SHOW, 'CAUSE I HAVE A FEELING.**
> —NIKKI M. JAMES

PLAYBILL
EUGENE O'NEILL THEATRE

THE BOOK OF MORMON

ACT 2 OPENING

"I AM JESUS. I'VE JUST BEEN CRUCIFIED ON THE OTHER SIDE OF THE WORLD, YOU GUYS."

BRIAN MACDEVITT: I INTRODUCED THIS PRODUCT THAT WE USE IN THE SCENERY ELEMENTS WHICH IS A REALLY THIN L.E.D. TAPE, AND WHEN WE FIRST PUT IT IN, IT LOOKED GREAT, BUT WE ALL ASSUMED THAT WE WERE GOING TO COVER IT BECAUSE IT KIND OF LOOKS LIKE ROPE LIGHT. IT LOOKS A LITTLE CHEESY. BUT THERE WAS A KIND OF EMBRACE OF THE THEATRICALITY OF IT. THERE'S A FINE LINE BETWEEN CLEVER AND KITSCH—A FINE LINE BETWEEN TASTELESS AND KNOWING. IT'S NEVER CAMP. EVER. AND I THINK ONE OF THE THINGS THAT MAKES THIS SHOW WORK IS THAT EVERYBODY PLAYS IT FOR KEEPS. WE REALLY WANT TO DELIVER A FIRST-CLASS, SERIOUS BROADWAY SHOW. IT'S CLEAR IN THE ACTING. THERE IS NOT ONE PERSON ON STAGE OR OFF WHO IS WINKING AT THE AUDIENCE, AND THAT'S WHAT THE DESIGN DOES TOO. WE MEAN IT, AND WE MEAN IT INSIDE OF A HOMEMADE, HANDCRAFTED AESTHETIC.

ANN ROTH: MY FIRST DRAWING OF JESUS DIDN'T TAKE VERY LONG. JESUS ALWAYS LOOKED LIKE CHERYL TIEGS TO ME, AND WHEN I HAD MY FIRST WIG DISCUSSIONS, I FOUND PHOTOGRAPHS OF CHERYL TIEGS SO THAT THE BRILLIANT JOSH MARQUETTE COULD STRIVE TO DO EXACTLY THAT. THANK GOD. I PUT LIGHTS UNDER JESUS INSIDE THE COSTUME BECAUSE I WANTED A GLOW ON HIM.

TREY PARKER: WE WENT TO PALMYRA, NEW YORK, ABOUT TWO YEARS AGO, BECAUSE THERE'S THIS BIG PAGEANT WHERE THEY BASICALLY PUT ON STORIES FROM THE BOOK OF MORMON, AND MORMONS FROM ALL OVER THE COUNTRY COME, AND IF THEY'RE DRESSED IN THE RIGHT COSTUME, THEY CAN BE PART OF THE CAST. IT'S THIS BIG, CRAZY THING I KEPT HEARING ABOUT. FINALLY TWO YEARS AGO, MATT AND BOBBY AND I ARE LIKE, OKAY, WE GOTTA GO. AND SO WE WENT, AND WE VISITED THE LITTLE CABIN THAT JOSEPH SMITH GREW UP IN. WE VISITED THE PRINTING PRESS THAT FIRST PRINTED THE BOOK OF MORMON, AND WE WENT TO THE PAGEANT, AND WE'RE LIKE, WOW, OKAY. WE GOTTA MAKE OUR MUSICAL BETTER THAN THIS ONE, AND THEY'VE BEEN WORKING ON THAT ONE A LONG TIME. BUT IT WAS THERE THAT WE GOT THE IDEA THAT WE SHOULD BOOKEND OUR MUSICAL WITH THE STORY OF MORMON AND THE HISTORY OF JOSEPH SMITH, AND DO OUR OWN MINIATURE VERSION OF THE HILL CUMORAH PAGEANT, WHICH IS HOW BOTH ACTS OPEN. AFTER YEARS OF WRITING, IT FINALLY TOOK ITS PROPER PLACE IN THE SHOW, AND NOW WHEN I WATCH IT I CAN'T EVEN IMAGINE THE SHOW WITHOUT IT.

ELDER CUNNINGHAM
Wait, no, I didn't lie...
I JUST USED MY IMAGINATION.
And it worked!

Cunningham's dad appears in Cunningham's imagination.

CUNNINGHAM'S DAD
YOU'RE MAKING THINGS UP AGAIN, ARNOLD.

ELDER CUNNINGHAM
Yeah, but it worked, Dad!

CUNNINGHAM'S DAD
YOU'RE STRETCHING THE TRUTH AGAIN, AND YOU KNOW IT.

Joseph Smith appears on another side of the stage.

JOSEPH SMITH
DON'T BE A FIBBING FRAN, ARNOLD.

ELDER CUNNINGHAM
Joseph Smith?

JOSEPH SMITH & DAD
BECAUSE A LIE IS A LIE.

> **YOU'RE MAKING THINGS UP, ARNOLD**

> "I'VE ALWAYS LOVED THE WHOLE NOTION OF MUSICALS. I REMEMBER SEEING *LES MIS* WHEN I WAS VERY YOUNG, AND BEING VERY IMPRESSIONABLE, AND WAS, LIKE, A FAT, LITTLE THIRD GRADER WHO WAS LIKE, I WANNA SING TOO, AND BE BRITISH, AND BE AT WAR WITH THE FRENCH. DOING THIS SHOW MAKES ME FEEL LIKE I GOT TO DO THAT."
> — JOSH GAD

HAVE YOU HEARD?
A baby cannot cure your illness, Joseph Smith—I shall give unto you...a frog...and thus Joseph laid with the frog and his AIDS was no more!"

BOBBY LOPEZ: IT WAS FUNNY, WE HAD JUST SEEN *SUNDAY IN THE PARK WITH GEORGE* IN LONDON DURING THE TIME THAT WE WERE WRITING THERE, AND I THINK TREY WAS SORT OF INFLUENCED BY IT—WHICH IS WEIRD BECAUSE I CONSIDER MYSELF THE SONDHEIM FREAK OUT OF EVERYONE. AND TREY JUST SAT DOWN AND STARTED PLUNKING OUT THIS GEORGES SEURAT RHYTHM, WHICH BECAME THE WHOLE MOTIF. I WAS LIKE, GREAT! WE GET TO WRITE A SONDHEIM SONG! I REMEMBER BEING IN THE STUDIO IN NEW YORK AND FINISHING THE NUMBER. I WAS SO EXCITED WHEN WE WROTE THOSE VOCALS OF THE MORMONS SINGING 'YOU'RE MAKING THINGS UP AGAIN' AND THE UGANDANS SINGING 'ELDER CUNNINGHAM, HOLY PROPHET MAN.' I LIKED THAT MOMENT. IT WAS A HUGE MOMENT OF HEART.

TREY PARKER: I ALWAYS WRITE SONGS BY SINGING—ALWAYS, EVER SINCE I WAS A KID WRITING SONGS, I WOULD JUST START SINGING SOMETHING, SINGING AS THE CHARACTER I'M TRYING TO WRITE. AND IT'S SORT OF THE SAME WAY THAT THE CHARACTERS' VOICES IN 'SOUTH PARK' COME INTO MY HEAD. OR LIKE, JOKES COME INTO MY HEAD. I'VE ALWAYS KNOWN THAT WHEN A MELODY OR A FUNNY IDEA FOR A SONG COMES INTO MY HEAD AND I JUST START SINGING IT—IT'S HOW I START TO ENVISION A CHARACTER—BY EXPERIENCING HOW THEY WOULD SING.

SPOOKY MORMON HELL DREAM

"DOWN DOWN TO SATAN'S REALM, SEE WHERE YOU BELONG!"

BOBBY LOPEZ: I LOVED IT WHEN WE FIGURED OUT PRICE'S INTRO TO THE SONG—WHERE HE RECOUNTS THE STORY OF, YOU KNOW, BEING FIVE AND EATING A DONUT AND BLAMING HIS BROTHER, WHICH IS WHAT HAPPENED TO ME WHEN I WAS FIVE. AND NOW MY DONUT INCIDENT IS IN OUR MUSICAL.

CASEY NICHOLAW: TREY WANTED THAT SORT OF TOP-HAT-AND-CANE IDEA AT THE END, TO MAKE THAT OUR BIG BROADWAY MOMENT, BUT WITH GENGHIS KHAN AND WITH JEFFREY DAHMER AND WITH, YOU KNOW, JOHNNIE COCHRAN. AND WE HAD TO WORK THOSE PEOPLE INTO A BROADWAY MUSICAL!

TREY PARKER: IN EARLIER VERSIONS WE HAD PRICE DYING AND GETTING SHOT IN THE FACE, AND THEN I REMEMBER SCOTT RUDIN WAS JUST LIKE, NO, HE'S GOT TO COME BACK. AND WE'RE LIKE, WELL, HOW'S HE GOING TO COME BACK? HE'S DEAD. HE WAS JUST SHOT IN THE FACE. AND SCOTT'S LIKE, I DON'T KNOW HOW HE'S COMING BACK, BUT HE'S COMING BACK. AND I WAS LIKE, HE'S IN HELL NOW. HE'S GOING TO FIGHT HIS WAY BACK FROM HELL.

ANN ROTH: THE DEVILS, THE LITTLE DEVILS, WERE A WEIRD SHAPE IN COSTUME. THEY ARE NOT YOUR NORMAL DANCER'S FITTED COSTUME. I HAD WANTED THEM TO LOOK LIKE LOST BOYS, OR BAD BOYS—REALLY BAD BOYS—AND SO I MADE THEM VERY WEIRD, WITH LONGER ARMS, AND FEET THAT CURLED UPWARDS. AT THE SAME TIME, THE ACTORS HAD TO GET OUT OF THE DEVIL JAMMIES AND INTO THEIR MORMON SHIRT, TIE, AND PANTS— WHICH WERE UNDERNEATH THE COSTUMES—IN LESS THAN 10 OR 15 SECONDS.

DID YOU BREAK RULE 72?

SCOTT PASK: IN HELL, WE REVEAL THIS PLACE THAT STILL HAS AS ITS REFERENCE THE WORLD THAT WE'VE BEEN LIVING WITH IN AFRICA— THE TATTERED DROP—BUT THERE'S ALSO THIS BUILT-IN PAINTING OF LAVA, AND EVEN SOME VAGUELY RENAISSANCE ARTWORK. THE WHOLE IDEA OF THAT KIND OF VORTEX IS THAT WE'RE ALMOST LOOKING AT IT FROM ANOTHER PERSPECTIVE, ALMOST FROM THE INSIDE OUT.

"IT'S A SONG ABOUT GUILT AND ABOUT, YOU BETTER BEHAVE OR ELSE SOME BAD SHIT'S GOING TO HAPPEN TO YOU. WHICH IS THE CORNERSTONE OF A LOT OF RELIGIONS. **ALL RELIGION, ACTUALLY…**"

—MATT STONE

CASEY'S TALE

CASEY NICHOLAW: I started as a kid in the San Diego Junior Theatre, which was a program for people eight to eighteen, and fell in love with it. I did *The Robber Bridegroom* at the Old Globe—I played Goat—when I was fifteen years old. That was basically my start, and what really got me excited about theater. I went to UCLA for a year, but I'd saved up all my money to go to New York on spring break.

I flew to New York. I thought, *I'm going to go audition for some things just to do it. This is totally cool.* So I auditioned for summer stock, I had no picture or résumé or anything. I just did it and got a job at New London Barn Playhouse for the summer, and fell in love with that, fell in love with all my new New York friends. Basically left school and moved to New York at nineteen, with fifty dollars and nowhere to live, and just stayed with friends.

I waited lots of tables, did lots of non-Equity theater, and then got my Equity card at Beef & Boards Dinner Theatre in Indianapolis. Painted the prop barn, stage managed, and just started working. First Broadway show as a performer was *Crazy for You*, and then I did seven more: *Best Little Whorehouse Goes Public*, *Victor/Victoria*, *Steel Pier*, *Scarlet Pimpernel*, *Seussical*, *Saturday Night Fever*, and *Thoroughly Modern Millie*. But I always choreographed, like at the New London Barn.

One of the choreographers quit because he couldn't take it, and so I jumped in and choreographed. I always knew I wanted to do that, but I sort of put it on the back burner until I could work as a performer in New York.

While I was acting, I had the joy of being able to watch these original musicals being made. I just sat by, at shows like *Seussical*, and learned and watched. I was that person who would think, *Well, maybe I would do it this way.* I was always looking to see what I would do if I was in that situation. I finally thought, *I don't want to hear myself do that anymore, so why don't I go do something?*

So I rented studio space Wednesdays and Saturdays between shows, and said, *I'm just going to be creative.* I didn't know what I was going to do. The first few weeks, it was me just sitting there, eating dinner, saying, *What am I doing here, this is stupid.* I spent all the money I had to rent studio space. But I ended up choreographing three pieces. I got twenty-five dancer friends together, and I basically invited every writer, director and producer that I'd worked with. They all came, and I got a job choreographing a show at the Fifth Avenue Theater in Seattle, *The Prince and the Pauper*. It was an original musical. Kevin McCollum co-produced it, he was the artistic director then, and that was that.

Then I went and did *Thoroughly Modern Millie*, and I did DanceBreak after that. The SDC—Stage Directors and Choreographers—has a program, they pay for six up-and-coming choreographers to showcase their work. So I did that, and most of the people that came to see my own presentation came to see that, too, and that sort of solidified it for them.

Des McAnuff, whom I'd never met, hired me to do the Sinatra show at Radio City, where I choreographed six numbers for the Rockettes. That was such a thrill, and so exciting, and that was basically how it started. I did some stuff for *Encores!,* including *Bye Bye Birdie* because Kathleen Marshall dropped out to do *The Music Man* on TV.

After *Bye Bye Birdie,* out of the blue I get a phone call from a general manager who says, *I have a meeting for you with Mike Nichols. He would like to talk to you about doing this new musical,* Spamalot. Completely out of the blue. So I go up to Mike's place, and I meet Diane Sawyer, and I say hi to everybody. I had my reel for my presentation, my résumé and stuff. Mike and I talked for like an hour, and then he said, *Well, you want the job?*

He hadn't seen any of my work! I cried the whole way in the cab back to my apartment. It was great, and that's kind of how it happened. He got my name from Jerry Mitchell, who was too busy to do it, and Jerry recommended me.

So I'm forever grateful to him for the generosity, because that's kind of what it's about, you know?

In July 2010, I was in San Diego doing *Robin and the 7 Hoods*, and I get another call out of the blue. Basically they said, *We'd like you to direct and choreograph* The Book of Mormon, *a six-week workshop starts in three weeks.* I was like, *What?* So I drove up to L.A. on my next day off to meet Matt and Trey and Anne Garefino. They said, *Great, we want you to do this.* So I was able to bring fresh eyes to the whole thing. I had them fly Glen Kelly, my dance arranger, to the Old Globe. We did our preproduction for the workshop in the mornings, *Robin* opened Saturday night, and we began the workshop Monday morning in New York.

Matt and Trey were like, *Hey, we don't know what this is*, but their comedy sense is so strong that it's theatrical. That's what makes it work. Maybe they didn't understand some of the logistics of Broadway—this was the first time either of them tried anything on the stage—but they really *got* theater, I could instantly see that they understood it. Everybody—Trey, Matt, Bobby, and me—worked seamlessly together. The whole experience was great, it really was a fantastic marriage. ♦

> **THE WHOLE EXPERIENCE WAS GREAT, IT REALLY WAS A FANTASTIC MARRIAGE.**

Casey's Script

"I HAVE A JOB TO DO AND A JOB I'M REALLY EXCITED ABOUT."
CASEY NICHOLAW

I BELIEVE

"THAT PLAN INVOLVES ME GETTING MY OWN PLANET."

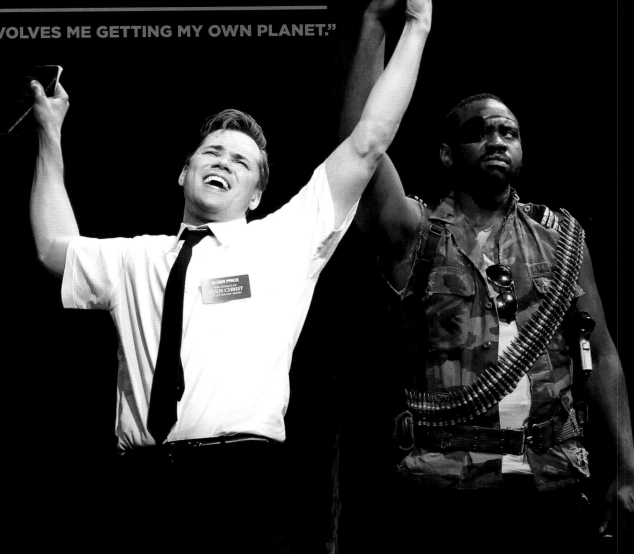

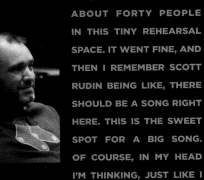

TREY PARKER: I REMEMBER EXACTLY WHEN AND HOW WE WROTE 'I BELIEVE.' WE WERE IN THE MIDDLE OF THE WORKSHOP PROCESS. WE DID A PERFORMANCE, A WORKSHOP, FOR ABOUT FORTY PEOPLE IN THIS TINY REHEARSAL SPACE. IT WENT FINE, AND THEN I REMEMBER SCOTT RUDIN BEING LIKE, THERE SHOULD BE A SONG RIGHT HERE. THIS IS THE SWEET SPOT FOR A BIG SONG. OF COURSE, IN MY HEAD I'M THINKING, JUST LIKE I ALWAYS AM, I DON'T WANT TO WRITE A SONG. I DON'T WANT TO WORK. THAT'S ALWAYS HOW IT IS WITH ANY-THING, LIKE, NO, I DON'T WANT TO GO WRITE ANOTHER SONG. AND RUDIN SAID, JUST GO TO THE STUDIO. WE GOT YOU A STUDIO ACROSS THE STREET. GO AND WRITE A SONG RIGHT HERE. PRICE NEEDS A SONG HERE. I REMEMBER GOING OVER TO THE STUDIO, KIND OF GRUMPILY, AND SITTING THERE, PISSED OFF, SAYING, I DON'T EVEN KNOW WHY HE'D SING A SONG HERE. AND EVEN IF HE DID IT COULD ONLY BE SOMETHING LIKE, YOU KNOW, AN AFFIRMATION OF WHAT HE BELIEVES IN. AND WITHIN 45 MINUTES BOBBY AND I HAD THE BEGINNING OF 'I BELIEVE.' IT WAS JUST ONE OF THOSE THINGS WHERE WE WERE LIKE, OKAY, THAT WAS PRETTY SWEET.

BOBBY LOPEZ: I'M MOST PROUD OF 'I BELIEVE' BECAUSE THERE ARE LITERALLY NO JOKES IN THAT SONG; IT'S JUST FACTS. IT'S JUST FUNNY WAYS TO DESCRIBE MORMON THINGS THAT THEY BELIEVE IN. IT'S ALL DIRECTLY FROM THE BOOK OF MORMON.

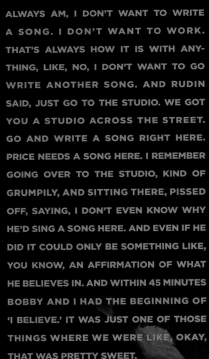

"I JUST FEEL LIKE THAT'S THE LITTLE ISLAND WE WANTED TO LAND ON, IN THE MIDDLE OF THESE TWO GIANT, EXTREMIST LAND MASSES."

— MATT STONE

I BELIEVE!
THAT IN 1978 GOD CHANGED HIS MIND ABOUT **BLACK PEOPLE!**

> **THE MORMON FRIENDS THAT I'VE HAD COME SEE THE SHOW SAY THAT THEY FIND THEMSELVES LAUGHING AT 'I BELIEVE,' BUT ALSO SURPRISINGLY TOUCHED BY IT, THAT IT IS SORT OF AN ANTHEM OF MORMONISM, BUT HILARIOUS AND INSANE AND COMPLETELY TRUE AND AUTHENTIC AT THE SAME TIME. IT'S THE MORMON DOCTRINE.**

— ANDREW RANNELLS

> **I DON'T THINK MATT AND TREY BELIEVE IN A MESSAGE. THEY'RE JUST DOING WHAT'S FUNNY AND WHAT HITS THEM, AND—AND THEY'RE USING TRUTH TO DO IT. SO IT'S ALMOST LOOKING AT OUR OWN HUMAN FOIBLES AND OUR OWN EXTREMISM, OUR OWN RELIGIOUS FERVOR AND TAKING SOME AIR OUT OF THAT.**

— MICHAEL POTTS

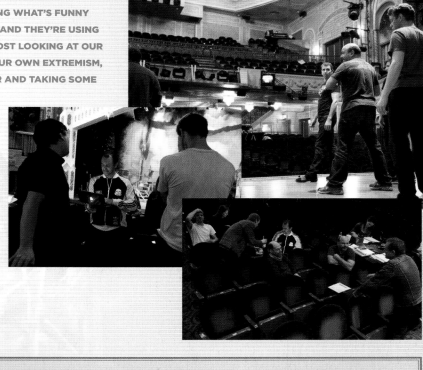

I'M DEFINITELY **OBSESSED** WITH MUSICALS

MATT STONE: I THINK THAT THERE'S A GROUP OF PEOPLE THAT ARE KIND OF IN THE MIDDLE OF THE TWO MOST EXTREME RELIGIOUS IDEOLOGIES, WHICH ARE RELIGIOUS FUNDAMENTALISTS WHO TAKE SCRIPTURE LITERALLY AND BELIEVE RELIGION HAS ALL THE ANSWERS, AND FUNDAMENTALIST ATHEISTS WHO JUST HATE RELIGION. ME AND BOBBY AND TREY ALWAYS FELT LIKE THERE WAS THIS MIDDLE THAT'S WHERE MOST OF US LIVE, MEANING THAT WE'RE EITHER LIGHTLY RELIGIOUS OR EVEN FAIRLY RELIGIOUS IN OUR PRIVATE LIVES, BUT IN OUR PUBLIC LIVES WE CAN BE SLIGHTLY ATHEISTIC. THERE'S A CATHARSIS IN BEING ABLE TO REALLY LAUGH AT SOME OF THE GOOFIER IDEAS OF RELIGION, WITHOUT NECESSARILY LAUGHING AT THE PEOPLE PRACTICING THEM. I THINK IT FEELS GOOD TO IN SOME WAYS ACKNOWLEDGE THAT CERTAIN ASPECTS OF RELIGION ARE JUST SILLY. BUT WHATEVER ANYBODY'S RELIGION IS, WE SHOULD BE ABLE TO LAUGH AT IT AND AT THE SAME TIME UNDERSTAND THAT WE SHOULD ACCEPT PEOPLE WHO BELIEVE AND HAVE FAITH, WITHOUT DISMISSING THEIR LIVES AS UNSERIOUS. I JUST FEEL LIKE THAT'S THE LITTLE ISLAND WE WANTED TO LAND ON, IN THE MIDDLE OF THESE TWO GIANT, EXTREMIST LAND MASSES. I THINK WE WERE SURPRISED TO FIND OUT THAT OUR LITTLE ISLAND WAS BIGGER THAN WE THOUGHT. THERE SEEM TO BE A LOT OF PEOPLE IN THE RADICAL MIDDLE. THAT WAS ALWAYS OUR INTENTION: WE NEVER WANTED THE MUSICAL TO PRETEND IT HAD ANY ANSWERS. WE WANTED TO BE FUNNY AND PUT ON GREAT NUMBERS AND GET SOME OF OUR IDEAS OUT THERE.

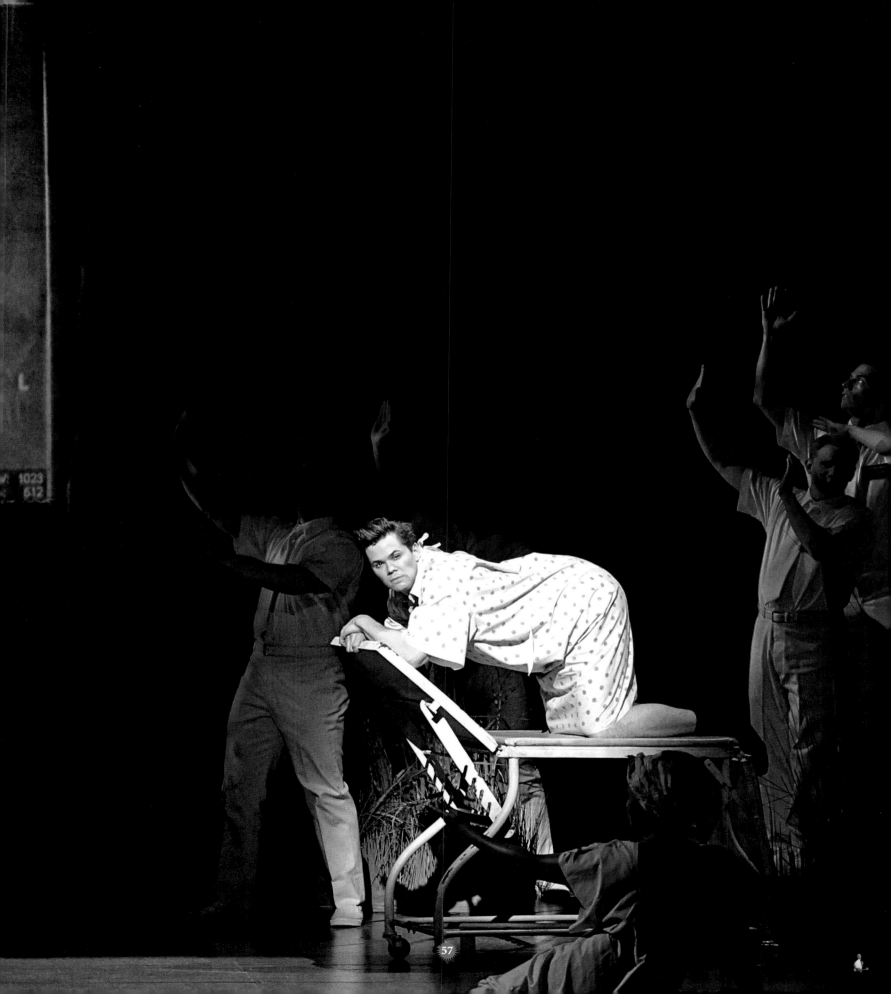

WORK IN DEVELOPMENT

BOBBY LOPEZ: We didn't know at the very beginning whether this was going to be an animated movie, or a live action movie, or a Broadway show. I was always pushing for it to be a stage piece because I thought that we've seen things like this in the movies. We've seen this level of hard-hittingness and language and all that stuff. But on Broadway people haven't really pushed the bounds of propriety quite so far, it's just a much more open field.

TREY PARKER: There's just nothing more perfect in the universe to me than a good musical. And a bad musical makes you want to kill yourself. But a good musical is to me so much more moving and powerful than a great movie or a great book, or anything.

BOBBY LOPEZ: We would sit and talk for a long time about what we wanted to write and come up with the big joke of it, little jokes that could be used along the way, and what needed to be accomplished by the characters in the story. And when we had enough brainstorming, we would go to our different spots. I would play something and say *What about this?*, and Trey would say *What about this?* He'd write some lyrics, Matt would, I would. Trey would go to the piano. I tend to be a little bit more tortured

in my process, and edit as I go. The fun thing for me was that they have a fun spirit of improvisation. Just let everything grow for a while. Follow the ideas. Chase the ideas down. Don't say *No, that's not right* before something has a chance to blossom. Chase down those ideas, don't stamp them out.

TREY PARKER: Even though we had to pick the project up and put it down because of *South Park*, we would always be able to sit someone down and play the CD of the four or five songs that we had. And they'd be like, *Oh, that's really cool,* and it would get us psyched again. And so then we'd go, *Oh, let's get together and write another song or two.*

BOBBY LOPEZ: We had a story and every time we'd meet, we'd talk through the story, and that would take a whole day. And when we thought we'd solved something, we'd make index cards and put them up on a bulletin board. By the next time we met, Trey would lose the index cards. So we'd be forced to talk it all through again and come up with a different solution. Usually, I think, the best ideas would stick in our heads. We'd be talking through a problem and say, *Wait, we solved this problem already, didn't we?*

JOSH GAD: The first time we did the show at the Vineyard, it ended with me singing "Man Up" by myself, no backup singers, nothing. And that was the end, black out. The second time we were told that we were going to be doing the second act, that they were starting to build this as a show. It was a two-week workshop and it was already the first weekend, and I said, *Will we be getting the second act anytime soon?* And they said, *Yeah, yeah, it'll be coming.* We started learning the songs, but there was no script. About two days before the invited audience, I go, *We will be getting the second act by the time that we read the second act, right?* They said, *Yeah, yeah, it's coming.* The morning of the performance, literally, we finally got the second act. And I was, like, *This is going to be a disaster, it gives us no time to fix anything that's problematic in the script.* Well, it turns out when you have Trey, Bobby and Matt writing the script, there isn't much that's problematic. After that point, I knew never to doubt these crazy bastards again because they're kind of like those kids who procrastinate studying for the test until the very last moment, and then do better than anybody else in the class. I think they figured out on *South Park* that they really work best under pressure. During previews they were at the peak of creative insanity. They would just come in with these ideas, like mad scientists throwing things out. You almost couldn't keep up with them sometimes, but you knew that they were always right.

TREY PARKER: When we finally found Andrew—and I knew immediately when he came in—it was like, *That's the guy.* And we started writing for him. It was just this Midwestern thing that I can't explain, he's from Nebraska. He's incredibly talented, great voice, really smart, but just kind of has that underlying little bit of cheesiness that could be Mormon.

Theater is different, because it is this living thing. You're surprised every night by something that didn't work the night before. You can't pinpoint why. You've got to be careful not to judge anything after one performance; if after eight it is not working, then cut it. ♦

IT'S TIME TO BE IMMERSED.

SCOTT PASK: I'D BRING THE RESEARCH TO TREY, MATT, AND CASEY AND SHOW THEM IMAGES I WAS DRAWN TO, BECAUSE THIS VILLAGE —WHERE THE UGANDANS LIVE—IT'S SO IMPORTANT. THE VILLAGERS ARE DEFENDING THEIR HOME AGAINST THE WARLORD, AND FAMINE, AND THE LACK OF WATER. THAT'S WHERE THE SOUL OF THE SHOW RESIDES—IT'S WHERE EVERYTHING REAL IS AT STAKE, AND THERE'S A MORAL OBLIGATION TO BE ACCURATE ABOUT IT. TO GET IT RIGHT.

HE WILL BAPTIZE ME!
HE'LL HOLD ME IN HIS ARMS
AND HE WILL BAPTIZE ME
RIGHT IN FRONT OF EVERYONE
AND IT WILL SET ME FREE.

> **"**I THINK THAT MY FAVORITE ELEMENT ISN'T THE COMEDY, 'CAUSE THE COMEDY I KNEW WOULD BE THERE, AND IT IS. IT'S ACTUALLY THE GENUINE EMOTION THAT THE SHOW HAS. IT'S THE FACT THAT YOU GO ON A JOURNEY, AND EVERY NIGHT IN THAT THEATER YOU HEAR SNIFFLES. 'BAPTIZE ME' IS A RIFF ON THAT LOSING YOUR VIRGINITY MOMENT, BUT IT SO QUICKLY TRANSCENDS THE JOKE—HOW COULD YOU NOT FALL IN LOVE WITH NIKKI IN THAT SCENE? I DO, EVERY NIGHT. I NEVER EXPECTED THAT. I NEVER IMAGINED THAT WE WOULD HAVE A SHOW THAT'S AS MOVING AS IT IS FUNNY. AND THAT TO ME IS THE MOST REWARDING PART OF IT. I GET UP THERE EVERY NIGHT JUST TO FEEL THAT, AND TO LOVE IT.**"** —JOSH GAD

LARRY HOCHMAN: I THINK I OFTEN SEE A BROADWAY SCORE PHRASE BY PHRASE, MOMENT BY MOMENT, AS ME TRYING TO PICTURE MYSELF AS THE CHARACTER. I TRY TO FOLLOW THE STORY, AND BE INSIDE THE STORY. AND SO YOU KNOW ON A NUMBER LIKE 'BAPTIZE ME,' I'M FOLLOWING WHAT HAPPENS IN THE SECOND VERSE, SO IT'S NOT JUST A REPEAT OF THE FIRST VERSE WITH A COUPLE MORE INSTRUMENTS. IT HAS TO DEVELOP THE WAY THE EVENTS DEVELOP. ARNOLD IS STILL BEING SHY BUT WE REALIZE WHAT NABULUNGI IS FEELING FOR HIM IN THAT MOMENT, AND YOU KNOW THERE ARE A LOT OF RELATIONSHIP DYNAMICS HAPPENING. THERE IS SUBTEXT GOING ON. FOR ME, THERE HAS TO BE A THROUGH-LINE. I HAVE TO FEEL I AM TELLING THE STORY, AND I HAVE TO FEEL MYSELF IN IT.

TREY PARKER: 'BAPTIZE ME' WAS ONE OF THOSE THINGS WHERE WE HAD ALREADY DONE WORKSHOPS, WE'D ALREADY BEEN LIVING WITH THE IDEA FOR A LONG TIME. AND THEN WE SAID, 'OH, WELL, MAYBE HE SHOULD BAPTIZE HER. AND IMMEDIATELY IT WAS ONE OF THOSE IDEAS THAT'S LIKE, WHY DIDN'T WE THINK OF THAT BEFORE? IT WAS LIKE, OH, OF COURSE. WHICH IS A NICE FEELING, BUT IT ALSO MAKES YOU FEEL KIND OF STUPID THAT YOU'VE BEEN HANGING OUT FOR FOUR YEARS NOT THINKING OF IT.

BAPTIZE ME

"I'M WET WITH SALVATION!"

I AM AFRICA

"I'M NOT A FOLLOWER ANYMORE. NO! NOW, I AM FRICKIN' AFRICA!"

MATT STONE: WE THOUGHT IF YOU COULD TELL THE STORY FROM INSIDE THEIR EXPERIENCE, THOSE CYNICAL LAUGHS COULD BE HARNESSED FOR A GREATER POWER. THE WHITEST GUYS SINGING ABOUT HOW THEY ARE AFRICA IS SO FUNNY TO ME, AND SO SWEET TOO. WE ALWAYS WANTED 'I AM AFRICA' TO BE THIS BIG, JOYOUS MOMENT RIGHT BEFORE THE SHIT HITS THE FAN. IT'S LIKE THE FANTASY OF BEING A MISSIONARY, WHERE YOU SOMEHOW THINK YOU HAVE BECOME THE PEOPLE THAT YOU'RE HELPING, AND THAT'S THE APEX OF SHOWING YOU CARE.

BOBBY LOPEZ: WE HAD THIS IDEA TO DO A SONG ABOUT WHITE PRESUMPTION AND AMERICAN IMPERIALISM, AND THE BELIEF AMONG WHITE PEOPLE THAT THEY HAVE ALL THE ANSWERS TO EVERYBODY'S PROBLEMS. SO WE DID OUR VERSION OF 'WE ARE THE WORLD' AND ALL THOSE SONGS THAT BASICALLY SAY, WE'RE BETTER THAN YOU AND SMARTER THAN YOU, SO WHY DON'T YOU LET US SAVE YOU? BUT YOU LOVE THE BOYS FOR THE EARNEST INNOCENCE OF WHAT IT MEANS TO THEM.

TREY PARKER: I'VE BEEN DREAMING ABOUT MUSICALS FOREVER. AND THEN ONCE WE WERE IN COLLEGE AND WE WERE LIKE, LET'S MAKE A MOVIE, I WAS LIKE, OKAY. I WANNA MAKE IT A MUSICAL, AND SO WE WROTE SONGS FOR THAT. AND THEN THE 'SOUTH PARK' MOVIE CAME, AND I WAS LIKE, OKAY, I WANNA MAKE A MUSICAL. I WANNA MAKE A 'SOUTH PARK' MUSICAL, AND SO WE WROTE SONGS FOR THAT. I WAS SO HAPPY DOING IT. SO WE'VE ALWAYS BEEN TRYING TO DO THIS, FOR SUCH A LONG TIME. IT'S A LONG PROCESS. BUT IT'S BEEN MORE REWARDING THAN ANYTHING WE'VE EVER DONE.

BRIAN MACDEVITT: WE ALL HAD THE IDEA THAT AFRICA—THE SET AND THE LIGHTING—SHOULD LOOK LIKE YOU COULD GET TETANUS FROM IT IF YOU BUMPED INTO ANYTHING ON THAT STAGE. BUT THERE IS A TRANSITION IN HOW WE PORTRAY AFRICA AS WE MOVE THROUGH THE SHOW. WE GO FROM OVERCAST AND DESTITUTE TO SUNLIGHT, TO JOY, AND DISNEY, AND MORMONS. THAT IDEA PEAKS IN 'I AM AFRICA,' WHERE WE SEE UGANDA AS THIS PLACE THAT'S ACTUALLY RICH AND BEAUTIFUL AND ROMANTIC AND REALLY POWERFUL.

{ WE ARE THE WINDS OF THE **SERENGETI,**
WE ARE THE SWEAT OF THE JUNGLE MAN.

"THE LIGHTING IS JUST SORCERY. IT'S MORE THAN JUST KEEPING US LIT. I DON'T KNOW HOW BRIAN DOES IT. BECAUSE SET DESIGNERS, THEY HAVE HISTORICAL DATA THEY CAN LOOK AT. THEY CAN GO TO THE MUSEUM, THEY CAN TAKE OUT BOOKS ON ARCHITECTURE. SO THEY HAVE REFERENCES. BUT LIGHTING, I MEAN, DO YOU GO TO UGANDA AND LOOK AT THE SKY AND THEN DECIDE WHAT GEL WILL GIVE YOU THE UGANDAN SKY AT THIS TIME OF DAY?"

—MICHAEL POTTS

HAVE YOU HEARD?

"The Prophet Joseph Smith died for what he believed in. But his followers, they kept heading west. And Brigham Young led them to Paradise. A sparkling land in Utah they named Salt Lake City."

{ **JUST LIKE** BONO!
I AM AFRICA!

MATT STONE: THE ENTIRE SHOW WAS KIND OF BUILT AROUND THE MOMENT WHERE ELDER PRICE FINALLY EXPERIENCES THE RELIGIOUS EPIPHANY HE'S BEEN WAITING FOR, AND IT HAPPENS IN THE MOST UNEXPECTED OF PLACES, WHICH IS BASICALLY A BLASPHEMOUS SEND-UP OF HIS OWN RELIGION. THE IDEA, WHICH WE REALLY BELIEVED IN, IS THAT ONE MAN'S BLASPHEMY IS ANOTHER MAN'S SCRIPTURE. PRICE KNEW WHAT THE BOOK OF MORMON STORIES WERE ABOUT LITERALLY, BUT CUNNINGHAM, IN HIS RIDICULOUS, GOOD-HEARTED WAY, REALLY KNEW WHAT THE BOOK OF MORMON ACTUALLY MEANT, WHICH ENDS UP BEING SO MUCH MORE IMPORTANT THAN WHAT IT SAYS.

TREY PARKER: WE ALWAYS THOUGHT, IT WOULD BE SO AWESOME TO DO OUR VERSION OF 'UNCLE TOM'S CABIN' FROM, YOU KNOW, *THE KING AND I*. AND SO WE TALKED ABOUT THAT A BUNCH AND THEN WE JUST DID THIS IMPROV WHERE WE PUT ON AFRICAN DRUM LOOPS AND JUST STARTED SINGING THESE AFRICAN MELODIES, WITH ME PLAYING ALL THE AFRICAN PARTS, AND WE HAD SUCH A GREAT TIME DOING IT. IT WAS RIDICULOUS. AND THEN I REMEMBER THAT WE SAID, OH, WE SHOULD MAKE THIS A BIGGER NUMBER. THIS CAN HANDLE BEING A BIGGER NUMBER. WE FINALLY, YEARS LATER, WE WENT BACK AND ACTUALLY WATCHED THE 'UNCLE TOM'S CABIN' SEQUENCE FROM *THE KING AND I* AND WERE LIKE, WOW, THIS IS REALLY LONG. BUT WE SAW HOW IT TOLD SUCH A HUGE STORY, HOW IT HELD A WHOLE NARRATIVE, AND THAT FIRST PASS WE HAD DONE WAS REALLY JUST KIND OF, NO, DON'T FUCK THE BABY. ALL THE MOST PROFANE STUFF, THE CLIT FACE, AND ALL THAT STUFF. BUT IT DIDN'T HAVE THEIR WHOLE STORY OF JOSEPH SMITH GETTING THE GOLD PLATES, AND THEN TRYING TO LEAD THE PEOPLE TO SALT LAKE CITY, AND THEN GETTING KILLED, AND BRIGHAM YOUNG TAKING THEM THE REST OF THE WAY. PLUS THE EMOTION, THE SUFFERING IN ALL OF THOSE EVENTS—NONE OF THAT WAS THERE AND SO WE WERE LIKE, LET'S FOLLOW THE TROPE IN *THE KING AND I*, AND REALLY TELL THIS STORY THAT MAKES CLEAR THAT IT HAD A MUCH DEEPER AND MORE PROFOUND MEANING TO THEM.

JOSEPH SMITH AMERICAN MOSES

"HIS NOSE WAS A CLITORIS"

ANN ROTH: I FOUND IN MY RESEARCH THAT JOSEPH SMITH WAS THIS HANDSOME, BLOND, SIX-FOOT GUY IN A DARK-BLUE JACKET AND TAN BRITCHES. WE WANTED, IN THE AFRICAN PAGEANT, FOR THE UGANDANS TO REPRESENT HIM NAIVELY AND CHARMINGLY— SO I HAD THEM MAKE A BLONDE WIG OUT OF LEAVES AND TWIGS AND BLONDE FEATHERS AND STRAW. THE JOSEPH SMITH JACKET WAS, I PRETENDED, FROM AN EASTERN AIRLINES PILOT WHO HAD CRASHED, AND THE UGANDANS TOOK HIS JACKET AND LEFT HIM WHEREVER HE WAS, AND THAT BECAME THE JACKET THAT AFRICAN JOSEPH SMITH WOULD WEAR. I SAW THAT IN RESEARCH: DEAD PEOPLE'S CLOTHES, SOMETIMES DEAD BY WAY OF BULLETS.

BOBBY LOPEZ: THAT WAS A GREAT MOMENT, WHEN WE REALIZED WE COULD SAY LIBERATION, ABOUT THE MORMONS, AND IT WOULD FEEL LIKE A VICTORY FOR THE AFRICANS, LIKE AN ACTUAL VICTORY. I WAS SO MOVED BY THAT. LIBERATION: I LOVED CONNECTING THOSE DOTS.

TREY PARKER: THEN WHEN WE DID THAT 'LIBERATION, EQUALITY,' THAT'S WHEN I THINK WE REALIZED, OKAY, THERE'S ANOTHER BIG IDEA FOR THE SONG. THIS IS THE HEART OF WHAT WE'RE WRITING ABOUT. THIS IS REAL.

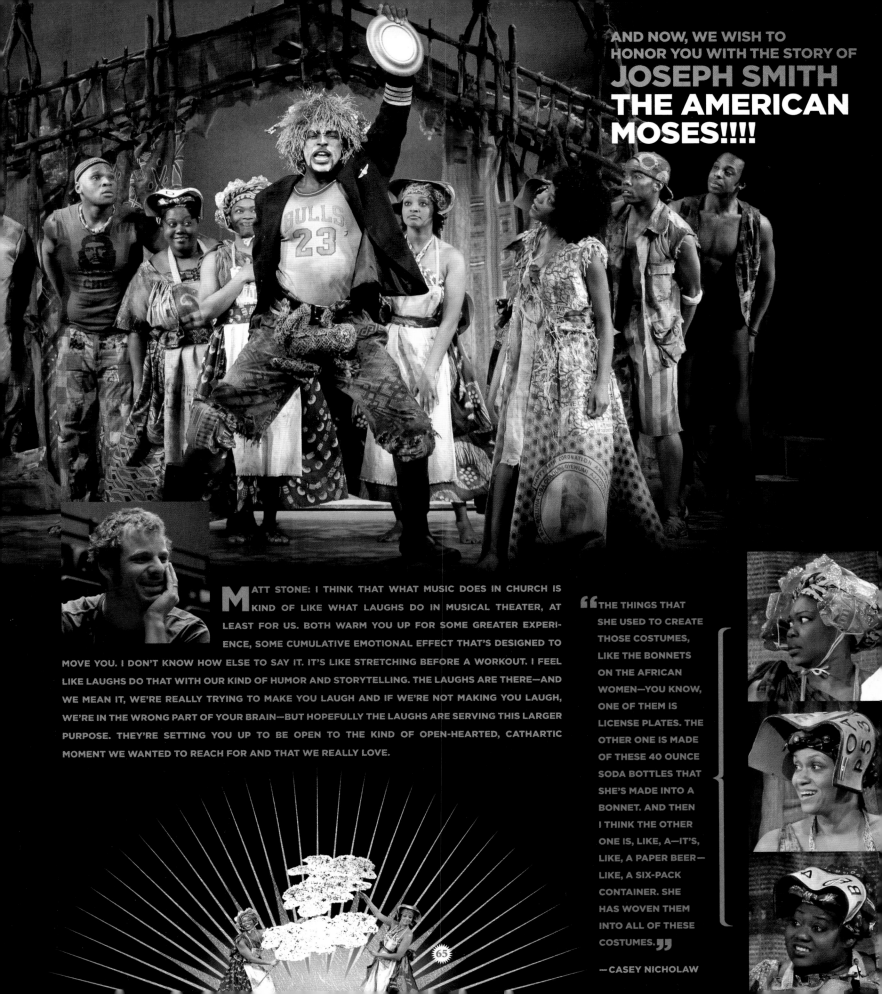

AND NOW, WE WISH TO HONOR YOU WITH THE STORY OF **JOSEPH SMITH THE AMERICAN MOSES!!!!**

MATT STONE: I THINK THAT WHAT MUSIC DOES IN CHURCH IS KIND OF LIKE WHAT LAUGHS DO IN MUSICAL THEATER, AT LEAST FOR US. BOTH WARM YOU UP FOR SOME GREATER EXPERIENCE, SOME CUMULATIVE EMOTIONAL EFFECT THAT'S DESIGNED TO MOVE YOU. I DON'T KNOW HOW ELSE TO SAY IT. IT'S LIKE STRETCHING BEFORE A WORKOUT. I FEEL LIKE LAUGHS DO THAT WITH OUR KIND OF HUMOR AND STORYTELLING. THE LAUGHS ARE THERE—AND WE MEAN IT, WE'RE REALLY TRYING TO MAKE YOU LAUGH AND IF WE'RE NOT MAKING YOU LAUGH, WE'RE IN THE WRONG PART OF YOUR BRAIN—BUT HOPEFULLY THE LAUGHS ARE SERVING THIS LARGER PURPOSE. THEY'RE SETTING YOU UP TO BE OPEN TO THE KIND OF OPEN-HEARTED, CATHARTIC MOMENT WE WANTED TO REACH FOR AND THAT WE REALLY LOVE.

"THE THINGS THAT SHE USED TO CREATE THOSE COSTUMES, LIKE THE BONNETS ON THE AFRICAN WOMEN—YOU KNOW, ONE OF THEM IS LICENSE PLATES. THE OTHER ONE IS MADE OF THESE 40 OUNCE SODA BOTTLES THAT SHE'S MADE INTO A BONNET. AND THEN I THINK THE OTHER ONE IS, LIKE, A—IT'S, LIKE, A PAPER BEER—LIKE, A SIX-PACK CONTAINER. SHE HAS WOVEN THEM INTO ALL OF THESE COSTUMES."
— CASEY NICHOLAW

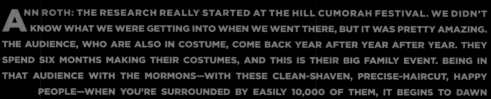

THE COSTUME DESIGN, I WOULD HOPE, IS CERTAINLY CONSCIOUS OF WHAT THE SHOW IS SAYING ABOUT THE WORLD.

ANN ROTH: THE RESEARCH REALLY STARTED AT THE HILL CUMORAH FESTIVAL. WE DIDN'T KNOW WHAT WE WERE GETTING INTO WHEN WE WENT THERE, BUT IT WAS PRETTY AMAZING. THE AUDIENCE, WHO ARE ALSO IN COSTUME, COME BACK YEAR AFTER YEAR AFTER YEAR. THEY SPEND SIX MONTHS MAKING THEIR COSTUMES, AND THIS IS THEIR BIG FAMILY EVENT. BEING IN THAT AUDIENCE WITH THE MORMONS—WITH THESE CLEAN-SHAVEN, PRECISE-HAIRCUT, HAPPY PEOPLE—WHEN YOU'RE SURROUNDED BY EASILY 10,000 OF THEM, IT BEGINS TO DAWN ON YOU. I'M NOT JUST DOING A BROADWAY SHOW. THIS IS SOMETHING ELSE.

WHEN I WORKED IN AFRICA, THE THING THAT STRUCK ME WAS THE UBIQUITY OF CERTAIN THINGS, LIKE THIS ONE WHITE PLASTIC CHAIR—THAT SAME WHITE PLASTIC LAWN CHAIR THAT YOU SEE EVERYWHERE IN THE WORLD. WHEN I SAW THAT CHAIR IN AFRICA, I THOUGHT, GOD, THAT THING REALLY IS EVERYWHERE. I WANTED THAT FEELING FOR THESE PEOPLE. IN OBSCURE PLACES—SUDDENLY YOU SEE A MICHAEL JORDAN BASKETBALL SHIRT—BECAUSE HE WAS A GREAT HERO TO EVERYONE EVERYWHERE. THERE'S A CONNECTEDNESS.

IT WAS ACTUALLY A FUN JOB. I DON'T THINK I'VE EVER SAID THAT IN MY LIFE—A FUN JOB. WELL, IT WAS. THE SHOW WAS JUST THAT GOOD.

MATT STONE: ANN ROTH WAS JUST ABOUT THE BEST THING TO HAPPEN TO THIS SHOW. SHE'S BEEN CREATING ICONIC COSTUMES FOR FIFTY YEARS. WE LEARNED SO MUCH ABOUT THINKING FOR THE STAGE FROM HER. THE MORMON COSTUMES SEEM SIMPLE, BUT THAT'S THE POINT—WHAT ANN DID WITH THEM IMMEDIATELY BECAME THIS BASELINE STYLE IDEA FOR THE SHOW. THAT'S OUR LOOK. AND THE AFRICANS—ANN BROUGHT THIS WHOLE BEAUTY AND MAJESTY AND SUCH WIT TO IT. AND THEN AS YOU WATCH THE MUSICAL, AND GET DEEPER INTO THE STORY, YOU START TO APPRECIATE THAT THESE AREN'T RAGS ON THE AFRICANS, THESE ARE THOROUGHLY CONCEIVED COSTUMES THAT HAVE A HUGE AMOUNT OF MEANING AND SPECIFICITY AND DETAIL. SHE LITERALLY HAS AN INDIVIDUAL STORY FOR EACH AND EVERY PIECE THAT THE AFRICANS WEAR. YOU KNOW, WHEREVER YOU ARE IN THE WORLD, YOU STILL WANT TO LOOK GOOD, AND YOU STILL WANT TO DO SOMETHING TO MAKE YOURSELF STAND OUT AND MAKE YOURSELF BEAUTIFUL NO MATTER WHAT MEANS YOU HAVE OR DON'T HAVE. THAT TOUCH IS IN THERE THROUGHOUT.

ANN ROTH: THIS IS NOT A BIG, NOISY MUSICAL—IT'S DIFFERENT. THERE'S A HOMEMADE ASPECT AT THE CENTER OF IT. YOU REALIZE THAT WHEN YOU GET TO THE AFRICAN PAGEANT; THE COSTUMES THE GIRLS ARE WEARING, THEIR ATTEMPT TO LOOK LIKE PIONEER WOMEN—THEY WANT BONNETS AND APRONS, THEY WANT TO LOOK LIKE THE PHOTOGRAPHS THEY SEE HANGING IN THE MORMON HEADQUARTERS' MISSION HALL IN UGANDA. THE JESUS IN THE PAGEANT, I LIKE HIM, WITH HIS HALO MADE OF A BABY-CARRIAGE WHEEL. THEY USE WHAT THEY HAVE. THE VILLAGERS HAVE MADE THEIR OWN PRIDEFUL STORY INSIDE OF A BROADWAY MUSICAL—WHEN WE GET TO THAT, YOU REALIZE YOU'VE BEEN WATCHING A MORMON VERSION OF THE AFRICAN PAGEANT ALL NIGHT.

CASEY NICHOLAW: ANN ROTH IS AMAZING. IF YOU COULD SEE MRS. BROWN IN HER *LION KING* OUTFIT—ANN DESIGNED IT ONLY WITH THINGS THAT ARE FOUND IN THE HOUSE. THE WHOLE THING IS WHISK-BROOMS AND SCRUBBIES. IT'S GOT PLASTIC TABLECLOTHS FOR THE RUFFLE. SHE'S GOT A LION BEACH TOWEL!

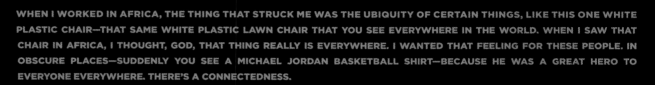

COSTUMES

"I'M NOT JUST DOING A BROADWAY SHOW. THIS IS SOMETHING ELSE"

TOMORROW IS A LATTER DAY

"I AM A LATTER-DAY SAINT! I HELP ALL THOSE I CAN!"

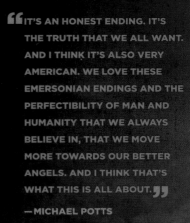

"IT'S AN HONEST ENDING. IT'S THE TRUTH THAT WE ALL WANT. AND I THINK IT'S ALSO VERY AMERICAN. WE LOVE THESE EMERSONIAN ENDINGS AND THE PERFECTIBILITY OF MAN AND HUMANITY THAT WE ALWAYS BELIEVE IN, THAT WE MOVE MORE TOWARDS OUR BETTER ANGELS. AND I THINK THAT'S WHAT THIS IS ALL ABOUT."

— MICHAEL POTTS

TREY PARKER: I KNEW WE WANTED THE BIG, JOYOUS CLOSING NUMBER. SO WE BASED IT ON THE NOTION OF CUNNINGHAM'S LULLABY KIND OF EXPANDING, AND THAT REALLY HELPED A LOT. WE LOVED THE IDEA OF THIS LULLABY THAT CUNNINGHAM'S MOM USED TO SING TO HIM BECOMING THIS HUGE, UNITING, WE-ARE-TOGETHER IDEA. I LOVE RETURNING TO AN IDEA AND TRANSFORMING WHAT IT MEANS, AND MAKING IT METAPHORICAL.

MATT STONE: IT WAS THE TAUTOLOGY SONG. IT'S BASED ON CUNNINGHAM'S RIDICULOUS, INSANE, HOPEFUL REFRAIN. HE'S ALWAYS SAYING, HEY, WELL, TOMORROW'S A LATTER DAY. AND THE SHOW KIND OF RIPS ON THAT FOR ALMOST THE WHOLE EVENING. IT POINTS OUT HOW RIDICULOUS THAT IS. AT THE END OF THE SHOW WE TURN IT AROUND AND IT'S ALMOST OUR ANTHEM FOR GOING FORWARD.

BOBBY LOPEZ: THE MOMENT WAS ABOUT SO MANY THINGS, BUT REALLY IT WAS ABOUT ONE THING: THAT RELIGIOUS STORIES ARE JUST STORIES. THAT'S ENOUGH. THEY DON'T NEED TO BE MORE.

BOBBY LOPEZ: WE'RE TELLING THE STORY OF A CHARACTER WHO LOSES HIS FAITH, AND WE GIVE HIS FAITH BACK TO HIM IN A BETTER, MORE ADULT, MORE INTEGRATED WAY AT THE END. AND I HOPE THAT THE EXPERIENCE OF THE AUDIENCE MIRRORS THAT, WHETHER IT'S A RELIGIOUS EXPERIENCE OR JUST FEELING ENTERTAINED. THAT IS PART OF WHAT A TRADITIONAL MUSICAL CAN DO. IT'S THIS MACHINE THAT'S DESIGNED TO BRING YOU DOWN AND RAISE YOU UP, AND TO GIVE YOU A POSITIVE, UPLIFTING EXPERIENCE.

THANK YOU GOD!
MA HA NEI BU, EEBOWAI!

"THERE'S A MOMENT IN THE SHOW WHERE WE SING 'THANK YOU GOD,' AND THERE'S A REAL EMOTIONAL SORT OF PRESENCE THAT HAPPENS TO ALL OF US ONSTAGE WHEN THE WHOLE CAST DOES THAT. WE ALL FEEL THIS—BECAUSE OF WHAT WE'VE GONE THROUGH, THE JOURNEY OF THE SHOW AND LOSING OUR FAITH AND GETTING IT BACK—IT DOES MAKE YOU BELIEVE IN SOMETHING GREATER. WHATEVER THAT IS."
— ANDREW RANNELLS

"THE SHOW REALLY IS, TO ME, ABOUT HOPE. AND I THINK THAT'S WHAT FAITH GIVES YOU. HOPE TO GO ON AND WAKE UP EVERY MORNING AND HAVE A REASON FOR LIVING. AND WHATEVER THAT MEANS TO YOU, IT'S A BEAUTIFUL THING WHEN YOU HAVE IT. AND IT'S ALSO ABOUT WHEN YOU HAVE IT AND YOU HAVE THAT FAITH AND IT'S REALLY—WHAT HAPPENS WHEN THE RUG IS PULLED OUT FROM UNDER YOU, AND WHAT HAPPENS WHEN YOU HAVE TO REBUILD IT ON YOUR OWN."
— RORY O'MALLEY

TOMORROW IS A **DOPER, PHATTER** LATTER DAY!

HAVE YOU HEARD?
So the Bible is actually a trilogy, and the Book of Mormon is Return of the Jedi.

HELLO (REPRISE)

"I WOULD LIKE TO SHARE WITH YOU THE MOST AMAZING BOOK!"

"THE SHOW IS WHAT WE WANTED IT TO BE."

> IT'S ABOUT FAITH. IT'S ABOUT RELIGIOUS FEELING AND
> # WHAT HOPE MEANS.
> IT'S ABOUT WHAT STORIES ARE DESIGNED TO DO.

TREY PARKER: THE BEST, MOST SURREAL, MOST GRATIFYING PART OF THE WHOLE EXPERIENCE HAS BEEN WATCHING LITTLE IDEAS GET TURNED INTO GIANT ONES. IT'S JUST BEEN SO SATISFYING TO BRING THIS SHOW TO LIFE, FROM WRITING THE MUSIC AND LYRICS IN THIS APARTMENT WITH MATT AND BOBBY TO WATCHING SOMEONE SING THE FIRST LITTLE SONG, TO YEARS OF READINGS AND WORKSHOPS, TO THAT FIRST DAY THAT YOU WALK INTO THE O'NEILL THEATRE ON 49TH STREET AND LISTEN TO EVERYONE SINGING WITH THE ORCHESTRA, AND YOU'RE JUST LIKE, WOW. THIS IS REAL. AND THERE WERE SO MANY MOMENTS IN THIS EXPERIENCE THAT WERE THE BIG, OH-MY-GOD-THIS-IS-REAL MOMENTS. THERE STILL ARE! THIS HAS BEEN, BY FAR, THE MOST COLLABORATIVE THING I'VE DONE, WHERE I'VE JUST BEEN SURROUNDED BY THE GREATEST PEOPLE WHO ALL WANTED THE SHOW TO BE AS GREAT AS I WANTED IT TO BE AND GAVE EVERYTHING OF THEMSELVES TO DO THAT.

MATT STONE: THE WHOLE TRICK FOR US WAS TO FIND AN ENDING THAT SATISFIED AS A STORY BUT THAT DIDN'T QUANTIFY ITSELF THEMATICALLY. WE NEVER LIKE TO MAKE A 'POINT,' PER SE. WE WANT TO FEEL THAT THE NARRATIVE IS CONCLUDING BUT WE WANT TO GIVE YOU ROOM TO FEEL WHAT THE SHOW IS SAYING TO YOU. WE DON'T WANT TO TELL ANYBODY WHAT THE POINT IS, OR WHAT THE POLITICS ARE. WE WANT TO GENTLY COME TO REST, LIKE THE SHOW IS FINALLY LANDING, BUT ON A PIECE OF PAPER—YOU THINK WE'RE LANDING THE WAY YOU EXPECT, AND THEN WE JUST KEEP GOING RIGHT ON THROUGH IT. AND IT'S UP TO YOU TO FIGURE OUT WHAT THE MATH OF IT IS, WHAT IT MEANT. SO THAT'S WHY I LOVE THAT THE SHOW ENDS WITH SOMEONE SINGING *I STILL HAVE MAGGOTS IN MY SCROTUM*—BECAUSE YES, NOW THEY HAVE FAITH AND HOPE, BUT THEY ALSO HAVE MAGGOTS IN THEIR SCROTUMS. THAT'S REAL LIFE, AND THAT'S A MUSICAL.

"I WANT THE MUSICAL TO SHOW PEOPLE THE DEPTHS OF HUMAN LOWS, AND THEN TO LIFT THEM BACK UP IN A REALLY TRUE WAY, PAST WHERE THEY WOULD NORMALLY GO."

BOBBY LOPEZ: I KNOW THAT MY PATH AS A CHORISTER CAME INTO PLAY WHEN WE WERE WRITING SOME OF THE MORE EMOTIONAL PASSAGES IN THE SCORE—SOME OF THE MORE RELIGIOUS-FEELING SONGS. I KNEW HOW TO GO FOR THAT FROM SINGING IN CHURCH EVERY SUNDAY, ALL THE WAY THROUGH HIGH SCHOOL AND COLLEGE AND MY QUARTER-LIFE CRISIS. RELIGIOUS MUSIC MEANS A LOT TO ME. IT STILL CONNECTS TO ME SPIRITUALLY, AS DOES MUSICAL THEATER.

I WANT THE MUSICAL TO SHOW PEOPLE THE DEPTHS OF HUMAN LOWS, THE—A NADIR OF HUMAN EXPERIENCE, A REAL NADIR, A REAL—TO MAKE PEOPLE FEEL THIS IN A REAL, TRUE WAY, AND THEN TO LIFT THEM BACK UP IN A REALLY TRUE WAY, PAST WHERE THEY WOULD NORMALLY GO. SO, FOR THIS MUSICAL, IT'S ABOUT FAITH. IT'S ABOUT RELIGIOUS FEELING AND WHAT HOPE MEANS. THAT'S WHAT STORIES ARE DESIGNED TO DO. THAT'S WHY WE LOVE STORIES.

CASEY NICHOLAW: IT'S SO LOVING. I'VE ALWAYS LOVED MUSICALS SINCE I WAS A KID, AND I JUST PICTURE MYSELF BEING A LITTLE KID WATCHING, AND I JUST WANNA LOVE IT, LOVE IT, LOVE IT. THAT'S WHAT I LOVE. IT'S THE ART FORM THAT I LOVE MORE THAN ANYTHING.

I JUST THINK THAT ANYONE CAN SEE THIS SHOW AND KNOW THAT IT'S ABOUT—IT DOESN'T MATTER WHAT YOU BELIEVE IN, IF YOU FEEL STRONGLY ABOUT IT AND YOU SHARE IT, WHETHER IT'S RELIGION OR, YOU KNOW, MUSICAL THEATER! EVERYONE CAN FIND SOMETHING THAT TOUCHES THEM—SOMETHING THAT MOVES YOU, OR SOMETHING YOU CAN USE IN YOUR LIFE ONE WAY OR ANOTHER. IT'S ABOUT WHAT BELIEF IS FOR, WHAT IT GIVES YOU, WHAT IT MEANS TO YOU.

> {
> I THOUGHT TO
> MYSELF, THAT'S
> **RIDICULOUS**
> AND I HAVE TO
> BE PART OF IT.

ELDER CUNNINGHAM

JOSH GAD

JOSH GAD: I REMEMBER READING AN ART-ICLE, BACK AROUND 2004, SAYING THAT TREY PARKER, MATT STONE AND BOBBY LOPEZ HAD DECIDED TO TEAM UP TO WRITE A SHOW ABOUT MORMONS. I THOUGHT TO MYSELF, *THAT'S FUCKING RIDICULOUS AND I HAVE TO BE PART OF IT.* THEN I COMPLETELY FORGOT ABOUT IT.

THREE YEARS LATER I DID A LITTLE SHOW CALLED *SPELLING BEE* ON BROADWAY, IT BECOMES MY BIG BREAK. I FINISH THAT AND DO SOME FILMS AND A TV SHOW. ONE DAY, OUT OF THE BLUE, I GET THIS PHONE CALL FROM BOBBY LOPEZ, WHO I DIDN'T KNOW. HE SAYS, *I'M DOING THIS NEW SHOW WITH TREY PARKER AND MATT STONE. WE'RE NOT SURE WHAT WE WANT TO DO WITH IT, IT COULD POTENTIALLY BE A SHOW OR A MOVIE. I WAS WONDERING IF YOU WOULD PLAY THIS CHARACTER?* THE WAY HE PITCHED IT TO ME WAS THAT ELDER CUNNINGHAM IS KIND OF LIKE A TRAIN WRECK, AND THE SECOND FIDDLE. BUT BY THE END OF THE FIRST ACT HE BECOMES THE LEAD OF THE SHOW. AND THAT WAS ALL HE KNEW. I WAS, LIKE, *OKAY, SO I'LL JUST BE THIS GOOFY SIDEKICK GUY.*

I GET THIS DEMO RECORDING AND THE FIRST SONG I LISTEN TO IS "HASA DIGA EEBOWAI." I PUT IT ON AND I HEAR THE WORDS, *FUCK YOU, GOD, IN THE ASS, MOUTH, AND CUNT* COME OUT OF MY SPEAKERS. I CALL UP MY AGENT AND SAY I CAN'T DO THIS. I MEAN, I'M NOT RELIGIOUS BUT THIS REALLY IS GOING TO BE POTENTIALLY DANGEROUS TO BE A PART OF. AND HE GOES, WELL, IT CAN'T BE THAT BAD AND I'M LIKE, YOU DON'T KNOW WHAT I'M LISTENING TO RIGHT NOW! HE SAW THE WORKSHOP AND CAME UP TO ME AFTER, AND HE GOES THIS IS THE MOST INCREDIBLY HYSTERICAL THING I'VE EVER SEEN! YOU CAN'T DO THIS!

BOBBY LOPEZ: WE LUCKED INTO JOSH GAD. IT WAS MORE THAN LUCK. IT WAS DIVINE INTERVENTION, BECAUSE I MIGHT NOT HAVE CAST HIM IF I HAD KNOWN WHAT HIS SINGING VOICE SOUNDED LIKE. WHAT HAPPENED WAS, I SAW A YOUTUBE OF HIM DOING AN INTERVIEW, AND I THOUGHT THIS GUY'S GREAT, BUT CAN HE SING? AND I KNEW HE HAD BEEN IN *SPELLING BEE* DOING THE "MAGIC FOOT" ROLE, BUT THAT DIDN'T NECESSARILY MEAN HE COULD SING. SO, I GOT A TRACK THE *SPELLING BEE* CAST DID FOR A BROADWAY CARES CHRISTMAS ALBUM. IT WAS A GROUP VOCAL WITH LITTLE SOLOS, AND I THOUGHT, *OH, HE'S GREAT, HE'S PERFECT!* BUT WHO I WAS LISTENING TO, I LATER FOUND OUT, WAS ACTUALLY BARRETT FOA! JOSH HAD THIS CRAZY VOICE. ELDER CUNNINGHAM WAS NOT INTENDED TO BE AS CRAZY AS JOSH ENDED UP MAKING HIM, BUT IT WAS ONE OF THE GREATEST SURPRISES FOR ME AND ONE OF THE HAPPIEST, MOST SERENDIPITOUS MOMENTS TO SEE HOW JOSH REALLY MADE THAT PART HIS OWN. HE BROUGHT SOMETHING TO IT THAT NONE OF US HAD ENVISIONED.

NIKKI M. JAMES: ELDER CUNNINGHAM AND JOSH GAD ARE SO ENTWINED, IT'S LIKE A PERFECT MARRIAGE. OVER TIME, THE WRITERS STARTED TO WRITE TOWARDS PEOPLE'S STRENGTHS; JOSH WAS BRAVE ENOUGH TO INFUSE HIS OWN SENSE OF COMEDY AND TIMING AND WEIRD LAUGHS. AND HIS VOCAL GYMNASTICS. 'CAUSE HE'S NOT A SINGER. BUT WHAT HE CAN DO WITH HIS VOICE AND THE COLORS THAT HE CAN FIND, HE CAN TURN A LINE THAT'S NOT THAT FUNNY INTO SOMETHING THAT'S NOT QUITE FUNNY BUT GETS A BIG LAUGH. BEING ON STAGE WITH JOSH IS LIKE SURFING, BECAUSE YOU DON'T REALLY KNOW WHAT TO EXPECT. HE IS VERY MUCH ALIVE AND ALMOST DANGEROUS. HE'S ALWAYS THIS CLOSE TO JUST GOING OVER THE EDGE.

I KNEW I REALLY WANTED TO BE A PART OF IT.

ANDREW RANNELLS: I FIRST HEARD ABOUT THE SHOW AFTER THE SECOND READING, WHEN CHEYENNE JACKSON WAS PLAYING ELDER PRICE. AND THEN I HEARD ABOUT IT AGAIN FROM MAIA WILSON, WHO I WAS DOING A SHOW WITH AT THE PAPER MILL PLAYHOUSE. SHE HAD JUST FINISHED DOING THE NEW 42 WORKSHOP, WITH DANIEL REICHARD PLAYING THE PART. IT CAME OUT THAT THEY WERE GOING TO BE RECASTING, AND WE WERE TRAPPED IN NEW JERSEY BETWEEN SHOWS ONE DAY. I ASKED HER WHAT SHE COULD TELL ME ABOUT IT, BECAUSE I KNEW I REALLY WANTED TO BE PART OF IT. THEN I SAW ON THE BREAKDOWN THAT HE'S SUPPOSED TO BE 19, AND AT THE TIME I WAS 31. AND I SAID TO MAIA, *I DON'T KNOW IF I CAN DO THIS.* SHE WAS LIKE, *JUST GO BE 19.*

THEY DIDN'T RELEASE THE SCRIPT, YOU HAD TO GO TO THE CASTING DIRECTOR'S OFFICE AND READ THE SCRIPT IN A CONFERENCE ROOM. I KIND OF COULDN'T BELIEVE THAT THEY WERE ACTUALLY GOING TO DO IT, BUT I WAS LIKE, *I HAVE TO BE A PART OF THIS.*

FOR MY LAST AUDITION, I WAS FLOWN OUT TO LOS ANGELES SO JOSH AND I COULD READ TOGETHER IN FRONT OF TREY AND MATT. I THINK THAT TREY IN PARTICULAR SORT OF SAW THAT ELDER PRICE WAS A VERY GOOD FIT FOR ME. I'M FROM NEBRASKA, THERE WAS SORT OF A MIDWESTERN-NESS THAT I BROUGHT TO IT THAT WAS A GOOD FIT; SHY OF CASTING AN ACTUAL MORMON, SOMEONE FROM NEBRASKA IS PRETTY CLOSE. JOSH HAD SORT OF DEVOURED THE PREVIOUS ELDER PRICES A LITTLE BIT. I QUICKLY REALIZED WHAT HE WAS BRINGING AND WHAT I WAS BRINGING, AND THERE WAS GOING TO BE NO COMPETING WITH HIM.

JOSH GAD: UP UNTIL THE FINAL WORKSHOP, THERE WAS A REAL QUESTION. MY CHARACTER WAS WORKING AMAZINGLY WELL— PROBABLY TOO WELL—AND IT WAS FRUSTRATING, BECAUSE YOU HAVE THIS BUDDY COMEDY AND MY CHARACTER IS KIND OF THIS WHIRLWIND. BUT WHO WAS I WHIRLING AROUND? AND ALONG CAME ANDREW RANNELLS, WHO THEY FLEW OUT TO L.A. AND HAD ME READ WITH. THIS GUY DOES THE SCENE WITH ME AND I'M, LIKE, *WHO THE HELL IS THIS? HE'S AMAZING!* FOR THE FIRST TIME, I WAS INTIMIDATED BY PRICE. FROM THAT POINT ON, THE SHOW CLICKED. ANDREW'S MIDWESTERN SENSIBILITIES INFORMED THE WRITERS THE REST OF THE WAY. THEY HAD THAT ANCHOR TO BALANCE MY INSANITY, AND ALSO TO CREATE A NEW DIRECTION FOR INSANITY. THERE'S THIS SENSE THAT AT ANY MOMENT THE FAÇADE IS GOING TO BREAK DOWN AND THIS MONSTER IS GOING TO POP OUT.

NIKKI M. JAMES

EVEN HAVE A SCRIPT AT THAT POINT, THEY WERE STILL FIDDLING AROUND WITH WHAT IT WAS GOING TO BE. AT THE END WE DID PRESENTATIONS FOR GUESTS, FRIENDS, AND COLLEAGUES. LITTLE BARE-BONES READINGS, WITH MUSIC STANDS; STAND UP WHEN IT'S YOUR TIME TO SING OR SAY SOMETHING, NO STAGING, STAGE DIRECTIONS READ BY THE STAGE MANAGER. AND I LOVED IT. I THOUGHT IT WAS TOTALLY BALLSY AND CRAZY OF THEM, AND ALSO REALLY WELL DONE—EVEN AT THAT LEVEL. THIS WAS A SHOW THAT WAS IN ITS INFANCY, AND IT ALREADY HAD THESE GREAT BONES. I DECIDED AT THAT MOMENT THAT I WANTED TO INVEST AS MUCH OF MYSELF AS I COULD SO THEY WOULD ALLOW ME TO STAY PART OF THE PROJECT. THAT WENT ON FOR ANOTHER THREE YEARS, ALMOST, UNTIL THE TIME IT OPENED ON BROADWAY.

ALONG THE WAY YOU'RE NEVER QUITE SURE IF YOU'RE THE RIGHT ACTRESS. YOU DO THE BEST WORK YOU CAN IN THE READING, THEN YOU WALK AWAY AND YOU TRY TO FORGET ABOUT IT. THEN YOU HEAR *I THINK THEY'RE DOING ANOTHER WORKSHOP* AND YOU HOPE THAT THEY CALL YOU, AND THEY DO. WE DID FOUR LITTLE MINI-PRODUCTIONS, EACH GOT BIGGER IN SCOPE AND CLOSER TO THE INEVITABLE GOAL. SO, IT WAS STRESSFUL. I NEVER AUDITIONED IN THE WAY PEOPLE USUALLY AUDITION FOR A SHOW. BUT IT WAS LIKE I WAS CONSTANTLY AUDITIONING. AT ANY POINT THEY COULD HAVE DECIDED SHE'S NOT THE VOICE WE WANT OR SHE'S NOT THE ACTRESS WE WANT OR IT'S NOT THE LOOK THAT WE WANT. OR I COULD HAVE BEEN UNAVAILABLE AT SOME POINT AND SOME OTHER ACTRESS COULD HAVE COME IN AND BLOWN ME OUT OF THE WATER. SO, IT'S SORT OF A LITTLE BIT OF KISMET AND LUCK. YOU GRAB ON, CLOSE YOUR EYES, AND HOPE THAT THEY TAKE YOU FOR THE RIDE.

NIKKI M. JAMES: I WAS DOING CLASSICAL THEATER UP AT THE STRATFORD FEST-IVAL IN CANADA, WHICH WAS AN AMAZING YEAR OF MY LIFE. AND I GOT A PHONE CALL FROM MY AGENT, WHO TELLS ME: *THEY WILL NOT SEND YOU A SCRIPT, THEY WON'T SEND YOU ANY MUSIC, THEY CAN'T TELL YOU THE PLOT, YOUR CHARACTER IS SOME SORT OF AFRICAN VILLAGER.* AND THAT'S ALL. IT WAS GOING TO BE A TWO-WEEK READING AT THE VINEYARD THEATER AND THOSE THINGS PAY ALMOST NOTHING. IF YOU BUY LUNCH EVERY DAY, IT COSTS YOU MONEY TO DO THOSE READINGS.

BUT THESE DEVELOPMENTAL READINGS ARE THINGS YOU DO WHEN YOU'RE A THEATRE ACTOR, BECAUSE THAT'S HOW YOU GET INVOLVED WITH THE PROJECTS THAT ARE GOING TO BE TOMORROW'S HITS. IN THIS INSTANCE I HAD NO IDEA WHAT TO EXPECT ON THE FIRST DAY OF REHEARSAL, EXCEPT I KNEW THAT THESE WERE PEOPLE I WANTED TO WORK WITH. SOMETIMES, THAT'S A BETTER REASON TO CHOOSE A PROJECT THAN ANYTHING ELSE. IT TURNS OUT THAT I WAS GOING TO SPEND THE NEXT FOUR YEARS OF MY LIFE WITH THESE PEOPLE, SO THANK GOODNESS THEY ARE PEOPLE I RESPECT AND LIKE.

SO, I SHOWED UP THE FIRST DAY. ACTUALLY, STEPHEN OREMUS—THE MUSICAL DIRECTOR—AND I GOT TOGETHER THE SUNDAY MORNING BEFORE. HE WANTED TO GET A SENSE OF KEYS, SO HE PLAYED THROUGH 'SAL TLAY KA SITI' AND A 'BAPTIZE ME,' THE TWO SONGS THAT I HAD THE MOST RESPONSIBILITY FOR. THEY WERE FUNNY, BUT I DIDN'T KNOW WHAT ELSE TO EXPECT.

THE FIRST DAY OF REHEARSAL, THEY PLAYED US THE DEMO OF BOBBY AND TREY AND MATT SINGING THE SONGS THAT WERE FINISHED. THE THINGS THAT ARE SHOCKING TO THE AUDIENCE TODAY WERE SHOCKING TO US THE FIRST TIME WE HEARD THEM. *FUCK YOU, GOD* IS A BIG DEAL. WE DIDN'T

THANK GOODNESS THEY ARE PEOPLE I RESPECT AND LIKE.

TREY PARKER: NIKKI PROBABLY HAD THE TOUGHEST JOB OF ANYONE, BEING DIRECTED IN EV-ERY POSSIBLE WAY. *TRY IT HAPP-IER! TRY IT SADDER! TRY IT LONELIER!* THINGS WENT BACK AND FORTH BETWEEN KEEPING HER SERIOUS—THE STRAIGHT MAN—AND KEEPING HER HAPPY-GO-LUCKY. WE DIDN'T WANT TO MAKE HER SO MISERABLE THAT SHE WASN'T FUN TO WATCH. AND WHEN WE GAVE HER SOMETHING SERIOUS, YOU REALLY BELIEVED IT. SHE HAD TO PULL OFF A CHARACTER WHO WAS SERIOUS, BUT STILL HAD A BIG SMILE ON HER FACE. ONE OF MY FAVORITE MOMENTS IS HER SAD REPRISE OF 'HASA DIGA.' AT ONE POINT EVERYONE WAS TRYING TO CONVINCE ME TO CUT IT, BUT IT'S MY FAVORITE THING THAT SHE DOES.

RORY O'MALLEY: I MOVED TO NEW YORK AT THE END OF 2006. ON THE DRIVE FROM LOS ANGELES, I STAYED WITH MY COUSIN WHO LIVES IN ST. GEORGE, UTAH. I HAD BEEN THERE A BUNCH OF TIMES; IT'S LIKE THE MOST BEAUTIFUL STATE IN THE COUNTRY. MY COUSIN IS NOT IN THE BUSINESS, BUT HE SAW ON SOME RUMOR BLOG THAT BOBBY LOPEZ, MATT AND TREY WERE WRITING A MUSICAL ABOUT MORMONS. THIS IS 2006, TWO YEARS BEFORE THE FIRST READING.

HE SAID, *RORY, YOU'VE GOT TO GET TO NEW YORK AND BE IN THIS, THIS IS THE SHOW THAT YOU SHOULD BE IN.* AND I WAS LIKE, *THAT SOUNDS LIKE IT WILL BE THE FUNNIEST MUSICAL OF ALL TIME BUT YOU JUST DON'T SHOW UP IN NEW YORK AND GET THROUGH THE LINCOLN TUNNEL AND SAY, 'YES, THIS IS THE SHOW I WOULD LIKE TO BE IN.'*

SO I WOUND UP IN NEW YORK. I WORKED IN *SPELLING BEE* WITH JOSH GAD—IT'S THE ONLY OTHER BROADWAY SHOW WE'VE DONE, EITHER OF US—AND THEN I WAS WORKING FOR A TEMP AGENCY AFTER THAT FINISHED. ONE DAY MY AGENT GOT A CALL FROM CARRIE GARDNER, THE CASTING DIRECTOR; I HAD AUDITIONED FOR HER A BUNCH OF TIMES, BUT NEVER BEEN HIRED. SHE SAID THERE'S A MUSICAL BEING WRITTEN BY THE SOUTH PARK GUYS AND BOBBY LOPEZ AND NO ONE CAN KNOW ANYTHING ABOUT IT, IT'S VERY SECRETIVE. THEY AREN'T EVEN HAVING AUDITIONS. WOULD YOU WANT TO PARTICIPATE? YOU KNOW, IT'S JUST FOR A WEEK AND IT'S FOR A REAL LITTLE AMOUNT OF MONEY, AND I DROPPED THE PHONE. I WAS LIKE, *YES, ABSOLUTELY, I KNOW WHAT THIS IS!* AND I KNEW THAT THERE WAS A CHANCE THAT I COULD BE PERFECT FOR IT; I'M VERY WHITE, AND AFTER PLAYING RICHIE CUNNINGHAM IN *HAPPY DAYS: THE MUSICAL* FOR GARRY MARSHALL, I KNEW THAT I HAD THE WHITE BREAD THING DOWN PAT. SO THAT WAS IN FEBRUARY 2008, AND I REMEMBER THE NIGHT BEFORE THE WORKSHOP I GOT A CALL FROM BOBBY LOPEZ. I'M AN OUT-OF-WORK ACTOR GETTING A CALL FROM BOBBY LOPEZ ON MY ANSWERING MACHINE, TO CALL HIM BACK! IT WAS UNREAL TO ME. HE WANTED TO TALK TO EVERY SINGLE ACTOR BEFORE WE SHOWED UP AND LET THEM KNOW THAT THERE IS A SONG IN THIS SHOW CALLED 'FUCK YOU, GOD,' AND WILL YOU BE OKAY WITH BEING A PART OF SOMETHING THAT SAYS THAT? AND I WAS LIKE, *DID YOU,*

MATT, AND TREY WRITE THIS SONG?, THEN I'M IN. I HAD COMPLETE FAITH WITHOUT EVER SEEING ANY OF THE MATERIAL. I WAS SUCH A HUGE *SOUTH PARK* FAN AND SUCH A HUGE *AVENUE Q* FAN THAT I KNEW THAT WHATEVER THESE GUYS CAME UP WITH WAS GOING TO BE GOLD.

AT THE FIRST READING, IT WAS HALF A SCRIPT AND MY CHARACTER DIDN'T EXIST. ACTUALLY, THERE WERE NO OTHER MORMONS IN UGANDA—JUST CUNNINGHAM AND PRICE. WE WERE JUST A DOZEN GUYS IN THE BEGINNING TO SING 'HELLO' AND 'TWO BY TWO,' AND IT REALLY DIDN'T HAVE A SECOND ACT AT THAT POINT. BUT JOSH WAS IN THE SHOW, WE WENT TO COLLEGE TOGETHER. WE SAW EACH OTHER AT THE FIRST READING, AND WE WERE LIKE, *WHAT ARE YOU DOING HERE?*

DURING THE FIRST THREE READINGS THEY STARTED WRITING THIS CHARACTER FOR ME LINE BY LINE, AND THEN HE BECAME A CLOSETED GAY, AND I WAS LIKE, *OH, MY GOD, THIS IS THE GREATEST THING EVER!* THEN THEY SAID BEFORE OUR FIRST WORKSHOP, *BY THE WAY, YOUR NUMBER'S GOING TO BE A TAP NUMBER,* AND I WAS LIKE, *OH, GOD, WHAT AM I GOING TO DO?* AND I STARTED GOING TO BROADWAY DANCE CENTER AND WAS TAKING TAP 1 WITH LIKE NINE-YEAR-OLD GIRLS. I NEVER THOUGHT ANYONE WOULD BE PAYING TO SEE ME TAP ON A STAGE, LET ALONE A BROADWAY STAGE, SO THAT WAS KIND OF THE BIG THING THAT I HAD TO OVERCOME.

TREY PARKER: FOR A LONG TIME THE SHOW WAS GOING TO BE ABOUT TWO KIDS WHO ENDED UP IN THE WRONG PLACE. THERE WAS NO MORMON MISSION. ALL ALONG WE HAD ONE GREAT SONG, 'TURN IT OFF.' THE IDEA IS THAT ONE OF THE LEADS THOUGHT HE WAS GAY. BUT WE CHANGED OUR MINDS, BECAUSE IT WAS A CLICHÉ, AND WE HAD NOWHERE TO FIT THIS GREAT SONG. STILL WE THOUGHT, *KEEP THAT NUMBER!* WHAT IF THEY'RE NOT ALONE, BUT WITH A BUNCH OF OTHER ELDERS? AT FIRST WE DIDN'T KNOW HOW TO MAKE IT WORK, IT DIDN'T MAKE SENSE WHY THE OTHER BOYS WERE THERE. IT DIDN'T MATTER, WE KNEW WE WANTED TAP DANCING MORMONS. WE KNEW IT WAS SOMETHING TO HOLD ON TO, AND WE'D MAKE THE SHOW WORK AROUND IT. THEY WERE JUST A BUNCH OF MORMON BOYS IN THE BACKGROUND. ONCE WE SAW RORY UP THERE DOING THE NUMBER, THOUGH, IT WAS OK! *WHAT ELSE CAN WE HAVE THIS BOY DO?* '*I AM AFRICA' HAS TO BE SUNG BY THIS GUY!* THE MISSION LEADER BECAME A PART, BECAUSE OF RORY.

MICHAEL POTTS

MAFALA HATIMBI

MICHAEL POTTS: MY MANAGER CALLED ME UP AND SAID THEY WANTED ME TO SING FOR THEM, AND HE TOLD ME ALL ABOUT THE PROVENANCE OF THE WHOLE THING, AND I SAID, *OKAY.* SO I WENT IN TO SING WITH NO EXPECTATION OF GETTING IT. I FIGURED EVERYONE IN NEW YORK WAS GOING TO WANT TO BE IN IT, AND PEOPLE WHO HAD TRAINED AS MUSICAL THEATER PERFORMERS HAD A MUCH BETTER SHOT. SO I WENT IN, BASICALLY, TO AVOID AN ARGUMENT WITH MY MANAGER; WE HAD AN ARGUMENT THE WEEK BEFORE BECAUSE OF SOMETHING ELSE HE WANTED ME TO GO IN FOR AND I PASSED.

SO I WENT AND SANG FOR THEM. THEY LIKED THAT, SO THEY ASKED ME TO WAIT OUTSIDE AND THEY BROUGHT SCRIPT PAGES AND THE MUSIC FOR 'HASA DIGA EEBOWAI.' AND THEY MADE PROFUSE APOLOGIES BEFOREHAND, LIKE, *WE KNOW THIS IS NOT FOR EVERYBODY, AND WE CAN UNDERSTAND IF YOU DON'T WANT TO SAY THIS, WE TOTALLY UNDERSTAND.* THEY JUST KEPT APOLOGIZING FOR IT, AND I'M GOING, *WELL, IT DOESN'T MATTER BECAUSE YOU'RE NOT GOING TO HIRE ME FOR THIS ANYWAY, YOU'RE GOING TO HIRE ONE OF THESE OTHER PEOPLE.*

> **"** THE BRILLIANT MICHAEL POTTS IS TOO GOOD FOR OUR SHOW. THIS MAN BELONGS IN THE HALLS OF SHAKESPEAREAN DRAMAS, AND HERE HE IS EVERY NIGHT SINGING 'FUCK YOU, GOD.' **"**
> — JOSH GAD

I WENT OUT IN A CORNER IN THE WAITING AREA TO READ IT, AND I STARTED HOWLING BECAUSE I JUST COULDN'T BELIEVE IT. *OH, NO, YOU'RE NOT GOING TO SAY THIS!* AND I LAUGHED UNTIL THEY CAME BACK AND GOT ME AND SAID, *IS IT OKAY?* AND I SAID, *IF YOU'RE GOING TO DO IT, IF YOU'VE GOT THE BALLS TO DO IT, I GUESS I CAN GROW THE PAIR TO SAY IT.* WE DID IT, AND THEY ASKED ME TO COME BACK THE NEXT DAY TO SING FOR BOBBY. I CAME BACK THINKING, *YOU'RE GOING TO HIRE SOMEBODY ELSE, BUT AT LEAST I'M HAVING FUN WITH IT.* SOME PEOPLE COULD HAVE TROUBLE DOING THIS MATERIAL, BUT I DIDN'T. WHICH IS FUNNY, BECAUSE MY FATHER WAS A MINISTER, MY STEP-FATHER'S A MINISTER, MY MOTHER'S AN OFFICIATE IN THE CHURCH, AND I'VE GROWN UP WITH ALL OF THIS. MAYBE BECAUSE I REALIZED IT WAS JUST A BIG JOKE, A SATIRE, AND SOMETHING THAT HAD NEVER DARED BEEN SAID ON BROADWAY, I COULDN'T RESIST. I HAD TO DO IT.

I DID *GREY GARDENS* A FEW YEARS AGO, AND I THOUGHT, *WELL, THAT WAS SORT OF AN ARTISTIC SUCCESS ON BROADWAY, A CRITICAL SUCCESS.* I WAS HAPPY WITH THAT, I THOUGHT, *WELL, I'VE ACHIEVED THIS, AND IT'S AS MUCH AS I CAN HOPE FOR.* NEVER IN MY MIND DID I THINK I'LL BE IN A SMASH HIT. SOMETHING THAT WOULD BECOME AN EVENT—IT'S AN EVENT. IT'S NOT JUST A BROADWAY MUSICAL ANYMORE. IT IS AN EVENT. THERE WAS NO EXPECTATION THAT PEOPLE WOULD GO SO CRAZY OVER THIS SHOW. IN MY MIND, I WAS JUST AN ACTOR ON A STAGE TRYING TO PLAY THIS ROLE. WHO KNEW THAT THIS SONG WOULD MAKE ME FAMOUS?

'HASA DIGA EEBOWAI' HAS MADE ME FAMOUS. YOU NEVER THINK TO MAKE HISTORY LIKE THAT. I GOT THE SONG THAT MADE HISTORY ON BROADWAY.

BOBBY LOPEZ: MICHAEL POTTS IS SUCH AN AMAZING ACTOR. I THINK FOR ANYONE WHO'S AS SMART AS HE IS, AND WHO'S AS FINELY TUNED AN ACTOR, IT WAS ABOUT *OKAY, THIS MATERIAL IS A LITTLE BIT RACY, I'M NOT SURE IF I TRUST IT.* BUT HIS INTELLIGENCE ALLOWED HIM TO FIGURE IT OUT. AND HE DID—HE'S ALWAYS FIGURED IT OUT, EVERYTHING THAT WE'VE HAD HIM DO. AND I THINK THE WAY HE SELLS IT ON BROADWAY IS THE PERFECT MIX OF REALISM, OF UNDERSTANDING WHAT HE'S SAYING, AND NOT GOING FOR CHEAP JOKES WHERE YOU SHOULDN'T AND ALSO GOING FOR CHEAP JOKES WHERE YOU SHOULD. HE DOES THAT. HE'S A HAM, TOO.

TREY PARKER: MICHAEL IS A GREAT DRAMATIC ACTOR, WITH A GREAT DRAMA BACKGROUND. WE KEPT TRYING TO KEEP HATIMBI FUN-LOVING, SAYING FUNNY THINGS. HIS LINES GOT FUNNIER AS WE WENT ALONG, BUT HE WAS ABLE TO RETAIN THE SERIOUSNESS. MICHAEL IS ABLE TO PULL OFF ANYTHING; WHATEVER HE DOES, YOU TOTALLY BUY IT.

IF YOU'RE GOING TO DO IT, IF YOU'VE GOT THE BALLS TO DO IT, I GUESS I CAN GROW A PAIR TO SAY IT.
— MICHAEL POTTS

ROLES:
JESUS, PRICE'S DAD, JOSEPH SMITH, MISSION PRESIDENT

LEWIS CLEALE: I AUDITIONED TWO MONTHS BEFORE REHEARSALS STARTED FOR BROADWAY. THEY HAD OTHER ACTORS IN MY PARTS OVER THE COURSE OF THE EVOLUTION, ALL PEOPLE THAT I LOVE AND ARE MY FRIENDS. BUT THE SHOW CHANGED AND THE ROLE GOT SNIPPED, AND THERE WASN'T REALLY MUCH LEFT. I THOUGHT, *I HAVE A MORTGAGE AND I LOVE MATT AND TREY, SO EVEN IF THE ROLE'S NOT MUCH IT COULD BE FUN TO BE IN THE ROOM.*

TO READ THE SCRIPT BEFORE AUDITIONING, YOU HAD TO GO TO LIKE A SAFE ROOM, SIGN IN AND LEAVE YOUR BELONGINGS. I STARTED READING IT. I CAN HANDLE PRETTY MUCH ANYTHING, AND MY JAW HIT THE FLOOR. I WAS REALLY HAPPY WITH MOST OF IT, BUT I COULDN'T BELIEVE *FUCK YOU, GOD.* I WAS ASTONISHED. BUT THE FIRST DAY THEY RAN IT IN REHEARSAL, I WAS IN TEARS. I WAS ABSOLUTELY MOVED BY THESE PEOPLE SAYING WHAT THEY WERE SAYING. IT WAS OUTRAGEOUS ON THE PAGE, BUT IN PERSON IT WAS DEVASTATING AND HEARTBREAKING. I MEAN, THEY ALL HAVE AIDS—AND IT'S TRUE, THERE ARE PEOPLE IN OUR WORLD WHO LIVE LIKE THAT RIGHT NOW. SO YES IT'S COMEDY; YES IT'S TREY, MATT, AND BOBBY; BUT TREY, MATT, AND BOBBY KNOW WHAT THEY'RE DOING. THEY'RE SKEWERING THINGS, THEY'RE ATTACKING THINGS, THEY'RE BREAKING DOWN RIDICULOUS RELIGIOUS BELIEFS. BUT IT WOULDN'T PLAY AS WELL AS IT DOES IF THERE WASN'T TRUTH AT THE CORE.

DURING REHEARSALS AND PREVIEWS, THINGS CHANGED. SONGS GOT ADDED, THEY LET ME BE ABSURD AND PLAY AROUND. LIKE IN THE HELL DREAM, WHAT JEFFREY DAHMER AND I DO. ENTRANCES LIKE THAT WEREN'T SET IN STONE, THEY JUST LET ME TRY WHATEVER I WANTED TO. SAME WITH JOSEPH SMITH, MY DANCE MOVES ON THE PLATFORM DURING 'ALL-AMERICAN PROPHET.' THEY JUST LET ME DO WHATEVER I WANTED. SO IT TURNED OUT TO BE GREAT.

BACK IN THE NINETIES, I DID A NATIONAL COMMERCIAL FOR BLOCKBUSTER IN MIAMI. THERE WERE TWO PRINCIPALS, CINDY CRAWFORD AND ME, AND A CHORUS OF TAP DANCERS FROM NEW YORK WHO WERE ALL PLAYING HOOKY FROM *CRAZY FOR YOU.* EVERY DAY WE WERE BROUGHT FROM OUR LITTLE HOTEL IN THE VAN. THERE WAS ONE DANCER WHO WAS ALWAYS IN THE MIDDLE, THEY ALL KIND OF SAT AROUND HIM, AND I THOUGHT, *WHO'S THIS GUY? THIS GUY'S GOT SOMETHING.* AND THAT WAS CASEY NICHOLAW. SO IN THIS BUSINESS, ALWAYS BE NICE TO EVERYBODY.

ROLES: GENERAL, SATAN

BRIAN TYREE HENRY: I'VE BEEN A FAN OF MATT AND TREY'S FOR SO LONG, I GREW UP WITH THEM. I WATCHED *SOUTH PARK* SINCE I WAS FOURTEEN YEARS OLD, ALL THE WAY THROUGH COLLEGE, ALL THE WAY THROUGH GRAD SCHOOL AT YALE. I GOT A CALL THAT THEY WANTED ME TO BE A PART OF A WORKSHOP, IT'S CALLED *THE MORMON MUSICAL*, AND SHE SAID IT'S WRITTEN BY TREY PARKER AND MATT—SHE DIDN'T EVEN FINISH, I WAS LIKE, *YES! OH GOD, YES, I'LL ABSOLUTELY DO IT.* I KIND OF LUCKED OUT 'CAUSE I DON'T HAVE TO DO A LOT OF SINGING AND DANCING, I JUST GET TO ACT. I'VE ALWAYS LOOKED UP TO MUSICAL THEATER ACTORS. HOW IN THE HELL DO YOU DO A PLAY WITH A BEGINNING, A MIDDLE, AN END, BUT START SINGING TO EACH OTHER IN THE MIDDLE OF IT? HOW DO YOU THEN CONVINCE THE AUDIENCE TO GO ALONG WITH YOU? SO I WAS NERVOUS GOING IN, LIKE *WHAT THE HELL AM I DOING HERE? I CLEARLY DON'T BELONG HERE.*

WHEN WE MOVED INTO THE THEATER, I HAD DONE THE LAST TWO WORKSHOPS BUT I STILL ONLY HAD ONE LINE. I WAS WAITING, JUST WAITING. I'M THE HUGEST DEVOTEE OF MATT AND TREY; I THOUGHT THEY HAVE TO KNOW THAT I KNOW WHAT I'M DOING WITH THIS PART, IF THEY JUST SEE THAT I REALLY BELIEVE IN THE GENERAL THEY'LL DO

SOMETHING. I WAS ACTING WITHOUT TALKING, AND I WAS GLAD THAT THEY NOTICED THAT. SO THEN THEY WERE LIKE, *HE'S OUT THERE ACTING HIS FACE OFF, LET'S JUST THROW HIM SOME LINES HERE, LET'S GIVE HIM A PART.* AND THEY DID.

WORKING WITH TREY AND MATT, IT'S THE JUICIEST MEAL I'VE EVER HAD. I JUST AM SO HAPPY TO WORK WITH THEM 'CAUSE THEY'RE LIKE MY COMIC GENIUSES. BEING A PART OF THIS EVERY DAY—AND BEING THE BAD GUY—IS JUST SO MUCH FUN. I LOVE HEARING THE AUDIENCE GASP AS SOON AS I WALK OUT, OR AFTER I SHOOT SOMEONE IN THE FACE. ONE OF THE BIGGEST THINGS THAT I HAVE TO REMIND MYSELF IS TO NEVER BREAK. IT'S HARD BECAUSE WE CRACK EACH OTHER UP ONSTAGE ALL THE TIME. I CAN NEVER SMILE; IF I SMILE ANYWHERE IN THE SHOW, THEN THE PAYOFF AT THE ENDING MEANS NOTHING.

THERE WAS ONE NIGHT I WAS LEAVING AFTER THE SHOW AND SOME GUY, HE WAS A FOREIGN GUY, HE SHOUTS, *HEY, BUTT-FUCKER.* AND I WAS LIKE, *OH IS THAT HOW I'M GOING TO BE KNOWN NOW? HEY, BUTT-FUCKER, YOU WERE GREAT, BUTT-FUCKER.* AND I THOUGHT, *THAT'S AWESOME.*

> **"THAT'S A REMARKABLE FEAT, TO LOOK AT THE NINETEENTH PERSON IN THE CAST AND GO, OH MY GOD, WHEN THEY SAID THAT LINE, HOW FUNNY WAS THAT?"**
> —JOSH GAD

GREATEST ENSEMBLE IN THE HISTORY OF MUSICAL THEATER.

—JOSH GAD

JOSH GAD: I TRULY THINK PEOPLE CAN AND WILL MAKE ARGUMENTS THAT THIS IS POTENTIALLY THE GREATEST ENSEMBLE IN THE HISTORY OF MUSICAL THEATER. I REALLY WOULD GO SO FAR AS TO SAY THAT. YOU HAVE THE BEST OF THE BEST SAYING THE SILLIEST THINGS, BUT COMMITTING TO IT IN A WAY THAT LETS THE AUDIENCE GO, *WOW, I GET IT*. WHEREAS YOU COULD HAVE A GROUP OF CRAZY FUNNY PEOPLE, BUT YOU WOULDN'T BE GETTING THAT SAME BIGGER PICTURE THAT YOU GET EVERY NIGHT. EACH PERSON BRINGS A SET OF UNIQUE CHARACTERISTICS THAT THE AUDIENCE RECOGNIZES, REMEMBERS, AND LEAVES TALKING ABOUT. THAT'S A REMARKABLE FEAT, TO LOOK AT THE NINETEENTH PERSON IN THE CAST AND GO, *OH MY GOD, WHEN THEY SAID THAT LINE, HOW FUNNY WAS THAT?*

STEPHEN OREMUS: SO MANY OF THE ENSEMBLE HAD BEEN WITH US FOR SO LONG, THROUGH THE READINGS, THAT THEIR PERSONALITIES BECAME APPARENT. AS NEW STUFF WAS WRITTEN AND EXPLORED, WE WERE ABLE TO REALLY FIT IT ON THESE ACTORS. THIS SHOW WAS NEVER CONCEIVED AS FIVE PRINCIPALS AND A BUNCH OF VILLAGERS; THE ENSEMBLE IS NEVER JUST FILLING THE STAGE, THEY ARE ALWAYS SERVING A PURPOSE. AND THEY ALL GET THEIR MOMENT TO BE FEATURED.

Scott Barnhardt

Roles:
Elder Harris, Elder Price's sister,
Elder Thomas ("Elder Pop Tarts"), Hobbit, Devil
Joined The Book:
Lincoln Center workshop, August 2010

✱ Justin Bohon ✱

Roles:
Elder Smith (who goes to France),
Price's Mom, Elder Zelder, Devil
Joined The Book:
3rd Vineyard Reading, July 2009

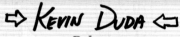

⇨ Kevin Duda ⇦

Roles:
Elder Young (who goes to Norway),
Cunningham's Dad, Eldery Neely, Hitler
Joined The Book:
1st Vineyard Reading, February 2008

ENSEMBLE:
THE MORMONS

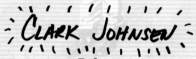

Clark Johnsen

Roles:
Elder Brown, Price's Brother, Elder Michaels,
Brigham Young, Devil, Mission President's assistant
Joined The Book:
Broadway, February 2011

Benjamin Schrader

Roles:
Elder White (who goes to France), Price's Brother,
Elder Schrader, Yoda, Jeffrey Dahmer, Mission President's Assistant
Joined The Book:
1st Vineyard Reading, February 2008

Brian Sears

Roles:
Elder Grant (who goes to Norway), Cunningham's Mom,
Elder Church, Hobbit, Devil
Joined The Book:
1st Vineyard Reading, February 2008

Jason Michael Snow

Roles:
Mormon (in Prologues), Elder Cross (who goes to Japan),
Price's brother, Elder Davis, Devil
Joined The Book:
3rd Vineyard Reading, July 2009

SCOTT BARNHARDT: I WORKED WITH CASEY NICHOLAW IN 2003 AT CITY CENTER, DOING *BYE BYE BIRDIE*. WE REALLY GOT ALONG. WHEN I GOT A CALL FOR THE FINAL *MORMON* WORKSHOP, I HAD NO IDEA WHY, AND I GOT THE JOB. LATER, CASEY AND I WERE CHATTING, AND HE SAID, *YOU KNOW HOW YOU GOT IN, RIGHT? I HAD JUST STARTED ON THE SHOW, I WAS IN A CAB ON EIGHTH AVENUE AND YOU WERE STANDING OUTSIDE A STARBUCKS. I THOUGHT: SCOTTIE WOULD BE GOOD FOR THIS.* SO I ONLY GOT THE JOB BECAUSE I WAS STANDING OUTSIDE STARBUCKS ON EIGHTH AVENUE.

JUSTIN BOHON: MY FAMILY IS STILL VERY RELIGIOUS. BUT AT THE FIRST INVITED AUDIENCE, PEOPLE SAT DOWN AND STARTED LISTENING, AND THEY JUST LOST THEIR MINDS—ALMOST IMMEDIATELY. I WATCHED THE AUDIENCE GO FROM SHOCK TO ENJOYMENT, AND WATCHED THEM REALIZE THAT THERE'S SO MUCH MORE TO THE SHOW THAN JUST THE SHOCK VALUE. IT SPEAKS GREATLY ABOUT RELIGION AND THE NEED FOR IT IN OUR LIVES. IT DOESN'T REALLY MATTER WHAT FORM IT COMES IN; WHAT'S IMPORTANT IS HOW IT GIVES YOU PEACE OR FAITH TO GET THROUGH ANOTHER DAY. YOU SEE PEOPLE'S FACES IN THE AUDIENCE AS THEY REALIZE THAT AND GO, *OH!*

JASON MICHAEL SNOW: THE FIRST TIME I HEARD 'HASA DIGA,' ALL THE BOYS WERE JUST WATCHING ME, AND I JUST SAID, *OH MY GOD!* IT WAS SO OFFENSIVE TO ME AND SO SHOCKING BECAUSE I'M SO VANILLA. I GREW UP CATHOLIC, AND YOU DON'T SAY THOSE THINGS. YOU DON'T EVEN THINK THOSE THINGS. AND IF YOU DO THINK THOSE THINGS YOU RUN TO CHURCH RIGHT AWAY AND APOLOGIZE FOR THINKING THEM. SO WHEN I FIRST HEARD 'HASA DIGA,' I WAS ON THE FLOOR 'CAUSE I COULDN'T BELIEVE THEY'D SANG IT. BUT LIKE THE AUDIENCE, I'M LAUGHING MY ASS OFF. SO THERE WAS AN AMAZING JUXTAPOSITION OF *THIS IS REALLY OFFENSIVE* AND *I'M FINDING MYSELF LOVING IT.*

BRIAN SEARS: EVERYONE EXPECTS THAT ALL WE'RE GOING TO DO IS JUST MAKE FUN OF THE RELIGION. AND THE SHOW DOES DO THAT, BUT AT THE SAME TIME IT SAYS, *WHATEVER WORKS FOR YOU, BELIEVE IN THAT.* PEOPLE GET A FEELING THAT THEY'VE LEARNED SOMETHING BY

WATCHING THE SHOW, WHICH I DON'T THINK ANYBODY EXPECTS WHILE COMING TO SEE *SOUTH PARK* OR AN *AVENUE Q*-TYPE SHOW.

JUSTIN BOHON: MY FAMILY IS STILL VERY RELIGIOUS, AND 'HASA DIGA EEBOWAI'—WELL, IT TOOK SOME GETTING USED TO. FOR ME, I DIDN'T HAVE TO SING IT; MAYBE I WOULD THINK ABOUT IT DIFFERENTLY IF I WERE THE ONE SAYING IT EVERY NIGHT. BUT IF YOU WERE THESE UGANDANS AND YOU WERE IN THIS POSITION, WOULD YOU NOT SAY THE SAME THING? THROUGHOUT THE BIBLE, PEOPLE CURSE GOD. WHEN YOU'RE IN DIRE CIRCUMSTANCES, IT MAKES PERFECT SENSE THAT YOU FEEL THAT WAY. WE ALL—WHEN BAD THINGS HAPPEN TO US—HAVE SAID, TO WHOEVER OUR GOD IS, *HOW COULD YOU DO THIS TO ME?*

JASON MICHAEL SNOW: AT THE STAGE DOOR SIGNING AUTOGRAPHS, YOU HEAR PEOPLE SAY, *I AM A MORMON AND I THINK THIS WAS RIGHT ON.* OR, *I'M REALLY RELIGIOUS AND I THOUGHT THAT IT'S PRO-FAITH.* BECAUSE AT THE END IT'S WHOLESOME. IF YOU'RE NOT RELIGIOUS IT DOESN'T MATTER, AND IF YOU ARE RELIGIOUS IT KIND OF SAYS THAT WHAT YOU BELIEVE IS OKAY. MATT AND TREY ARE SO DAMN BRILLIANT WITH HOW THEY CAN MAKE FUN OF A RELIGION AND AT THE VERY END SAY, *BUT RELIGION'S ACTUALLY PRETTY OKAY.*

BEN SCHRADER: EVERYONE FROM ATHEISTS TO AGNOSTICS TO PRIESTS TO RABBIS, EVERYONE WHO'S SEEN THE SHOW WALKS OUT WITH A STRONGER SENSE OF WHAT THEY BELIEVE. I THINK IT'S BEEN A SURPRISE FOR EVERYONE. ANYONE WHO CRITICIZES THE HANDLING OF RELIGION, THEY HAVEN'T SEEN THE SHOW.

KEVIN DUDA: THE DRESSING ROOM BUZZ AT THE FIRST READING AT THE VINEYARD WAS, *OH WE'RE GOING RIGHT TO BROADWAY, THIS IS GOING TO HAPPEN!* AFTER THAT, THOUGH, YOU HAVE LIKE A WEEK OR TWO WHERE YOU DON'T HEAR ANYTHING AND YOU TALK YOURSELF OFF THE LEDGE.

CLARK JOHNSEN: I WOULD SAY THAT THE MOST ACCURATE THING IN THE SHOW IS THE PORTRAYAL OF THE MISSIONARIES. THAT SORT OF INFECTIOUS ENTHUSIASM—THAT POSITIVE TAKE ON HOW TO HANDLE DIFFICULTIES—IS EXTREMELY TRUE TO LIFE. MY WHOLE LIFE, PEOPLE HAVE ALWAYS SAID, *YOU'RE JUST SMILING TOO MUCH, YOU'RE TOO HYPER, TOO ENERGETIC,* BECAUSE I WAS SHAPED WITHIN THIS FAITH. THIS RELIGION REALLY STRESSES OVERCOMING OBSTACLES, AND OPTIMISM.

> "EVERYONE FROM ATHEISTS TO AGNOSTICS TO PRIESTS TO RABBIS, EVERYONE WHO'S SEEN THE SHOW WALKS OUT WITH A **STRONGER SENSE OF WHAT THEY BELIEVE.**"
> —BEN SCHRADER

Roles:
Sadaka, Skeleton, Coffee Cup
Joined The Book:
Lincoln Center Workshop, August 2010

Asmeret Ghebremichael

Roles:
Asmeret (Ugandan Woman), Devil
Joined The Book:
3rd Vineyard Reading, July 2009

John Eric Parker

Roles:
General's Guard #2, Mutumbo, Devil, Joseph Smith (African Pageant)
Joined The Book:
1st Vineyard Reading, February 2008

!Michael James Scott!

Roles:
Gotswana (Doctor), Devil, Brigham Young (African Pageant)
Joined The Book:
1st Vineyard Reading, February 2008

ENSEMBLE:
THE AFRICANS

Lawrence Stallings

Roles:
Ugandan Man (who is shot), Middala, Skeleton, Moroni (African Pageant)
Joined The Book:
Lincoln Center Workshop, August 2010

Rema Webb

Roles:
Mrs. Brown, Kimbay, Uhura, Skeleton, Coffee Cup
Joined The Book:
1st Vineyard Reading, February 2008

Maia Nkenge Wilson

Roles:
Kalimba, Genghis Kahn
Joined The Book:
1st Vineyard Reading, February 2008

Tommar Wilson

Roles:
General's Guard #2, Ghali, Darth Vader, Skeleton, Jesus (African Pageant)
Joined The Book:
Broadway, February 2011

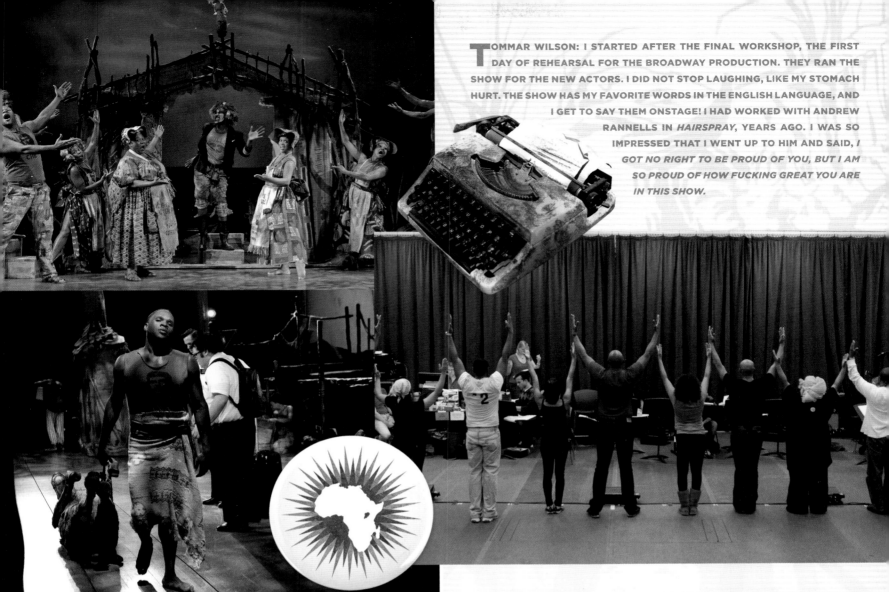

TOMMAR WILSON: I STARTED AFTER THE FINAL WORKSHOP, THE FIRST DAY OF REHEARSAL FOR THE BROADWAY PRODUCTION. THEY RAN THE SHOW FOR THE NEW ACTORS. I DID NOT STOP LAUGHING, LIKE MY STOMACH HURT. THE SHOW HAS MY FAVORITE WORDS IN THE ENGLISH LANGUAGE, AND I GET TO SAY THEM ONSTAGE! I HAD WORKED WITH ANDREW RANNELLS IN *HAIRSPRAY*, YEARS AGO. I WAS SO IMPRESSED THAT I WENT UP TO HIM AND SAID, *I GOT NO RIGHT TO BE PROUD OF YOU, BUT I AM SO PROUD OF HOW FUCKING GREAT YOU ARE IN THIS SHOW.*

ASMERET GHEBREMICHAEL: A LOT OF PEOPLE WONDERED WHAT THE MORMON COMMUNITY WOULD THINK ABOUT IT. THOSE OF US WHO PLAY UGANDANS WERE LIKE, *YEAH, BUT WHAT ABOUT THE BLACK COMMUNITY?* THIS IS REALLY CONTROVERSIAL. WE'RE RESPONSIBLE FOR SHARING ALL THE OUTRAGEOUS INFORMATION IN THE SHOW. SO I DIDN'T KNOW HOW PEOPLE WERE GOING TO RESPOND TO US SAYING *FUCK YOU, GOD.* I ALSO WONDERED WHAT MY PARENTS WERE GOING TO THINK, BECAUSE THEY'RE AFRICAN. I THOUGHT THEY WOULD EITHER FIND IT ABSOLUTELY HYSTERICAL OR BE OFFENDED. BUT THEY LOVED IT. WHEN WE ALL FREEZE AND SING *FUCK YOU GOD IN THE ASS, MOUTH, AND CUNT,* I JUST HAPPENED TO BE RIGHT IN FRONT OF MY MOTHER. I WAS LOOKING OVER HER HEAD, BUT THEN I JUST GLANCED DOWN TO SEE HOW SHE WAS GOING TO RESPOND. WE SANG THE LINE AND SHE WAS DOUBLED OVER IN LAUGHTER. SHE SAID AFTERWARDS, *YOU COULDN'T EVEN SAY 'SHUT UP' GROWING UP, AND NOW YOU CAN SAY ALL THE BAD WORDS.*

MAIA NKENGE WILSON: I GOT A PHONE CALL FROM BOBBY LOPEZ, AND HE WAS LIKE, *WE'RE DOING A NEW SHOW, BUT BEFORE YOU SAY YES WE WANT TO LET YOU KNOW WHAT YOU WOULD BE SINGING.* I WAS JUST LIKE, *OKAY.* AND WHEN HE SAID *FUCK YOU IN THE ASS* AND EVERYTHING, I WAS JUST LIKE, *OH MY GOODNESS, YES I'LL DO IT!* I LOVE SHOCK VALUE, I LOVE GETTING PEOPLE TO THINK. I THOUGHT TO BE A PART OF THAT WOULD BE GREAT.

JOHN ERIC PARKER: I COME FROM A FAMILY OF MINISTERS, DEACONS, DEACONESSES, AND GOSPEL SINGERS, SO I WAS A LITTLE NERVOUS ABOUT WHAT I LIKE TO CALL GRATUITOUS GOD JOKES. AND I WAS A LITTLE NERVOUS ABOUT WHETHER THE THINGS THAT MATUMBO HAS TO SAY WERE GROUNDED IN SOMETHING. BUT THE WAY MATT, TREY AND BOBBY WRITE, IT'S ALL GROUNDED AND TIED INTO SOMETHING REAL AND TANGIBLE. EVEN IF YOU THINK IT'S JUST A JOKE, IT TAKES YOU RIGHT BACK TO SOMETHING THAT IS REAL AND TANGIBLE. SO THERE WAS A LITTLE APPREHENSION AT FIRST, BUT WHEN I GOT TO SEE HOW THEY WORK FIRSTHAND, I WAS NOT NERVOUS AT ALL.

I LOVE SHOCK VALUE.
I LOVE GETTING PEOPLE TO THINK.

MAIA NKENGE WILSON

LAWRENCE STALLINGS: THE AFRICAN ENSEMBLE CAN FEEL THE AUDIENCE ENJOYING THE SHOW IN 'HELLO' AND 'TWO BY TWO.' WE FEEL THEM STARTING TO LOVE THESE CHARACTERS. AND THEN WE COME ON, AND WE FEEL EVERYBODY'S GUARD SHOOT UP WHEN 'HASA DIGA' IS TRANSLATED. IN THE BEGINNING IT WAS LIKE, *OH MAN, WHY DON'T WE GET THE SAME KIND OF APPLAUSE THAT THE MORMONS GET?* BECAUSE I THINK PEOPLE, EVEN WHEN THEY ENJOY IT, ARE THINKING, *SHOULD WE CLAP FOR THIS, IF WE APPLAUD ARE WE CONDONING IT?* YOU CAN FEEL IT, BUT YOU CAN ALSO FEEL THE ONES WHO GET IT IMMEDIATELY, AND THEY GIVE PERMISSION TO EVERYONE ELSE TO JUST RELAX AND NOT TAKE IT SO SERIOUSLY. THAT'S ALSO TRANSFORMATIVE, BECAUSE YOU SEE PEOPLE IN THE AUDIENCE WHO LOOK LIKE *I CANNOT TAKE ANOTHER OFFENSE.* AND THEN YOU SEE THOSE SAME PEOPLE AT THE END OF THE SHOW JUMP TO THEIR FEET BECAUSE THEY GOT IT, THEY UNDERSTOOD WHAT THE SHOW WAS ABOUT. SO YOU FEEL LIKE YOU'RE A PART OF SOMETHING TRANSFORMATIVE.

MICHAEL JAMES SCOTT: TO BE ABLE TO GET TO DO WHAT I'M DOING IN THE SHOW, I KIND OF DON'T REALLY BELIEVE IT SOMETIMES. IT'S LIKE AN ACTOR'S DREAM TO RUN DOWN CENTER AT THE END OF THE ACT AND STAND THERE WITH YOUR HANDS OUT, BELTING *I HAVE MAGGOTS IN MY SCROTUM.* IT'S SO OUT OF CONTEXT FOR ME THAT I FEEL LIKE IT'S IMAGINARY, LIKE IT'S NOT REAL THAT I ACTUALLY GET TO DO THAT. WHEN I'M WALKING ON THE STREET, THAT'S THE NUMBER ONE QUESTION FROM EVERYBODY WHO RECOGNIZES ME FROM THE SHOW: *HEY, HOW'S YOUR SCROTUM?*

DARLESIA CEARCY: I'M A SPIRITUAL PERSON, I KNOW THERE ARE MOMENTS WHEN YOU'RE GOING TO HAVE CONFLICT ABOUT HOW THINGS ARE GOING. THE HUMAN PART OF YOU WILL PROBABLY LASH OUT FROM TIME TO TIME. SO THE LANGUAGE DIDN'T BOTHER ME, IT WAS ACTUALLY QUITE INTERESTING. MATT SAYS, *I THINK GOD HAS A SENSE OF HUMOR,* AND I WOULD AGREE WITH THAT.

REMA WEBB: I'VE BEEN WITH THE SHOW SINCE THE FIRST READING AT THE VINEYARD. I WAS IN *THE LION KING*, WORKING ON BOTH DURING THE READINGS AND WORKSHOPS. I ALSO BOOKED *SPIDER-MAN* AT THE SAME TIME, BUT MY HEART WAS WITH *MORMON.* I DIDN'T KNOW WHERE IT WAS GOING, BUT DIDN'T CARE. NONE OF US CARED, WE JUST LOVED THE PROJECT SO MUCH, WE JUST WANTED TO STAY WITH IT. WE WORKED ON THE SHOW SO LONG TOGETHER THAT WE DEVELOPED OUR OWN RELATIONSHIPS; EVERY CHARACTER HAS A RELATIONSHIP WITH EACH OTHER. I AM THE AUNTIE OF THE VILLAGE; MICHAEL JAMES SCOTT—THE DOCTOR—AND I DECIDED THAT WE WERE HAVING A SECRET AFFAIR THAT NONE OF THE OTHER CHARACTERS KNEW ABOUT.

{ IT'S A HIT! }

JOSH GAD: During the first week of previews, something strange started to happen. We have a daily ticket lottery, and on the first day maybe sixty people showed up, which was huge. We were, like, *Wow!* Then second day, about a hundred people. *Okay, that's kind of crazy.* By the end of the first week there were no less than three hundred people waiting for this lottery. The word of mouth spread so fast and furious, it was unlike anything I've ever seen before. Originally, I thought this is going to be a big show for the twenty-somethings who grew up with *South Park*, who love that kind of humor. Everybody else may eventually discover it. That idea was shattered early on. We started to see seventy-year-olds, eighty-year-olds. Within the first month there was a hundred-year-old man sitting in the balcony and I was, like, *What is going on here?*

ANDREW RANNELLS: I knew that it was going to be big. Either because it was going to be protested and people were going to be livid, or it would be some cool underground thing. But when we had an audience at the end of our workshop, there was something about it I was like *This is actually bigger than we think it is.* So I was pretty confident that we would be okay. I didn't think that it was going to be as widely received as it has been. It's definitely a surprise to see the demographic is a wide one. It's strange, the mix of people. Hillary Clinton came with Chelsea Clinton and her new husband and Nana Rodham on her ninetieth birthday, so it was the four of them sitting there. It was a very strange picture to see each of their reactions to what

was being performed in front of them. I felt bad for that son-in-law—a little awkward sitting next to your new mother-in-law.

JOSH GAD: One night I was sitting at home browsing the internet. I have Piers Morgan on in the background, and I hear Kevin Smith—the film director—go on this five-minute monologue about how *The Book of Mormon* has completely changed the game for every comedic personality out there, for every creative director, actor, et cetera. And I look up and I see pictures of me on the TV and I'm like, *This thing, it's not a show, it's a pop cultural phenomenon.* When we first got started, I knew it was something special; but I didn't know what the implications would be, and it's transcended all of them.

RORY O'MALLEY: People ask me if I get tired of it, or if it's difficult to do the same thing over and over again, and I say it is sometimes like *Groundhog Day.* But it's *Groundhog Day* of the greatest day of your life, over and over again, so you can't really complain.

JOSH GAD: I think that it's a remarkable thing that every day people leave the theatre and come up to me and say, *not only did I laugh but I cried, and I never expected to do that.* That to me says that this is something greater than just a biting comedy. This is something that is thought-provoking and really has the ability to change your life. And that's a pretty cool thing. Maybe the last show to do that was *Cats*? ♦

> **THE SHOW IS WHAT WE WANTED IT TO BE. IT IS THE SHOW WE FANTASIZED ABOUT, WHAT WE HOPED FOR AND DREAMED OF. WHATEVER YOU THINK ABOUT IT, IT'S WHAT WE WANTED IT TO BE...**
>
> **TO WORK ON SOMETHING FOR SEVEN YEARS—AND THEN CATCH MYSELF ALL THE TIME THINKING, OH, YOU KNOW WHAT WOULD BE REALLY COOL IS IF WHEN THEY GET TO—OH, NO. WAIT. WHY AM I THINKING ABOUT THIS ANYMORE? IT'S DONE. I CAN'T CHANGE IT ANYMORE. AND IT'S REALLY HARD AFTER SPENDING SEVEN YEARS WORKING ON IT, AND ALL THE LOVE YOU FEEL FOR IT—IT'S HARD TO SAY, STOP THINKING ABOUT THAT!**

TREY PARKER
MARCH 24, 2011
OPENING NIGHT

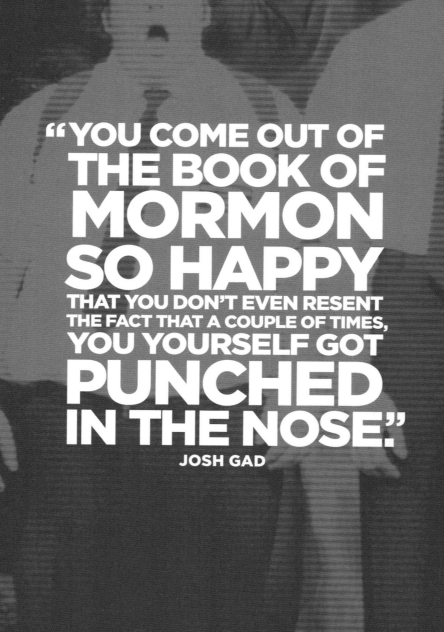

"YOU COME OUT OF THE BOOK OF MORMON SO HAPPY THAT YOU DON'T EVEN RESENT THE FACT THAT A COUPLE OF TIMES, YOU YOURSELF GOT PUNCHED IN THE NOSE."

JOSH GAD

PART 3
THE BOOK

Reading the Script

by

MARK HARRIS

About five minutes into the *The Book of Mormon*, the jaw of the woman sitting to my left dropped, her arched eyebrows took up residence about one inch higher than their usual position, and her face remained thus frozen for the rest of the show, an ossified mask of utter shock, what an Easter Island statue might look like if another Easter Island statue suddenly farted. Conversely, the woman sitting to my right was so convulsed with laughter that she had to cover her mouth so she wouldn't miss the next line. And the man in front of me was wiping away a tear during the final song, perhaps because he was unexpectedly moved, or maybe out of sheer adrenalized elation that yes, they had really pulled it off—a great pastiche of classic musical comedies that, by sheer force of talent, brains, commitment and originality, had become a great musical comedy itself. It is one of the many triumphs of *The Book of Mormon* that these various reactions are equally appropriate, and the fact that if you're lucky, you can experience all three of them—shock, delight and joy—at the

> **❝CONVERSELY, THE WOMAN SITTING TO MY RIGHT WAS SO CONVULSED WITH LAUGHTER THAT SHE HAD TO COVER HER MOUTH SO SHE WOULDN'T MISS THE NEXT LINE.❞**

same time is a testament to the spectacular feat that Trey Parker, Matt Stone, and Robert Lopez have pulled off.

And what better way to kill all that fun than by taking away the music, the great performances, the dazzling design and choreography and just looking at the script? Ordinarily, I'd warn people away from spoiling their own fun this way, but reading *The Book of Mormon* turns out to be a wholly entertaining and edifying experience on its own—a mellower moment in which to appreciate that the exuberant, anarchic spirit of what the *South Park* guys and the gentleman from *Avenue Q* have created was not accomplished casually. The subtlety and suppleness of the architecture of this piece is the product of exacting, even painstaking work. It's almost impossible to make it look this easy, but that's what musical theater has to do. And there's no condescension to the form in this amazing work—rather, there's a reverent understanding that the genre is rich and roomy enough to accommodate acid social commentary and high-energy dance breaks, Jesus, Hitler, and Starbucks, classic heartfelt moments and things that I'd be tempted to call unsayable except that they say them. All of them. Often in rhymed couplets.

Some people—not many—have contended that what you're about to read is deeply unfair to Mormons (it's not nice to make fun of somebody's religion). A few others have suggested that the show is deeply unfair to Africa (it's not nice to make fun of somebody's continent). And these two arguments are another very good reason to read the script. While you do, it might be helpful to keep in mind G. K. Chesterton's famous maxim that "wit is a sword; it is meant to make people feel the point as well as see it." But you don't need a copy of *Bartlett's Familiar Quotations* (or, okay, Google) to understand, from these pages, that Parker, Stone and Lopez are certainly not interested in taking a flamethrower to the Church of Jesus Christ of Latter-Day Saints, or in evincing any contempt for or indifference to the plight of Africans. As is always true of the best satirists, they are merciless but never mean.

Ultimately, they're determined to go for the jugular only when it comes to one particular target. That target is us. What the creators of *The Book of Mormon* understand so brilliantly is an essential and underexplored contradiction in the American character: they revel in the conundrum that we love learning about mystical faraway places—whether Uganda, Orlando or Sal Tlay Ka Siti—but at the same time, we're so creeped out by anything or anyone that isn't just like us that we have to make up fairy tales about them (and sometimes about ourselves) to make everything feel okay again. But the simple primitive people are not so simple—and neither, it turns out, are the simple primitive missionaries. In song after song and scene after scene, this show knows how to find that exquisitely uncomfortable sweet spot, the precise place where sunny optimism shades into privileged smugness, where blind faith becomes oblivious cultism, where charity crosses the line into sanctimony. I'd be more than happy to explain how, in songs like "I Believe" and "I Am Africa" and "You and Me (But Mostly Me)," they pull it off. But first of all, I have no idea, and second, in this case, explanations are completely superfluous. The point is, they do it, and do it impeccably. You come out of *The Book of Mormon* so happy that you don't even resent the fact that a couple of times, you yourself got punched in the nose. That's not just great theater. That's great writing. ◆

MARK HARRIS is a journalist and the author of *Pictures At A Revolution: Movies* and *The Birth Of The New Hollywood.*

Opening Night

The Book of Mormon opened on Broadway on March 24, 2011 at the Eugene O'Neill Theatre, where it was presented by Anne Garefino, Scott Rudin, Roger Berlind, Scott M. Delman, Jean Doumanian, Roy Furman, Important Musicals LLC, Stephanie P. McClelland, Kevin Morris, Jon B. Platt, Sonia Friedman Productions, and Stuart Thompson. It was directed by Casey Nicholaw and Trey Parker with choreography by Casey Nicholaw. The set design was by Scott Pask, the costume design was by Ann Roth, the lighting design was by Brian MacDevitt, the sound design was by Brian Ronan; the musical direction and vocal arrangements were by Stephen Oremus, the orchestrations were by Larry Hochman and Stephen Oremus, the dance music arrangements were by Glen Kelly; the music coordinator was Michael Keller, the production stage manager was Karen Moore. The cast was (in order of appearance):

Mormon . . . . *Jason Michael Snow*
Moroni. . . . . *Rory O'Malley*
Elder Price . . . . *Andrew Rannells*
Elder Cunningham. . . . . *Josh Gad*
Price's Dad . . . . *Lewis Cleale*
Cunningham's Dad. . . . . *Kevin Duda*
Mrs. Brown . . . . *Rema Webb*
Guards . . . . *John Eric Parker, Tommar Wilson*
Mafala Hatimbi . . . . *Michael Potts*
Nabulungi. . . . . *Nikki M. James*
Elder McKinley . . . . *Rory O'Malley*
General . . . . *Brian Tyree Henry*
Doctor . . . . *Michael James Scott*
Ensemble. . . . . *Scott Barnhardt, Justin Bohon, Darlesia Cearcy,*
Kevin Duda, Asmeret Ghebremichael,
Clark Johnsen, John Eric Parker,
Benjamin Schrader, Michael James Scott, Brian Sears,
Jason Michael Snow, Lawrence Stallings,
Rema Webb, Maia Nkenge Wilson, Tommar Wilson

HELLO
I WOULD LIKE TO SHARE WITH YOU THE MOST AMAZING BOOK.

ACT 1

THE BOOK OF MORMON

– PROLOGUE –
THE HILL CUMORAH

The Mormon theme blares out of trumpets. Upstage there is a large picture frame, depicting a biblical scene from the Book of Mormon.

NARRATOR
Long ago, in the year of our Lord 326 AD, a great prophet is leader of the Nephite people in ancient Upstate New York. His name...is Mormon. ❶

MORMON
I am Mormon. My people sailed here from Israel to create a new civilization. These golden plates tell of our people and how we met...with Jesus Christ.

Christ appears to Mormon.

JESUS
I am Jesus. Take care of your golden plates, Mormon, for soon, your entire civilization will be gone and nobody will remember you.

Christ leaves and Mormon begins to write and then dig.

NARRATOR
Just before the Nephite people were wiped out, Mormon gave the plates to his son, Moroni.

MORONI
I am Moroni, the last of my kind. I shall BURY the golden plates, father, and perhaps one day, someone very special will find them... ❷

NARRATOR
And lo, Moroni buried the golden plates high on a hill. Centuries later, the golden plates were found, giving birth to the fastest growing religion today! A church that even now sends missionaries out... All over the world...

❶ **TREY PARKER:** For a long time, "Hello" was going to be the beginning of the show. People who have met (*Continued on p. 102*)
❷ **RORY O'MALLEY:** (*Continued on p. 102*)

(continued from p. 101)
Mormons, their first contact is usually someone ringing the doorbell and saying "Hello." It was literally the first song we wrote, it helped us to set up what the show was going to be about. Just before we started the third workshop, we went to the Hill Cumorah Pageant, on Joseph Smith's old farm in upstate New York. As soon as we saw the pageant, we thought: *we want to do this!* We had all these facts about the Mormon religion, we were constantly trying to decide how much information to put in. The pageant does it so well.

(continued from p. 101)
2 RORY O'MALLEY: Sometimes the audience acts like they are coming to a rock show, they are there to scream and holler. As soon as the lights go out, they're already cheering. And there are other nights when they can't believe what they're seeing, and their jaws are on the ground. We start the show with that little tableau about ancient America. There are two laughs: *"ancient Upstate New York"* and Jesus being up on the stage. It's a recorded voice-over by Trey, so it's the same delivery every night. I'm up there as Moroni, and I can always tell what kind of audience we're going to have by what kind of laughs we get. Sometimes they're a little more shocked that Jesus is on a stage with a '70s glamour wig on, with the blonde locks; and sometimes you simply can't hear the line, because they've been cheering since the lights went down. So I know right off the bat if it's going to be that rock star audience, or if it's going to be that shocked audience. But then we know what our job is. We know that we're going to be in a rock show and we have to make sure that we wait it out for some of the jokes, or we know we've got to bring the audience with us a little bit more. And those are usually the audiences that are on their feet fastest at the end of the show.

– MISSIONARY TRAINING CENTER –

ELDER KEVIN PRICE, a young, dashing Mormon missionary in a white shirt and black tie, walks up with a big smile on his face, holding the Book of Mormon. He pantomimes ringing a doorbell, and we hear DING DONG!

HELLO!

ELDER PRICE
HELLO,
MY NAME IS ELDER PRICE,
AND I WOULD LIKE TO SHARE
    WITH YOU
THE MOST AMAZING BOOK.

A different Mormon missionary now steps forward on another part of the stage and pretends to ring a bell. (DING DONG)

ELDER GRANT
HELLO,
MY NAME IS ELDER GRANT,
IT'S A BOOK ABOUT AMERICA
    A LONG LONG TIME AGO.

(DING DONG) Yet another kid at a different area of the stage.

ELDER PRICE
IT HAS SO MANY AWESOME PARTS –

(DING DONG) A new missionary rings, but no answer.

ELDER PRICE
YOU SIMPLY WON'T BELIEVE
    HOW MUCH THIS BOOK
    CAN CHANGE YOUR LIFE!

(DING DONG, DING DONG, DONG DONG) Same kid with no answer, tries more.

ELDER GREEN
HELLO,
MY NAME IS ELDER GREEN.
AND I WOULD LIKE TO SHARE WITH
    YOU THIS BOOK OF JESUS CHRIST.

(DING DONG)

ELDER YOUNG
HELLO, MY NAME IS ELDER
    YOUNG.

ELDER HARRIS
HELLO!

ELDER YOUNG
DID YOU KNOW THAT JESUS
    LIVED HERE IN THE USA?

ELDER GRANT
YOU CAN READ ALL ABOUT IT NOW.

ELDER CROSS

HELLO!

ELDER GRANT

IN THIS NIFTY BOOK, IT'S FREE!
NO YOU DON'T HAVE TO PAY.

ELDER YOUNG

HELLO!

ELDER SMITH

HELLO,
MY NAME IS ELDER SMITH,
AND CAN I LEAVE THIS BOOK WITH YOU
FOR YOU TO JUST PERUSE?

ELDER BROWN

HELLO!

ELDER GREEN

HELLO!

ELDER HARRIS

HELLO!

ELDER SMITH

I'LL JUST LEAVE IT HERE.
IT HAS A LOT OF INFORMATION
YOU CAN REALLY USE.

ELDER PRICE

HELLO!

ELDER HARRIS

HI!

ELDER PRICE

MY NAME IS –

ELDER GREEN

JESUS CHRIST!

ELDER GRANT

YOU HAVE A LOVELY HOME

ELDER CROSS

HELLO!

ELDER YOUNG

IT'S AN AMAZING BOOK

ELDER SMITH

BONJOUR!

ELDER WHITE

HOLA!

ELDER HARRIS

NI HAO!

ELDER WHITE

ME LLAMO ELDER WHITE.

ELDER GRANT

ARE THESE YOUR KIDS?

ELDER GREEN

THIS BOOK GIVES YOU THE SECRET
TO ETERNAL LIFE.

ELDER CROSS

SOUND GOOD?

ELDERS

ETERNAL LIFE!

ELDER GREEN

WITH JESUS CHRIST!

ELDERS

IS SUPER FUN!

ELDER WHITE

HELLO!

ELDER YOUNG

DING DONG!

ELDERS

AND IF YOU LET US IN WE'LL SHOW
YOU HOW IT CAN BE DONE!

ELDER GRANT

NO THANKS?

ELDER GREEN

YOU SURE?

ELDER GRANT

OH WELL.

ELDER GREEN

THAT'S FINE.

ELDER GRANT

GOODBYE!

ELDER GREEN

HAVE FUN IN HELL.

ELDER GRANT & ELDER CROSS
Hey now!

ELDERS

YOU SIMPLY WON'T BELIEVE

③ ANNE GAREFINO: When Trey, Matt, and Bobby were first meeting to work on their undefined project about Mormons, Trey would send me things that they had written. The very first thing he sent me was the song, "Hello." I got chills when I listened to it. I knew whatever this was going to be, it was going to be special.

Y GUARANTEE

THAT

OK WILL

NGE

R LIFE

HOW MUCH THIS BOOK WILL
   CHANGE YOUR LIFE,
THIS BOOK WILL CHANGE YOUR LIFE,
THIS BOOK WILL CHANGE YOUR LIFE!
THIS BOOK WILL CHANGE YOUR LIFE!
THIS BOOK WILL CHANGE YOUR LIFE!

Shy, nerdy ELDER ARNOLD CUNNINGHAM walks up and with a big gesture rings a fake doorbell. DWANG, DONG, DWOONG!!!

ELDER CUNNINGHAM
Hello?! Would you like to change religions, I have a free book written by Jesus!

Silence. All the Elders glare at him. Now a big, booming VOICE comes out of the darkness.

VOICE
NO, NO, ELDER CUNNINGHAM! That's NOT how we do it. You're making things up again. JUST STICK TO THE APPROVED DIALOGUE. Elders, show him.

The music starts again and the Elders all sing around Arnold, who tries to keep up.

ELDERS
   HELLO!

ELDER CUNNINGHAM
Hello...

ELDERS
   MY NAME IS

ELDER CUNNINGHAM
Elder Cunningham?

ELDERS
   AND WE WOULD LIKE TO SHARE
      WITH YOU
   THIS BOOK OF JESUS CHRIST!

ELDER PRICE
   HELLO!

ELDER GRANT
   HELLO!

ELDER GREEN
   DING DONG!

ELDER WHITE
   HEIGH HO!

ELDER SMITH
   JUST TAKE THIS BOOK!

ELDER YOUNG
   IT'S FREE!

ELDER PRICE
   FOR YOU!

ELDER HARRIS
   FROM ME!

ELDER GRANT
   YOU SEE?

ELDERS
   YOU SIMPLY WON'T BELIEVE
      HOW MUCH THIS BOOK WILL
         CHANGE YOUR LIFE!
   HELLO
   THIS BOOK WILL CHANGE YOUR LIFE!
   HELLO
   SO YOU WON'T BURN IN

ELDER WHITE
   HEL - LO!

ELDERS
   YOU'RE GONNA DIE SOMEDAY!
   BUT IF YOU READ THIS BOOK
      YOU'LL SEE
      THAT THERE'S ANOTHER WAY.
   SPEND ETERNITY WITH FRIENDS
      AND FAMILY.
   WE CAN FULLY GUARANTEE YOU
      THAT
   THIS BOOK WILL CHANGE YOUR LIFE
   HELLO!
   THIS BOOK WILL CHANGE YOUR LIFE!
   HELLO!
   THIS BOOK WILL CHANGE YOUR LIFE!
   THE BOOK OF MORMON!
   MORMON!
   HELLO!!!

The same booming voice is heard–

VOICE
Alright, Elders, that was very good indeed. You have been training for three months and you are now...READY TO GO OUT AND SPREAD THE WORD!

The Elders all look at each other and jump around with excitement.

ELDERS
Alright! / Yes! / We graduated! / Etc.

VOICE

In a moment you will be assigned your mission companions and locations!

More excitement and CHATTER from the Elders.

ELDER PRICE

Oh boy! Oh boy this is IT, guys!

ELDER YOUNG

I can't believe the day is here! We get to go out and see the world!

ELDER SMITH

Do you have any idea where they're sending you, Elder Price?

ELDER PRICE

Well... Of course, we don't REALLY have final say over where we get sent... But I have been PRAYING to be sent to my favorite place in the world...

ELDER GRANT

Well, if YOU prayed for a location I'm sure Heavenly Father will make it happen! You're like the smartest, best, most deserving Elder the center has ever seen!

ELDERS

Yeah! / That's right! / Etc.

ELDER PRICE

Aw, come on guys...

The Elders all turn and talk to each other as Price steps forward and addresses the crowd.

TWO BY TWO

ELDER PRICE

THE MOST IMPORTANT TIME OF
  A MORMON KID'S LIFE
  IS HIS MISSION.
A CHANCE TO GO OUT AND HELP
  HEAL THE WORLD,
THAT'S MY MISSION.
SOON I'LL BE OFF IN A DIFFERENT
  PLACE,
HELPING THE WHOLE HUMAN
  RACE.
I KNOW MY MISSION WILL BE
  SOMETHING INCREDIBLE.

VOICE

Elders, form a line and step forward when your name is called! Elder Young!

Young runs to center stage.

ELDER YOUNG

Yes, sir!

VOICE

Your mission brother will be... ELDER GRANT!!!

Grant steps out of the crowd.

ELDER GRANT

That's...that's me!

Elder Grant runs out to stand next to Young and they high-five each other.

ELDER GRANT

Hey brother!

They shake hands.

VOICE

And your mission location is... NORWAY!

ELDER YOUNG

Oh wow, NORWAY!

ELDER GRANT

Land of gnomes and trolls!!

ELDER GRANT & ELDER YOUNG

TWO BY TWO WE'RE MARCHING
  DOOR TO DOOR!
'CAUSE GOD LOVES MORMONS
  AND HE WANTS SOME MORE!
A TWO-YEAR MISSION IS OUR
  SACRIFICE
WE ARE THE ARMY OF THE
  CHURCH OF JESUS CHRIST!
[OF LATTER-DAY SAINTS]

ELDERS

TWO BY TWO AND TODAY WE'LL
  KNOW
    WHO WE'LL MAKE THE
    JOURNEY WITH AND WHERE
    WE'LL GO.
WE'RE FIGHTING FOR A CAUSE BUT
    WE'RE REALLY REALLY NICE,
WE ARE THE ARMY OF THE
  CHURCH OF JESUS CHRIST!
[OF LATTER-DAY SAINTS]

2 KEVIN DUDA: I'm Elder Young in the opening. Brian Sears and I are the first couple to get assigned—we're sent to Norway. Then I rush to don the fat suit and play Elder Cunningham's schleppy father. Once we're in Africa, I play Elder Neeley. I don't have much to say in Africa because I play so many different roles. At the top of Act Two, I play Jesus, and Hitler in Hell, and also Cunningham's Dad again in "Making Things Up Again."

①SCOTT BARNHARDT: Clark and I aren't not sent anywhere. Every now and then we'll just come up with different places where we're going, like Bakersfield, California.

②BOBBY LOPEZ: It was Somalia at first. We started in Somalia and I think it was between Africa and maybe Japan. If it had been Japan, it would have been white guys coming to a beautiful Zen country with lovely, wonderful traditions—and through their naïveté, kind of ruining it like in *Pacific Overtures*. But I was more attracted to the Africa story, I think we all were. Matt knows more about Africa than anyone I know. He had all these facts about atrocities and really terrible stuff, the kind of stuff that challenges anyone's belief in God and we tend not to talk about. And I thought, *What better challenge for these two guys with one of the silliest religions going to one of the bleakest places, like an epic struggle.* That's something to write about.

VOICE
Elder White and Elder Smith!

White and Smith now take center stage.

ELDER SMITH
I KNEW we'd get paired together!

VOICE
Your location will be FRANCE!

ELDER WHITE
FRANCE! Land of pastries and turtlenecks!

ELDER SMITH & ELDER WHITE
TWO BY TWO I GUESS IT'S YOU
AND ME.
WE'RE OFF TO PREACH ACROSS
LAND AND SEA!

ELDER WHITE
Satan has a hold of France!

ELDER SMITH
We need to knock him off his perch!

ELDERS
WE ARE THE SOLDIERS OF THE ARMY
OF THE CHURCH!
[OF JESUS CHRIST OF LATTER-DAY
SAINTS]

VOICE
Elder Cross and Elder Green!

The new two take center stage.

VOICE
You will be serving in JAPAN!

ELDER GREEN
Oh boy, Japan!

ELDER CROSS
Land of soy sauce —

ELDER GREEN
And Mothra!

VOICE
Elder Harris and Elder Brown...

Now our hero, Elder Price, steps forward into a spotlight, having a moment to himself as the action continues in the dark behind him. ①

ELDER PRICE
HEAVENLY FATHER, WHERE WILL I

GO ON MY MISSION?

ELDERS
ON MY MISSION

ELDER PRICE
WILL IT BE CHINA OR OL' MEXICO
ON MY MISSION?

ELDERS
MY MISSION...

ELDER PRICE
IT COULD BE SAN FRAN BY THE BAY,
AUSTRALIA WHERE THEY SAY
"G'DAY!"
(crossing his fingers)
BUT I PRAY I'M SENT TO MY
FAVORITE PLACE –
ORLANDO!

ELDERS
ORLANDO

ELDER PRICE
I LOVE YOU

ELDER PRICE & ELDERS
ORLANDO!

ELDER PRICE
SEA WORLD AND DISNEY AND

ELDER PRICE & ELDERS
PUTT PUTT GOLFING

VOICE
Elder Price!

Price is snapped out of his moment and runs back to center stage.

ELDER PRICE
Yes, sir!!!

VOICE
Your brother will be...ELDER Cunningham!

The nerdy Cunningham comes bouncing out.

ELDER CUNNINGHAM
That's! That's ME!

He struts out to Price and gives a big dorky wave.

ELDER CUNNINGHAM
HELLO!!!

ELDER PRICE
Oh... Hi...

VOICE
And your mission location is... UGANDA!!!! ❷

MUSIC STOPS.

ELDER PRICE
...Uganda?

ELDER CUNNINGHAM
UGANDA! COOL! WHERE IS THAT?!

VOICE
AFRICA!

Price looks visibly upset, but then bucks up and tries to rally himself.

ELDER CUNNINGHAM
Oh BOY–Like *Lion King*!

The other Elders all dance forward, but Price still looks a little shocked.

ELDERS
(Price still perplexed)
TWO BY TWO –
AND NOW IT'S TIME TO GO.
OUR PATHS HAVE BEEN REVEALED
SO LET'S START THE SHOW!
OUR SHIRTS ARE CLEANED AND
    PRESSED
AND OUR HAIRCUTS ARE PRECISE
WE ARE THE ARMY OF THE
    CHURCH,
WE ARE THE ARMY OF THE
    CHURCH,
WE ARE THE ARMY OF THE CHURCH
    OF JESUS CHRIST!
[OF LATTER-DAY SAINTS!] ❺

Even through the rest of the song, Price seems a bit confused and is still reeling from not getting sent to Orlando.

ELDERS
TWO BY TWO
WE MARCH FOR VICTORY
ARMED WITH THE GREATEST BOOK
    IN HISTORY
WE'LL CONVERT EVERYONE ALL
    ACROSS THE PLANET EARTH!
THAT IS THE BEAUTY OF

THE ESSENCE OF
THE PURPOSE OF
THE MISSION OF
THE SOLDIERS OF
THE ARMY OF THE CHURCH
    OF JESUS CHRIST!
[OF LATTER-DAY SAINTS]

VOICE
Alright Elders, go home and pack your things! Tomorrow, your missions begin!

The other Elders all happily walk off in their pairs, ad libbing happy conversation and patting each other on the back, leaving Price and Cunningham alone. Price looks a little uncomfortable, Cunningham looks thrilled.

ELDER CUNNINGHAM
I am SO STOKED we got paired together Elder Price!

ELDER PRICE
Yeah, so am I. This is...fantastic.

ELDER CUNNINGHAM
You know what? I PRAYED to Heavenly Father that we would get paired together. HE REALLY DOES LISTEN!

ELDER PRICE
(confused)
He ANSWERED your prayer, huh?

ELDER CUNNINGHAM
Yup! My mom always said if Heavenly Father is proud of you he'll always give you what you ask! YOU AND ME, FOR TWO YEARS IN UGHAN-DAH! THIS IS GONNA BE AWESOME!!

ELDER PRICE
Yes, I'm sure the Book of Mormon will do those Africans a lot of good.

ELDER CUNNINGHAM
(laughs in his face)
AHH HA HA HAA!!

Cunningham realizes he laughed at the wrong time.

ELDER CUNNINGHAM
Well, see ya tomorrow, companion. TOMORROW IS A LATTER DAY!!!

Cunningham pounces offstage and Price is left staring up at his God.

❸ **CASEY NICHOLAW:** I got to dig into all of my theme park fantasies. This was particularly easy for me because I am that kind of cheesiness in life. I staged that in a room by myself, before I arrived for the workshop. It really was me in my living room in San Diego by myself, no one around, and I kind of enjoyed that.

– SALT LAKE CITY AIRPORT –
❶ ❷ ❸

Elder Price and Elder Cunningham have their suitcases and are each surrounded by their families.

Note that Price's mom is most likely going to have to be played by a male, so we can put a guy in drag and just have him sobbing into a hanky.

PRICE'S DAD
Goodbye, son, we are SO proud of you!

PRICE'S BROTHER
Oh, I can't believe Kevin is going to Africa for TWO YEARS! I'm gonna miss my brother so much!

ELDER PRICE
I know, I'm going to miss you guys, too! Maybe we should see if there's any way I can get assigned somewhere a little closer to home. Like... Florida... or...

PRICE'S DAD
(chuckling)
Ho! Don't worry, son. Heavenly Father has a hand in everything.
(pointing up)
He knows what's best... He always knows!

ELDER PRICE
You're right, dad... I'm sure I'll have an amazing time.

Now we focus on Cunningham with his family.

CUNNINGHAM'S DAD
Alright, son, remember, just do whatever Elder Price tells you. He is a great Mormon. The kind of kid any parent would be proud of.

ELDER CUNNINGHAM
Right! And I'm a FOLLOWER!

CUNNINGHAM'S DAD
That's right. Do your best. Maybe your new companion can help make you not so weird.

ELDER CUNNINGHAM
Yeah, we're gonna have the most amazing time together! It's like... *(stepping out to audience)* It's like I'm finally gonna have a best friend...

CUNNINGHAM'S DAD
And REMEMBER, Arnold, what we talked about in regards to your... little PROBLEM.

ELDER CUNNINGHAM
Don't worry, dad, my little problem is IN CHECK! Not gonna be an issue!

Price has overheard this–

ELDER PRICE
Uh, what's the – "little problem"?

CUNNINGHAM'S DAD
Our little Arnold can sometimes be...Well... He has a very ACTIVE imagination.

ELDER CUNNINGHAM
I LIE A LOT!

CUNNINGHAM'S DAD
NO! He – he just sometimes MAKES THINGS UP when he doesn't know what to say.

ELDER CUNNINGHAM
Bishop Donahue says it's because I have no self-esteem and desperately want to fit in with my peers!

PRICE'S DAD
Well, alright everyone! I think it's time we leave these two to their work! That's right, you boys have a lot of catching up to do now that you're companions! This is it, Elders. You're heading... TO AFRICA!!!!!

The families make it offstage. The lights go dark and a spot comes up on a Lion King— like character who enters stage.

LION KING CHARACTER
HEY NA DA HEY NA! AYA BUBBU ❹
TAYA TAYAAAAAAAAAA!
HAIYAAAA TAYAAA MALA
ENNYAAAAA! HEY NAAA NAAA
NAAA DA HAYAAA!

Finally the lights come up, the families are back, and we are STILL at the airport.

PRICE'S DAD
How did you like THAT, boys?! A real LION KING SEND-OFF!!! We got Mrs. Brown to sing like an African for you.

ELDER PRICE
That's great, Dad, thanks.

LION KING CHARACTER
(waving)
Good luck, boys! I've never been to Africa, but I'm sure it's a hoot!

CUNNINGHAM'S DAD
Goodbye, son! Please be careful!

PRICE'S DAD
Get out there and baptize those Africans, boy!

ELDER PRICE
Bye, Mrs. Brown.

MRS. BROWN
Bye, baby.

Mrs. Brown walks off. The families walk off as well. The boys sit down next to each other.

ELDER CUNNINGHAM
Well... It's just you and me now, companion.

ELDER PRICE
Yup, that's right, Elder.

ELDER CUNNINGHAM
From this point on, according to missionary rule number seventy-two we are never to go anywhere without each other, except the bathroom!

ELDER PRICE
Yes, that's right.

ELDER CUNNINGHAM
It's so awesome because my friends always end up leaving me, but YOU CAN'T! HA HA HAAA!!

Price looks sad.

ELDER CUNNINGHAM
OKAY! Favorite movies! Are you a *Star Wars* guy or a *Star Trek* guy?! I wanna know EVERYTHING ABOUT YOU. Personally I like *Star Wars* but I'm willing to like *Star Trek* more if YOU think it's better.

Price stares at him a minute, then closes his eyes, takes a breath and tries a new strategy.

ELDER PRICE
Elder... I like to have fun just as much as the next guy. But things are different now, you know? We're MEN now. This is OUR TIME to PROVE that we are worthy.

ELDER CUNNINGHAM
Worthy of what?

ELDER PRICE
Of everything we've been promised in the afterlife...

Slow music starts.

YOU AND ME (BUT MOSTLY ME)

ELDER PRICE
I'VE ALWAYS HAD THE HOPE,
    THAT ON THE DAY I GO TO
    HEAVEN,
HEAVENLY FATHER WILL SHAKE
    MY HAND AND SAY
"YOU'VE DONE AN AWESOME JOB,
    KEVIN,"
NOW IT'S OUR TIME TO GO OUT

ELDER CUNNINGHAM
MY BEST FRIEND

ELDER PRICE
AND SET THE WORLD'S PEOPLE
    FREE.
AND WE CAN DO IT TOGETHER,
YOU AND ME,
BUT MOSTLY ME.

Price takes Cunningham under his wing.

ELDER PRICE
YOU AND ME – BUT MOSTLY ME –
ARE GONNA CHANGE THE WORLD
    FOREVER.
CUZ I CAN DO MOST ANYTHING!

ELDER CUNNINGHAM
AND I CAN STAND NEXT TO YOU
    AND WATCH.

ELDER PRICE
EVERY HERO NEEDS A SIDEKICK –
EVERY CAPTAIN NEEDS A MATE.

ELDER CUNNINGHAM
AYE AYE!

ELDER PRICE
EVERY DINNER NEEDS A SIDE DISH –

1 CASEY NICHOLAW: One of the funniest things to me is the moment where Andrew's singing, "Something incredible, I'll do something incredible"—blah, blah, blah. We were going to have him in a pin spot, and Josh was going to pop his head in and say, "My best friend." When we were in tech rehearsal, we were starting to iris in the flat. Josh was standing there, and I said, *Josh, step back, step back, step back.* He was in the way and I thought he was going to get hit. He was like, *What, what?* And the thing closed on him, and Trey and I looked at each other and laughed so hard and we said, *Keep it in! We have to do it!*

2 MICHAEL JAMES SCOTT: Originally in the stage directions it said, *A man walks onto the stage, takes a dump, and leaves.* I remember us being like, *Oh my God, this is crazy.* At our first reading, they had a set sketch showing very skinny Africans, emaciated, and there was one person with a dead carcass, and it just became my thing. It sets up the ridiculousness of the Ugandan world. Not only are you seeing the set, you're seeing that we're now in a very different world from Utah. I was going to have the donkey throughout the entire number, I was going to drag it and dance with it. It was just too big, we couldn't really do that at all; so it became just the cross at the opening. For my next entrance, right before "All-American Prophet," I had a dead dog on my shoulder for the first week of previews. They cut it; it was just too much.

ELDER CUNNINGHAM

ON A SLIGHTLY SMALLER PLATE!

BOTH

AND NOW WE'RE SEEING EYE TO
EYE,
IT'S SO GREAT WE CAN AGREE
THAT HEAVENLY FATHER HAS
CHOSEN YOU AND ME

ELDER PRICE

JUST MOSTLY ME!

Price steps away from Cunningham, ignoring him again and leaving him in the background. **1**

ELDER PRICE

SOMETHING INCREDIBLE... I'LL DO
SOMETHING INCREDIBLE...
I WANT TO BE THE MORMON WHO
CHANGED ALL OF MANKIND

ELDER CUNNINGHAM

MY BEST FRIEND

ELDER PRICE

IT'S SOMETHING I'VE FORESEEN.
NOW THAT I'M NINETEEN,
I'LL DO SOMETHING INCREDIBLE,
THAT BLOWS GOD'S FREAKING
MIND!

BOTH

AND AS LONG AS WE STICK
TOGETHER

ELDER CUNNINGHAM

AND I STAY OUT OF YOUR WAY

ELDER PRICE

OUT OF MY WAY

BOTH

WE WILL CHANGE THE WORLD
FOREVER

ELDER CUNNINGHAM

AND MAKE TOMORROW A LATTER
DAY!

ELDER PRICE

MOSTLY ME!

BOTH

SO STOP SINGING ABOUT IT, AND DO
IT!
HOW READY AND PSYCHED ARE WE?!
LIFE IS ABOUT TO CHANGE FOR YOU
AND –

LIFE IS ABOUT TO CHANGE
FOR ME AND –
LIFE IS ABOUT TO CHANGE
FOR YOU AND –
ME –

ELDER PRICE

BUT ME MOSTLY.
AND THERE'S NO LIMIT TO
WHAT WE CAN DO –
ME AND YOU.
BUT MOSTLY MEEEEEEE!

– A SMALL VILLAGE IN NORTHERN UGANDA –

As the boys walk out onto the stage with their bags, the music starts to slow down, fall apart ...and finally stop.

The boys look around in horror at the poverty they see.

A man walks in front of them dragging a donkey carcass. The boys just watch him pass. **2 3**

ELDER CUNNINGHAM
Wow! Here we are, huh, buddy?! We made it!

ELDER PRICE
(obviously a little freaked out and grossed out)
Yeah, that was...that was ONE LONG TRIP.

Cunningham takes out his video camera and points it at Price.

ELDER CUNNINGHAM
(narrating for camera)
Here we are, in KIT-GU-LI UGANDA! What'dya think about Uganda, Elder?!

ELDER PRICE
I think it's really DIFFERENT!

ELDER CUNNINGHAM
YEAH!! IT'S DIFFERENT!!!

Two very bad-ass guards with sunglasses and machine guns walk up threateningly to the boys.

GENERAL'S GUARD #1
YA! YA! WHAT WE GOT HERE, MAYBE?! GERMAN?! BRITISH?!

ELDER PRICE
Hello!

GENERAL'S GUARD #1
AMERICAN.

ELDER PRICE
Uh, we are supposed to meet
(reading note)
a mister Mafala Hatimbi.

GENERAL'S GUARD #1
YOUR BAGS!

ELDER PRICE
Oh sure. We don't have anything illegal, sirs.

The guards take the bags, rip them open and start tearing through everything inside.

ELDER PRICE
We are from the Church of Jesus Christ of Latter-Day Saints.

ELDER CUNNINGHAM
(still videotaping)
Here are some men with guns looking through our bags!

GENERAL'S GUARD #2
SHUT UP!

After they finish going through the bags, they close them up again.

GENERAL'S GUARD #2
We take these bags!

ELDER CUNNINGHAM
WHAT?!

GENERAL'S GUARD #1
This is your TARIFF to The General!

ELDER PRICE
The General? HEY WAIT A MINUTE!

Suddenly, the guards PUMP their shotguns and M-16s and shove them in the Elders' faces.

GENERAL'S GUARD #1
YOU SHUT THE FUCK UP YOU WANNA DIE?!

ELDER PRICE
Oh my gosh! Okay! Okay!

ELDER CUNNINGHAM
JUST take the bags! WHY ARE YOU DOING THIS?!

The guards walk away. That's when another Ugandan man, MAFALA HATIMBI, comes walking in happily.

MAFALA
(big and happy)
AHHH! There you are! I have been looking for you! I am Mafala Hatimbi. I've been hired to show you to your building.

ELDER PRICE
Oh, thank goodness! Some men just took our bags!

MAFALA
Oh, yes, you must be very careful around here! Now let's get going!

He starts to lead the boys away.

ELDER PRICE
Well, no, first shouldn't we talk to the police about getting our bags back?

MAFALA
The police?! Ha, ha! The police are in Kampala! Two days' drive away!

ELDER PRICE
But a lot of important stuff was in those bags!

MAFALA
Oh well, "Hasa Diga Eebowai!"

ELDER CUNNINGHAM
Excuse me?

BOBBY LOPEZ: In every reading we did, Africa was represented by black people coming on stage. And it just hit this note of uncomfortableness in every single version. All those times, "Hasa Diga" felt very harsh, and we lost a lot of people in that song. People who got what we were going for loved it, but other people just said, *This show's too extreme for me.* But once we put that set in and had the dead donkey actually being dragged across the stage, and the tin corrugated roofs and the sound effects of flies buzzing, people understood that there was a grain of truth behind this, and it wasn't just racism. It wasn't just excessive gratuitous profanity. They got that this is something to say "fuck you, God" about. Why should human beings have to live in such poverty and crisis and degradation when we have drive-thru McDonald's and the Internet and air conditioning? It's just not fair.

MICHAEL POTTS: I'm not on for the first twenty-five minutes. Normally when I'm heading down to the stage, one of the other actors is coming up from the stage, so we have this moment of going, *So, how are they?* And he'll say, *Oh, they're good!*

MICHAEL POTTS: This moment is absolute joy. It's thrilling because of the whole idea; singing the first part of the song without the audience knowing, without tipping your hand a bit, and letting them believe we're going in a totally different direction. And then springing it on them and just listening to the response—it is probably the most thrilling moment I have in the show. That big grin reflects my joy. You didn't know we were going there, did you? *You didn't know it was going to be this kind of show. Here it is, buckle up. This is only the beginning, and if you can get past this, then you'll be okay.*

HASA DIGA EEBOWAI

MAFALA
You're in NORTHERN Uganda now!

MUSIC kicks in.

MAFALA
And in this part of Africa, we ALL have a saying – whenever something bad happens, we just throw our hands up to the sky and say HASA DIGA EEBOWAI!

ELDER CUNNINGHAM
Hasa Diga Eebowai?

MAFALA
It's the only way to get through all these troubled times. There's war, famine...but having a saying makes it all seem better...

MAFALA
THERE ISN'T ENOUGH FOOD TO
EAT.

UGANDANS
HASA DIGA EEBOWAI!

MAFALA
PEOPLE ARE STARVING IN THE
STREET.

UGANDANS & MAFALA
HASA DIGA EEBOWAI!
HASA DIGA EEBOWAI!
HASA DIGA EEBOWAI!

ELDER PRICE
Hey, that's pretty neat!

ELDER CUNNINGHAM
Does it mean no worries for the rest of our days?

MAFALA
Kind of!
WE'VE HAD NO RAIN IN SEVERAL
DAYS.

UGANDANS
HASA DIGA EEBOWAI!

MAFALA
AND EIGHTY PERCENT OF US HAVE
AIDS.

UGANDANS
HASA DIGA EEBOWAI!

MAFALA
MANY YOUNG GIRLS HERE GET
CIRCUMCISED,
THEIR CLITS GET CUT RIGHT OFF.

UGANDANS
WAY OH!

WOMEN
AND SO WE SAY UP TO THE SKY:

UGANDANS
HASA DIGA EEBOWAI!
HASA DIGA EEBOWAI!
HASA DIGA EEBOWAI!

MAFALA
Now you try. Just stand up tall, tilt your head to the sky, and list all the bad things in YOUR life.

Elder Cunningham steps up.

ELDER CUNNINGHAM
SOMEBODY TOOK OUR LUGGAGE
AWAY!

UGANDANS

HASA DIGA EEBOWAI!

ELDER PRICE

THE PLANE WAS CROWDED AND
THE BUS WAS LATE!

UGANDANS

HASA DIGA EEBOWAI!

MAFALA

WHEN THE WORLD IS GETTING
YOU DOWN,
THERE'S NOBODY ELSE TO BLAME.

UGANDANS

WAY OH!

MAFALA

RAISE A MIDDLE FINGER TO THE SKY,
AND CURSE HIS ROTTEN NAME.

ELDER PRICE
Wait, what?

*Elder Cunningham is out of earshot, jamming
with some Ugandans.*

UGANDANS & ELDER CUNNINGHAM

HASA DIGA EEBOWAI!

ELDER CUNNINGHAM
Am I saying it right?

UGANDANS

HASA DIGA EEBOWAI!

ELDER PRICE
Excuse me, what EXACTLY does that phrase
mean?

MAFALA
Well, let's see…"Eebowai" means "God", and
"Hasa Diga" means "FUCK YOU". So I guess in
English it would be, "Fuck you, God!"

UGANDANS

HASA DIGA EEBOWAI!

ELDER PRICE
What?!!

MAFALA

WHEN GOD FUCKS YOU IN THE BUTT

UGANDANS

HASA DIGA EEBOWAI!

MAFALA

FUCK GOD BACK RIGHT IN HIS CUNT!

UGANDANS

HASA DIGA EEBOWAI!

ELDER CUNNINGHAM

HASA DIGA EEBOWAI!
WHAT A NIFTY PHRASE!

UGANDANS

WAY OH!

ELDER CUNNINGHAM

HASA DIGA EEBOWAI!
HASA DIGA EEBOWAI!
HASA DIGA EEBOWAI!

(He keeps going –)

ELDER PRICE
(overlapping –)
Elder Cunningham. Elder Cunningham. Stop –
Elder Cunningham. ELDER CUNNINGHAM!

ELDER CUNNINGHAM
What, what, what?

ELDER PRICE
Don't say that!

ELDER CUNNINGHAM
What? Hasa Diga –

ELDER PRICE
Don't say it! It means something very bad.

ELDER CUNNINGHAM
What?

ELDER PRICE
They're saying F you to Heavenly Father!

ELDER CUNNINGHAM
F you, Heavenly Father?! Holy Moly! I said it
like thirteen times!

UGANDANS

HASA DIGA EEBOWAI!
FUCK YOU, GOD!
HASA DIGA EEBOWAI!
FUCK YOU, GOD!

Price and Cunningham approach Mafala.

2 RORY O'MALLEY: I thought
the ushers would have a standard
routine of what to do when fifty
audience members get up and leave.
I thought, *Well of course there's going
to be a mass exodus, but that's fine.
That's what it's supposed to be.* But I
can maybe count on my two hands
how many times people have left
our show, and I can probably count
many more times in other shows
I've been in that more people have
left. It wasn't because of the material
being offensive, it was just not good.

3 CASEY NICHOLAW: I had
a problem at first saying, Okay,
let's take it from *"fuck you, God."* I
didn't like hearing myself say that
over and over, especially coming
from doing the musical *Elf* where
I was saying, *Let's take it from
"Sparklejollytwinklejingley."* But you
just get used to it.

HA
DIO
EEBO

① **ANDREW RANNELLS:** There are certain points in the show where I can look in the audience and just basically mimic someone's face who is horrified by what's going on. And if I start to get numb to the material, all I have to do is watch the audience for a little while and then it's like, *Oh yes, this is what it's like to hear this for the first time.*

② **REMA WEBB:** When we started down at the Vineyard, it was difficult to sing "Hasa Diga Eebowai." They could see in everyone's eyes that we were conflicted, so they sat us down early on. They asked us what was going on in our heads, we discussed what was going on in the Ugandan village at that time. Things were hard for us, missionaries would come to help but then leave, all we had is ourselves so we thought *No more of this God stuff.* It was important for us to be committed, important for the audience to see how bad things really were, and how excited we were when someone came along and tailored their bible to our needs. We knew all along it was a metaphor; we were never dumb. It doesn't matter what the Book says; what matters is that it gives our characters hope in ourselves and something to look forward to. We began to understand the context of what Trey, Bobby and Matt wrote.

ELDER PRICE
Sir, you really should not be saying that. Things aren't always as bad as they seem.

MAFALA
Oh really? Well, take this fucking asshole MUTUMBO. He got caught last week trying to RAPE A BABY. ①

ELDER PRICE
What? Why?

MAFALA
Some people in his tribe believe having sex with a virgin can cure their AIDS. There aren't many virgins left, so some of them are turning to babies!

ELDER PRICE
But...but that's HORRIBLE?!

MAFALA
I know!

UGANDANS
HASA DIGA EEBOWAI!

MAFALA
HERE'S THE BUTCHER, HE HAS AIDS.
HERE'S THE TEACHER, SHE HAS AIDS.
HERE'S THE DOCTOR, HE HAS AIDS –
HERE'S MY DAUGHTER, SHE HAS A...

They hang on his words...

MAFALA
...WONDERFUL DISPOSITION.
SHE'S ALL I HAVE LEFT IN THE
WORLD.
AND IF EITHER OF YOU LAYS A
HAND ON HER –
I WILL GIVE YOU MY AIDS.

ELDER CUNNINGHAM
No!!!

The Ugandans laugh and party.

UGANDANS
IF YOU DON'T LIKE WHAT WE SAY ②
TRY LIVING HERE A COUPLE DAYS.
WATCH ALL YOUR FRIENDS AND
FAMILY DIE.
HASA DIGA EEBOWAI! FUCK YOU!
HASA DIGA EEBOWAI!
FUCK YOU GOD IN THE ASS, MOUTH,
AND CUNT-A,
FUCK YOU GOD IN THE ASS, MOUTH,
AND CUNT-A,
FUCK YOU GOD IN THE ASS, MOUTH,
AND CUNT-A,
FUCK YOU IN THE EYE.
HASA –
DIGA EEBOWAI
HASA –
FUCK YOU IN THE OTHER EYE.
HASA DIGA EEBOWAI!
HASA DIGA EEBOWAI!
FUCK YOU,
FUCK YOU GOD!
FUCK YOU,
FUCK YOU GOD!
HASA DIGA,
FUCK YOU GOD!
IN THE CUNT!

After the inevitable thunderous applause, we can start the music up again as the set changes and MAFALA'S DAUGHTER leads the boys as if walking them down some village street.

– MORMON MISSIONARIES'
LIVING QUARTERS –

The daughter leads the two boys up to the very small and humble little apartment building. Price is still in a bit of a daze from what he heard the Ugandans singing.

NABULUNGI
This is where my father asked me to bring you. The others like you should be inside.

ELDER CUNNINGHAM
Thank you so much, Jon Bon Jovi.

NABULUNGI
Nabulungi.

ELDER CUNNINGHAM
Nab... Bon Jovi. ③ ④

ELDER PRICE
I'm sorry, we appreciate your help, Nabulungi. Look, uh, maybe sometime, Elder Cunningham and I could talk to you about things. Sort of tell you a little about the Church of Jesus Christ of Latter-Day Saints.

Cunningham again realizes he has laughed inappropriately.

NABULUNGI
I have to get back to the village. But I am always

there – if you want to talk to me.

She turns to go but then turns back.

NABULUNGI

Just one piece of advice. No matter how hot you get at night, keep your windows closed. It is the only way to protect against the scorpions... And the mosquitoes. And the lions. And the murderers and the robbers and the AIDS and the snakes and the safari ants which can actually plant their eggs under your skin and eat you from the inside out.

She walks away. Cunningham stares after her but Price turns away and wipes his forehead.

ELDER PRICE
(big sigh, wipes his brow)
Oh man, Elder, can you believe this?

ELDER CUNNINGHAM

I know, right... She is such a hot shade of black. She's like a latte.

ELDER PRICE

Let's just go inside and meet the other missionaries, alright?

The two walk in the mission door and find an empty room inside the living quarters.

ELDER PRICE
Hello?

Suddenly, six bright crisp white Elders jump out from various positions.

ELDER MCKINLEY
The new recruits are here!

ALL ELDERS
(way too excited)
Oh boy!!!! / Yeah!!! / Alright! / Etc.

ELDER MCKINLEY
WELCOME, Elder Price and Elder Cunningham! I am Elder McKinley, current district leader for this area of the Uganda Mission.

ELDER PRICE
Great to meet you.

ELDER CHURCH
My name is Elder Church. Originally from the great city of Cheyenne, Wyoming!

ELDER MICHAELS
Elder Michaels. From Provo.

ELDER THOMAS
Elder Thomas! But the Elders here all call me Elder Pop Tarts because I love 'em so much! **5**

ELDER MCKINLEY
And that's Elder Neeley and Elder Davis.

ELDER CUNNINGHAM
Whew! That's a lot to remember!

ELDERS
(cheesy laughter)

After all the laughter has died out, Cunningham finally chimes in with a badly timed laugh of his own.

ELDER MCKINLEY
Sit, please.

ELDER PRICE
Thank you.

They sit and there is an awkward pause.

ELDER MCKINLEY
Well! We've all been here about three months now. Spreading the word of Christ, and saving the souls of the fine Ugandan people through baptism.

ELDER PRICE
How many have you baptized so far?

ELDER MCKINLEY
Uhhh...zero.

Everyone looks a little ashamed.

3 BOBBY LOPEZ: Josh Gad is a force of nature, sort of a Zero Mostel kind of guy. He threw in certain things, like getting Nabulungi's name wrong. I think that started as a joke that Trey wrote. He just wrote some kind of ooga-booga word for Nabulungi, but Josh kept spinning that and turning it into all sorts of things.

4 JOSH GAD: One night I called her Sharon. That was my favorite. It was Scott Rudin's favorite too, but the boys didn't care for that one too much. But that's my all-time favorite, Sharon. And Linda.

5 SCOTT BARNHARDT: Elder Pop Tarts is my claim to fame. I remember when I got the line at the workshop, I was like, *Oh I really hope I get to keep this 'cause it's so silly and funny*, it felt like a match. I feel like if I were a Mormon missionary, I would be Elder Pop Tarts.

① BOBBY LOPEZ: One night they were doing that hubbub moment at the Mission, when Elder McKinley says that the Elders have done zero baptisms and they make embarrassed crowd noises. Josh threw in, *That's practically nothing.*

② CLARK JOHNSEN: "Turn It Off" is just an amazing insight. It's funny and it's hilarious, but it is literally pulled out of my own life. I just had so many fears about being a gay person and how I was going to handle my homosexuality. I was in the church for years as an out gay man, and I told my parents, I told my ecclesiastical leaders, I told everyone: *I'm gay, but I'm celibate and I'm following the rules and I'm obeying the law of chastity and I do plan to hopefully get married to a woman someday. God willing, I'll be able to find my natural tendencies towards women.*

I was constantly anxious inside, but I wasn't displaying any of that anxiety because I was turning it off. Everyone who knew me would have assumed that I was just a happy-go-lucky person, and just optimistic and positive, because I was making the choice to be very positive. So the song could not be more on the nose.

When you're growing up and you are being taught about sexual temptation, if you're having inappropriate thoughts about the opposite sex—or the same sex in my case—then what you're supposed to do is hum your favorite hymn. You get those thoughts out of your head by picking a better thought, a different thought.

From the outside, it probably looks like total repression. But Mormons wouldn't say, *I'm repressed.* They would say, *I'm being careful about what I choose to think about, and if I'm thinking about something that's unpleasant or inappropriate, I'm going to hum a hymn. That hymn will invoke within me certain memories of my faith and my fervor and I will feel better.*

ELDERS
Yeah, zero. / Zip. / None, yeah. / Etc.

ELDER CUNNINGHAM
That's practically nothing...

ELDER PRICE
(stands and walks away)
Oh boy...

ELDER CUNNINGHAM
(follows Price)
Hey, you alright, partner?

ELDER PRICE
Yeah, I'm just a little CONFUSED right now, okay?

ELDERS
Oooooh, confuuused!! / Confused, yeah... / Etc.

ELDER MCKINLEY
Well, Elder, that is NATURAL. There are certainly a lot of things here in Uganda that can be... disturbing. But your mission has officially started, which means you need to do what WE have all done...

TURN IT OFF ②

ELDER MCKINLEY
I'VE GOT A FEELIN',
  THAT YOU COULD BE FEELIN' –
A WHOLE LOT BETTER THAN YOU
  FEEL TODAY.
YOU SAY YOU'VE GOT A PROBLEM?
WELL THAT'S NO PROBLEM,
IT'S SUPER EASY NOT TO FEEL THAT
  WAY.
WHEN YOU START TO GET
  CONFUSED
BECAUSE OF THOUGHTS IN YOUR
  HEAD –
DON'T FEEL THOSE FEELINGS –
HOLD THEM IN – IN – STEAD!
TURN 'EM OFF!
LIKE A LIGHT SWITCH,
JUST GO "CLICK"
IT'S A COOL LITTLE MORMON TRICK.
WE DO IT ALL THE TIME.
WHEN YOU'RE FEELING CERTAIN
  FEELINGS
  THAT JUST DON'T SEEM RIGHT,
TREAT THOSE PESKY FEELINGS LIKE A

READING LIGHT

ELDER MICHAELS
AND TURN 'EM OFF!
LIKE A LIGHT SWITCH!

ELDER CHURCH
JUST GO BAP!

ELDER NEELEY
REALLY, WHAT'S SO HARD ABOUT
  THAT?

ELDER MCKINLEY
TURN IT OFF!

ALL ELDERS
TURN IT OFF!

Now another Elder steps in to sing. This whole time, Price looks confused and Cunningham seems to be enjoying himself.

ELDER CHURCH
WHEN I WAS YOUNG, MY DAD
  WOULD TREAT MY MOM
  REAL BAD
EVERY TIME THE UTAH JAZZ
  WOULD LOSE.
HE'D START A'DRINKIN' AND I'D
  START A'THINKIN'
HOW'M I GONNA KEEP MY MOM
  FROM GETTING ABUSED?
I'D SEE HER ALL SCARED AND MY
  SOUL WAS DYIN'!
MY DAD WOULD SAY TO ME,
  "NOW DON'T YOU DARE START
  CRYIN'!"
TURN IT OFF!

ELDERS
LIKE A LIGHT SWITCH.
JUST GO FLICK!
IT'S OUR NIFTY LITTLE MORMON
  TRICK!

ELDER CHURCH
TURN IT OFF!

ELDERS
TURN. IT. OFF!

ELDER THOMAS
MY SISTER WAS A DANCER ③ ④
BUT SHE GOT CANCER.

THE DOCTOR SAID SHE STILL HAD
  TWO MONTHS MORE.
I THOUGHT SHE HAD TIME,
SO I GOT IN LINE FOR THE
  NEW iPHONE AT THE APPLE STORE.
SHE LAID THERE DYING WITH
  MY FATHER AND MOTHER.
HER VERY LAST WORDS WERE
  'WHERE IS MY BROTHER?'

ELDERS
TURN IT OFF!

ELDER THOMAS
YEAH!

ELDERS
BID THOSE SAD FEELINGS ADIEU!

ELDER THOMAS
THE FEAR THAT I MIGHT GET
  CANCER, TOO.

ELDER MCKINLEY
WHEN I WAS IN FIFTH GRADE,
  I HAD A FRIEND, STEVE BLADE –

ELDERS
STEVE BLADE

ELDER MCKINLEY
HE AND I WERE CLOSE AS TWO
  FRIENDS COULD BE.

ELDERS
WE COULD BE CLOSE OOOH

ELDER MCKINLEY
ONE THING LED TO ANOTHER,
AND SOON I WOULD DISCOVER

ELDERS
WOW

ELDER MCKINLEY
I WAS HAVING REALLY STRANGE
  FEELINGS FOR STEVE.

ELDERS
FEELINGS FOR STEVE

ELDER MCKINLEY
I THOUGHT ABOUT US ON A

DESERTED ISLAND,

ELDERS
WE'RE ALL ALONE

ELDER MCKINLEY
WE'D SWIM NAKED IN THE SEA
  AND THEN HE'D TRY AND –
WHOA! TURN IT OFF!
LIKE A LIGHT SWITCH.
THERE, IT'S GONE.

ELDER CHURCH
Good for you!

ELDER MCKINLEY
MY HETERO SIDE JUST WON.
I'M ALL BETTER NOW.
BOYS SHOULD BE WITH GIRLS,
  THAT'S HEAVENLY FATHER'S
  PLAN.
SO IF YOU EVER FEEL YOU'D RATHER
  BE WITH A MAN –
TURN IT OFF.

ELDER PRICE
Well, Elder McKinley, I think it's okay to have gay thoughts. So long as you never act upon them.

ELDER MCKINLEY
No,
  BECAUSE THEN YOU'RE JUST
    KEEPING IT DOWN.
  LIKE A DIMMER SWITCH ON LOW...

ELDERS
ON LOW

③ CASEY NICHOLAW: When I first came onboard, there was the chorus about the Utah Jazz and being abused, and then everything else was about being gay. It felt like the song was dominated by that. One time we met halfway between San Diego and L.A., at some hotel with a golf course somewhere. We sat in the room and Trey came up with *"My sister was a dancer but she got cancer"* on the spot, and it cracked me up.

④ SCOTT BARNHARDT: There used to be an extra verse, right before I sing "my sister was a dancer." It went, "when I see Katie Couric on TV, my no-no parts get tingly."

TURN
LIKE A LIG[HT]
JUS[T]
CL[ICK]

ELDER MCKINLEY

> THINKING NOBODY NEEDS TO KNOW.

ELDERS

> UH-OH

ELDER MCKINLEY

> BUT THAT'S NOT TRUE.
> BEING GAY IS BAD BUT LYING IS
>   WORSE.
> SO JUST REALIZE YOU HAVE A
>   CURABLE CURSE –
> AND TURN IT OFF.
> TURN IT OFF.
> TURN IT OFF.
> TURN IT OFF!

There is a short tap dance break.

ELDERS

> TURN IT OFF!

ELDER MCKINLEY
Now how do you feel?

ELDER PRICE
The same.

ELDER MCKINLEY

> THEN YOU'VE ONLY GOT YOURSELF
>   TO BLAME.
> YOU DIDN'T PRETEND HARD
>   ENOUGH.
> IMAGINE THAT YOUR BRAIN IS
>   MADE OF TINY BOXES
> THEN FIND THE BOX THAT'S GAY
>   AND CRUSH IT!!

Okay...

ELDER PRICE
Wait...I'm not having gay thoughts!!!!!

ELDER CUNNINGHAM
Alright! It worked!

ELDERS
Hurray!!!

ELDERS

> HE TURNED IT OFF
> TURN IT OFF
> TURN IT OFF
> TURN IT OFF
> TURN IT OFF
> TURN IT OFF
> LIKE A LIGHT SWITCH

> JUST GO CLICK
>   CLICK, CLICK
> WHAT A COOL LITTLE MORMON
>   TRICK.
> TRICK, TRICK
> WE DO IT ALL THE TIME.

ELDER MCKINLEY

> WHEN YOU'RE FEELIN'
> CERTAIN FEELINGS THAT JUST
>   DON'T SEEM RIGHT,

ELDERS

> DON'T SEEM RIGHT

ELDER MCKINLEY

> TREAT THOSE PESKY FEELINGS
>   LIKE A READING LIGHT

ELDERS

> READING LIGHT

ELDER MCKINLEY

> AND TURN 'EM OFFFFFFF!

ELDERS

> LIKE A LIGHT SWITCH ON A
>   CORD
> NOW HE ISN'T GAY ANY...
> TURN IT TURN IT TURN IT TURN IT
> TURN IT TURN IT TURN IT TURN IT
> TUUUUUURN IT

ELDER MCKINLEY

> TURN IT OFF!

ELDERS

> OFFFFFFFF!!!!!!

ELDERS
Alright! / Yeah! / Great job, guys! / Etc.

ELDER MCKINLEY
(quieting them down)
Alright, Elders, alright – our two new missionaries must be EXHAUSTED from all their travels. Let's show them their room. A SIX, SEVEN, EIGHT!

The Elders all exit.

Price and Cunningham are brought into their tiny room, where two humble beds are RIGHT NEXT to each other. Price looks surprised but Cunningham LEAPS onto his bed, sits down, and starts jumping up and down on it.

ELDER CUNNINGHAM
ALRIGHT! CHECK THIS OUT!! WE GETTA SLEEP RIGHT NEXT TO EACH OTHER!!!

ELDER MCKINLEY
Get settled in, Elders. According to the missionary rules, lights out promptly at ten and we all wake UP at exactly 6:30. We've heard a lot of great things about you, Elder Price. Really hoping you can turn things around here.

ELDER CUNNINGHAM
Oh we will!

ELDER MCKINLEY
Elders... We're glad you're here.

McKinley closes the door, and walks away.

ELDER PRICE
ZERO baptisms? This is going to be a WHOLE LOT harder than we thought, huh?

ELDER CUNNINGHAM
Yeah! I can see this is gonna be a LOT like *Lord of the Rings*! You're Frodo and I'm Samwise fighting against impossible odds!

ELDER PRICE
This just all isn't what I was expecting. I've gotta admit, I'm really starting to feel... I don't wanna say "ripped off" but just... overwhelmed.

ELDER CUNNINGHAM
Well, I've got something to admit, too... Remember when I told you that I sometimes make things up, and Bishop Donahue said it's because I have no self-esteem?

ELDER PRICE
Yeah?

ELDER CUNNINGHAM
It's not true. There is no Bishop Donahue. I made him up.

Elder Price looks very confused.

ELDER PRICE
Elder, I really think you should just think about the big day we have ahead tomorrow, okay? Remember why we are here. Can you do that for me?

ELDER CUNNINGHAM
I would do anything for you – I'm your best friend.

ELDER PRICE
Alright, let's get to sleep.

ELDER CUNNINGHAM
Yeah!

The two boys get into their tiny beds and pull up the sheets. Cunningham happily watches Price as Price just rolls over and pulls the blanket around him. After a while, Elder Cunningham leans over and gently starts to sing.

I AM HERE FOR YOU

ELDER CUNNINGHAM
(singing gently)
SLEEP NOW LITTLE BUDDY,
PUT YOUR CARES AWAY.
NAPPY WITH A HAPPY FACE,
TOMORROW'S A LATTER DAY

Elder Price's eyes open.

ELDER PRICE
What are you doing?

ELDER CUNNINGHAM
That's what my mom used to sing to make ME feel better.

ELDER PRICE
I feel FINE. But our focus needs to be on our WORK now, Elder. Do you understand how difficult this is going to be? The missionaries here have yet to bring a SINGLE PERSON to the church.

ELDER CUNNINGHAM
Well, if they had already baptized a bunch of Africans here, then it wouldn't be so incredible when YOU did it, now would it?

Price looks at Cunningham and smiles.

ELDER PRICE
I guess...I guess that's kind of true...

ELDER CUNNINGHAM
Don't forget what you told me, Elder. You are AWESOME. Together we're gonna bring lots of Africans to the church. And then my dad will finally feel proud of me – instead of just feeling "stuck" with me...

 **ANNE GAREFINO:** Trey, Matt, and Bobby worked so hard to figure out Price's character; whenever they tried something new to define Price, this scene had to change again. My personal favorite was a version where everything Cunningham did got on Price's nerves. There was a lot of Cunningham being ridiculously awkward, and Price rolling his eyes out of his head. But the version that stuck is sweeter, it shows the potential of their relationship.

ELDER PRICE
You know what, Elder? I think he's got plenty to be proud of already.

ELDER CUNNINGHAM
Really?!

ELDER PRICE
Yeah.

ELDER CUNNINGHAM
EVENING STAR SHINES BRIGHTLY.
GOD MAKES LIFE ANEW!
TOMORROW IS A LATTER DAY
AND I AM HERE FOR YOU.

ELDER PRICE
I AM HERE FOR YOU, TOO.

BOTH
WE ARE HERE
FOR US.

ELDER CUNNINGHAM
Good night, best friend.

ELDER PRICE
Good night, PAL.

Cunningham takes the blanket from Price.

– THE VILLAGE –
The people of the village are milling about, working as they sing.

UGANDANS
HEY NAH HEYY AHH... HAYAAAA...

Nabulungi is happily returning home. She is carrying a large, clunky old typewriter and looking at it like a new prize.

MAFALA
Nabulungi! Where have you been?!

NABULUNGI
Baba! Look what I got at the market!

MAFALA
What have I told you about wandering off?! The market is NOT SAFE!

NABULUNGI
But, Baba, I finally found one! A TEXTING device! Now I can text all my friends!

MAFALA
Listen to me! Do not go to the market again!

The General is MUTILATING girls in the next village over!

NABULUNGI
I'm sorry, Baba...

MAFALA
Nabulungi, if we want to stay alive our village needs to LAY LOW and not attract any attention.

On the other side of the stage, closer to some of the houses, the two Mormons happily march in holding their Books of Mormon.

ELDER PRICE & ELDER CUNNINGHAM
TWO BY TWO WE MARCH FROM
    DOOR TO DOOR!
CUZ GOD LOVES MORMONS AND HE
    WANTS SOME MORE!

ELDER PRICE
Okay, let's try and get some placements.

ELDER CUNNINGHAM
Right! What's a placement again?

ELDER PRICE
Look, just... Let ME do the talking, alright? You just sort of...SUPPORT what I'm talking about by going "Oh wow" and stuff like that.

ELDER CUNNINGHAM
Oh, yeah! Like the lady in INFOMERCIALS that always says, "Wow, what an incredible offer!" I'm like THAT lady!

ELDER PRICE
Okay fine. Whatever. Why don't we try this little house. Just walk up and do it like at the missionary training center.

ELDER CUNNINGHAM
Okay!

Cunningham looks all around the door.

ELDER CUNNINGHAM
OH NO!!! There's no doorbell!

ELDER PRICE
What?

ELDER CUNNINGHAM
(freaking out)
THEY'VE GOT NO DOORBELLS!!! WHAT DO WE DO WHAT DO WE DO!?!?!?

ELDER PRICE
CALM DOWN!

A Ugandan woman, Kalimba, comes out the door.

ELDER PRICE
Oh hello, ma'am! Have you ever felt that there's an emptiness in your life?

Kalimba looks around as if to say, "What the fuck are you talking about?"

KALIMBA
What?

ELDER PRICE
When you go to sleep at night do you sometimes feel a power STIRRING inside you?

A Ugandan man in the background raises his arm and takes a step forward.

GOTSWANA
Yes! That's how I feel!

ELDER PRICE
Alright YOU, sir! Step on up here!

Gotswana steps up to Price as some other Ugandan people start to gather around. Price puts his arm around the man.

ELDER PRICE
Do you find yourself asking questions about that strange feeling inside?

GOTSWANA
YES!

ELDER PRICE
And it's because you want to believe in something more, isn't it?!

GOTSWANA
No, it's because I have maggots in my scrotum.

ELDER CUNNINGHAM
YOU'VE GOT WHAT?!

GOTSWANA
I have maggots in my scrotum! You can help?

ELDER PRICE
Wul, no you should probably see a doctor.

GOTSWANA
I AM the doctor.

ELDER PRICE
Uh... Yes... Ladies and gentlemen. We would like to tell you ALL about a VERY SPECIAL BOOK! A book that tells you how to find PARADISE. Through Christ!

UGANDANS
(they've heard this before)
Awww...

Now Nabulungi enters, arms folded.

NABULUNGI
They've HEARD of the Bible. We ALL have.

ELDER CUNNINGHAM
Bon Bon Jovi! Hey girl.

NABULUNGI
People come and tell us about Jesus and him dying for our sins once a year!

KALIMBA
They always come, tell us the story and then leave. And nothing gets better. Your BIBLE doesn't work.

ELDER PRICE
Of COURSE it didn't work. Those were CHRISTIAN missionaries. We're MORMONS.

NABULUNGI
What's the difference?

ALL-AMERICAN PROPHET

ELDER PRICE
YOU ALL KNOW THE BIBLE IS MADE
    OF TESTAMENTS OLD AND NEW.
YOU'VE BEEN TOLD IT'S JUST THOSE
    TWO PARTS,
OR ONLY ONE IF YOU'RE A JEW.
BUT WHAT IF I WERE TO TELL YOU
THERE'S A FRESH THIRD PART OUT
    THERE
WHICH WAS FOUND BY A HIP NEW
    PROPHET
WHO HAD A LITTLE
    DONNY OSMOND FLAIR...

Price does a flashy Osmond-style dance.

ELDER CUNNINGHAM
(impressed)
Woo hoo!!

❷ MATT STONE: "All-American Prophet" was the last song we wrote. It was the hardest and it went through many iterations. The song has so many jobs to do, and we wrote ourselves into this corner. The song has to tell the story of Joseph Smith; it has to be Price's big missionary moment; it needs to tell an Exodus story to Nabulungi; and it has to be dismissed by the Africans. We circled it and circled it, and then Bobby said "All-American" and it stuck. That phrase, "All-American" holds all these ideas. Mormons present themselves as the cleanest-cut of the cleanest-cut and the best in their class. The thing we knew we wanted was the sheer stupidity of Mormons in pioneer dress, dancing around in a dusty poor part of Africa. "All-American" gave that ridiculousness a form.

❸ JASON MICHAEL SNOW: Andrew had all these intros that he had to learn, they always kept changing. Eventually they cut them all. Now he just literally looks out at the audience, goes into the splits, and starts the song.

① JASON MICHAEL SNOW: They are such genius writers. A number doesn't work, we go to sleep, they pull an all-nighter and show up the next day with a brand new number. You read it and you're like, *God damn it, you guys are brilliant.*

② STEPHEN OREMUS: The original number was called "The Bible Is a Trilogy." The chorus listed famous trilogies: The Mighty Ducks, Spider-Man, The Matrix. Parts of that song have been retained in "All-American Prophet." Michael Scott, who plays the village doctor, kept stopping the song to sing, *I think the third Matrix was the worst one.* As the song changed, they took away the movie references—and instead of Michael's line about The Matrix they somehow came up with *"I have maggots in my scrotum."*

ELDER PRICE

HAVE YOU HEARD OF THE ALL-
AMERICAN PROPHET, ①
THE BLONDE-HAIRED, BLUE-EYED
VOICE OF GOD?
HE DIDN'T COME FROM THE
MIDDLE EAST,
LIKE THOSE OTHER HOLY MEN;
NO, GOD'S FAVORITE PROPHET WAS
ALL-AMERICAN

I'm gonna take you back to Biblical times, 1823. An American man named Joe livin' on a farm in the Holy Land of Rochester, New York!

Cunningham steps forward like he's doing an infomercial, over-acting and supporting Price.

ELDER CUNNINGHAM
You mean the Mormon prophet Joseph Smith?

ELDER PRICE
That's right, that young man spoke to God.

ELDER CUNNINGHAM
He spoke to God?

ELDER PRICE
And God said, "Joe, people really need to know that the Bible isn't two parts. There's a part three to the Bible, Joe! And I, God, have anointed you to dig up this part three, which is buried by a tree on the hill in your backyard."

ELDER CUNNINGHAM
Wow, God says, "Go to your backyard and start digging"? That makes perfect sense!

ELDER PRICE

JOSEPH SMITH WENT UP ON THAT
HILL
AND DUG WHERE HE WAS TOLD!
DEEP IN THE GROUND JOSEPH
FOUND
SHINING PLATES OF GOLD!

JOSEPH SMITH
What are these golden plates? Who buried them here, and why?

ELDER PRICE

THEN APPEARED AN ANGEL.
HIS NAME WAS MORO-NI!

MORONI
I am Moroni

THE ALL-AMERICAN ANGEL
MY PEOPLE LIVED HERE LONG,
LONG AGO!
THIS IS A HISTORY OF MY RACE
PLEASE READ THE WORDS WITHIN
WE WERE JEWS WHO MET WITH
CHRIST.
BUT WE WERE ALL-AMERICAN
BUT DON'T LET ANYBODY SEE
THESE PLATES EXCEPT FOR YOU.
THEY ARE ONLY FOR YOU TO SEE.
EVEN IF PEOPLE ASK YOU TO SHOW
THE PLATES TO THEM,
DON'T.
JUST COPY THEM ONTO NORMAL
PAPER.
EVEN THOUGH THIS MIGHT MAKE
THEM QUESTION
IF THE PLATES ARE REAL OR NOT.
THIS IS SORT OF WHAT GOD IS
GOING FOR.

ELDER PRICE

JOSEPH TOOK THE PLATES HOME
AND WROTE DOWN WHAT HE
FOUND INSIDE.
HE TURNED THOSE PLATES INTO A
BOOK
THEN RUSHED INTO TOWN AND
CRIED:

JOSEPH SMITH

HEY, GOD SPOKE TO ME
AND GAVE ME THIS BLESSED
ANCIENT TOME.
HE HATH COMMANDED ME TO
PUBLISH IT
AND STICK IT IN EV'RY HOME

ELDER CUNNINGHAM

Wow! So the Bible is actually a trilogy, and Book of Mormon is *Return of the Jedi*?! I'M interested!

ELDER PRICE

Now, many people didn't believe the prophet Joseph Smith. They thought he'd made up this part three that was buried by a tree on a hill in his backyard.

MORMONS

Liar!

ELDER PRICE

SO JOE SAID,

JOSEPH SMITH

THIS IS NO LIE,
I SPEAK TO GOD ALL THE TIME
AND HE'S TOLD ME TO HEAD WEST!
SO I'LL TAKE MY PART THREE
    FROM THE HILL WITH THE TREE,
FEEL FREE IF YOU'D LIKE TO COME
    ALONG WITH ME,
TO THE PROMISED LAND!

MORMONS

The PROMISED LAND?

JOSEPH SMITH

Paradise! On the west coast,
    NOTHING BUT FRUIT AND FIELDS
        AS FAR AS THE EYE CAN SEE!

ALL

HAVE YOU HEARD OF
THE ALL-AMERICAN PROPHET?
HE FOUND A BRAND, NEW BOOK
    ABOUT JESUS CHRIST?
WE'RE FOLLOWING HIM TO
    PARADISE,
WE CALL OURSELVES MORMEN,
AND OUR NEW RELIGION IS –
    ALL-AMERICAN.

ELDER CUNNINGHAM

Wow! How much does this all cost?!

ELDER PRICE

THE MORMONS KEPT ON SEARCHING
    FOR THAT PLACE TO SETTLE DOWN
BUT EV'RY TIME THEY THOUGHT
    THEY FOUND IT
THEY GOT KICKED OUT OF TOWN
AND EVEN THOUGH PEOPLE

WANTED
TO SEE THE GOLDEN PLATES
JOSEPH NEVER SHOWED 'EM!

GOTSWANA

I HAVE MAGGOTS IN MY SCROTUM

The song comes to a halt as Price stares at the man.

ELDER PRICE

Okay–anyway...

ELDER PRICE

NOW COMES THE PART OF OUR
    STORY
    THAT GETS A LITTLE BIT SAD.
ON THE WAY TO THE PROMISED
    LAND,
    MORMONS MADE PEOPLE MAD.
JOSEPH WAS SHOT BY AN ANGRY
    MOB
AND KNEW HE'D SOON BE DONE

TOWNSPEOPLE

OOOOOO –
OOOO –
WAHH
SOON BE DONE

JOSEPH SMITH

YOU MUST LEAD THE PEOPLE NOW
MY GOOD FRIEND BRIGHAM
    YOUNG.

Joseph Smith is left alone to die.

JOSEPH SMITH

OH GOD WHY ARE YOU LETTING
    ME DIE
WITHOUT HAVING ME SHOW
    PEOPLE THE PLATES?
THEY'LL HAVE NO PROOF
    I WAS TELLING THE TRUTH OR
    NOT
THEY'LL HAVE TO BELIEVE IT JUST
    CUZ
OH. I GUESS THAT'S KIND OF WHAT
    YOU WERE GOING FOR.
BLARGGGH

ELDER PRICE

The Prophet Joseph Smith died for what he believed in. But his followers, they kept heading west. And Brigham Young led them to Paradise. A sparkling land in Utah they named

⑤ MICHAEL JAMES SCOTT:
In the original song, "The Bible Is a Trilogy," there were some lines about the Matrix movies, and I had a line that I thought the third was the worst one. We were in the studio one day and Trey came up to me privately and said, *So you're going to say, "I have maggots in my scrotum."* I was like, *Okay.* They used to give me all kinds of stuff to do, they knew that I'm not fazed by it. Trey was like, *You're cool with it, right?* Then the producer Anne Garefino pulled me aside, *You're okay with saying that, right?* Trey literally whispered it to me, none of the cast knew until I actually said it. When we finally got to Broadway and they were doing rewrites, the new scene they added before "All-American Prophet" introduced my character, the doctor, with "I have maggots in my scrotum." So it became my recurring line, but that's where it really started.

WE CALL O

MORMEN

NE

RELIGIO

AMER

OURSELVES
AND OUR

W

N IS ALL-
RICAN.

1 **BRIAN TYREE HENRY:** Originally my character didn't have a name, it was Warlord and then General. They kept playing with the name. One day Trey decided to add fucks to everything I said. He was just like, *Add fuck there, we're just going to put fuck there. Fuck there, just say it.* And then he got to General Butt-Fucking Naked. It was fun telling my mother who I play. She seems to need to be reminded every time. *Ooh, who're you playing again?* General Butt-Fucking Naked, mom, *Butt-Fucking Naked.*

2 **ANNE GAREFINO:** One of the things we wrestled with the most was the General's character. We did not want a Disney scenario where he was going to take Nabulungi as his bride. So then, what was the threat of the General? It was near the end of the Lincoln Center workshop when Trey, Matt and Bobby told me they had an idea they wanted to run by me: to have the General threaten to cut off all of the women's clitorises. Up until then, the only mention of women getting their "clits cut off" was a joke in "Hasa Diga." I think they thought I'd freak out at the idea of clitoridectomies as a sub-plot. I actually thought it was a great idea. I felt like it was offensive when it was just a joke, but to make it a threat—which it is in some parts of Africa—grounded it and the show. It gave all of the clit references some meaning. They were stunned and, I think, a little disappointed that I wasn't totally offended.

SALT LAKE CITY. And there the Mormons multiplied! And made big Mormon families!! Generation to generation until finally... They made me!!! And now it's my job to lead you where those early settlers were led so long ago!!!!

TOWNSPEOPLE & ELDER CUNNINGHAM

HOOOOOO –
HOOOO –
AHH

The imaginary pioneers gather around Price.

MORMONS

HAVE YOU HEARD OF THE ALL -
AMERICAN PROPHET?

ELDER CUNNINGHAM

Kevin Price!!!

MORMONS

THE NEXT IN LINE TO BE THE
VOICE OF GOD?!

ELDER PRICE

My best friend!

MORMONS

HE'S GONNA DO SOMETHING
INCREDIBLE!
AND BE JOSEPH SMITH A-GAIN!
CUZ KEVIN PRICE THE PROPHET IS
ALL, ALL, ALL, ALL,
ALL-AMERICAN!

ELDER CUNNINGHAM

And if you order now, we'll also throw in a set of steak knives!

MORMONS

ALL-AMERICAN!

ELDER PRICE

Alright, now who would like their very own copy of the Book of Mormon?!

UGANDAN WOMAN

What the fuck is a steak knife?

All the Ugandan people look at each other for a beat, and then walk away making groans and making "blow off" gestures with their hands. As they all leave, Nabulungi is obviously hesitating and intrigued.

ELDER PRICE

What were you DOING?!

ELDER CUNNINGHAM

Just doing my part! You know, cuz we're supposed to be a team.

ELDER PRICE

There's nothing in the Book of Mormon about STEAK KNIVES!

ELDER CUNNINGHAM

I'm sorry. I actually never read it.

ELDER PRICE

YOU WHAT?!

ELDER CUNNINGHAM

It's just so boring!

THE GENERAL

JUMAMOSI!!!!!

UGANDANS

(shouts and screams)

SADAKA

(frightened)

He's here! THE GENERAL! HE'S HERE!!

In a big entrance, we see the guards from before, and then The GENERAL breaks through with OMINOUS MUSIC.

THE GENERAL

What is THIS? Some kind of party?! Who didn't invite me?!

Everyone cowers and keeps their heads down. The General walks over to the boys and looks them up and down.

THE GENERAL

My NAME...is GENERAL BUTT-FUCKING NAKED. Because when I KILL...AND DRINK BLOOD FOR POWER–I DO IT BUTT-FUCKING NAKED!!!! This village belongs to ME. **1**

UGANDAN MAN

We don't belong to anyone! You only lead a gang of THUGS who mutilate women for no reason!

THE GENERAL

For no REASON?! The CLITORIS is an ABOMINATION! Its wicked pleasure for women has brought a WRATH UPON UGANDA AND IT MUST BE CAST OUT!

Nabulungi looks at him, scared.

UGANDAN MAN
My wife's body is none of your business! And YOU are no general.

The General, walks over to the man –

THE GENERAL
By the end of the week ALL females in this village WILL BE CIRCUMCISED. OR I WILL GET BUTT-FUCKING NAKED AND DO THIS!!! ❷

– and shoots the man in the face. A very realistic and large squib blows blood and brain matter all over Elder Price. All the villagers scream and run away. Mafala grabs Nabulungi and pulls her out.

– NABULUNGI'S HOUSE –

Mafala rushes Nabulungi inside.

MAFALA
Alright, I think he's gone. You have to stay indoors, Nabulungi! Keep the light off and the windows closed! ❸

NABULUNGI
No, Baba, I don't want to spend another night hiding under my bed!

MAFALA
It is the world we live in! We don't have a choice!

NABULUNGI
Baba – Baba, the white boys! They said they know the answers to our problems!

MAFALA
I have to check on the others –

NABULUNGI
LISTEN TO ME, BABA! The Mormon boys talked about people who were miserable like us, but they all found somewhere to GO! Somewhere WONDERFUL!
(picking up her typewriter)
I'm going to text them right now and tell them we are interested!

MAFALA
(taking the typewriter from her)

PUT THAT STUPID THING DOWN!
(he sets it down)
JUST STAY INSIDE AND DO NOT OPEN THE DOOR FOR ANYONE!

Her father runs out, slamming the door. She is left alone.

She can hear more SCREAMING coming from the distance outside. She picks up her typewriter again, and looks at it sadly.

Music starts.

SAL TLAY KA SITI ❹ ❺

NABULUNGI
MY MOTHER ONCE TOLD ME
   OF A PLACE WITH WATERFALLS
   AND UNICORNS FLYING
WHERE THERE WAS NO SUFFERING,
   NO PAIN
WHERE THERE WAS LAUGHTER
   INSTEAD OF DYING.

I ALWAYS THOUGHT SHE'D MADE IT
   UP
   TO COMFORT ME IN TIMES OF PAIN.
NOW I KNOW THAT PLACE IS REAL.
NOW I KNOW ITS NAME.
SAL TLAY KA SITI,
   JUST LIKE A STORY MAMA TOLD
A VILLAGE IN OOH-TAH,
WHERE THE ROOFS ARE THATCHED
   WITH GOLD.
IF I COULD LET MYSELF BELIEVE,
I KNOW JUST WHERE I'D BE
RIGHT ON THE NEXT BUS TO
   PARADISE.
   SAL TLAY KA SITI.

I CAN IMAGINE WHAT IT MUST BE
   LIKE,
THIS PERFECT HAPPY PLACE.
I BET THE GOAT MEAT THERE IS
   PLENTIFUL
AND THEY HAVE VITAMIN
   INJECTIONS BY THE CASE.
THE WARLORDS THERE ARE
   FRIENDLY.
THEY'D HELP YOU CROSS THE
   STREET.

❸ **TREY PARKER:** This scene got written over and over. We had to see a protective father, with his daughter. We had to see it was not fun and games anymore.

❹ **NIKKI M. JAMES:** It's a smart moment. The show is funny, funny, funny, funny, then someone gets shot in the face. Then comes "Sal Tlay Ka Siti," in which they tell this sweet story and give us a moment of both levity and a little bit of gravity.

❺ **MATT STONE:** One thing I think Casey and Trey did very well is give each number its own feeling and texture, and reason for being. I feel like a lot of shows have numbers that sort of mush into one another. I remember the two of them always talking about what could be different about each number, what could be unique, what you would remember after the show.

AND THERE'S A RED CROSS ON
   EVERY CORNER
WITH ALL THE FLOUR YOU CAN
   EAT.

SAL TLAY KA SITI,
THE MOST PERFECT PLACE ON
   EARTH.
WHERE FLIES DON'T BITE YOUR
   EYEBALLS
AND HUMAN LIFE HAS WORTH.
IT ISN'T A PLACE OF FAIRY TALES.
IT'S AS REAL AS IT CAN BE.
A LAND WHERE EVIL DOESN'T
   EXIST.
SAL TLAY KA SITI.

AND I'LL BET THE PEOPLE ARE OPEN-
   MINDED,
AND DON'T CARE WHO YOU'VE
   BEEN
AND ALL I HOPE IS THAT WHEN I
   FIND IT,
I'M ABLE TO FIT IN.
WILL I FIT IN?
SAL TLAY KA SITI,
A LAND OF HOPE AND JOY.
AND IF I WANT TO GET THERE,
I JUST HAVE TO FOLLOW THAT
   WHITE BOY.
YOU WERE RIGHT, MAMA,
   YOU DIDN'T LIE.
THIS PLACE IS REAL, AND I'M
   GONNA FLY.

I'M ON MY WAY.
SOON LIFE WON'T BE SO SHITTY.
NOW SALVATION HAS A NAME
SAL TLAY KA... SITI.

The scene fades down on her looking outwards longingly.

– MORMON MISSIONARIES' LIVING QUARTERS –

The Elders are studying scripture. Elder McKinley rushes in, freaking out. **1**

ELDER MCKINLEY
O-M GOSH, you guys! I AM FREAKING OUT!!!

ELDER DAVIS
What is it?

ELDER MCKINLEY
I just got off the phone with the District Leader.

The MISSION PRESIDENT wants a WRITTEN PROGRESS REPORT from us THIS WEEK!!!!

ELDER MICHAELS
A progress report?! But we don't have any baptisms!!!!

ELDER MCKINLEY
I KNOW THAT! WHAT ARE WE GONNA DO?!

ELDERS
We're gonna look like failures! / This is terrible! / Oh gosh, oh no! / My dad's gonna beat me! / Etc.

ELDER CHURCH
Okay, okay, HOLD ON! I mean... We COULD... SAY that we had some baptisms.

The other Elders stare at him.

ELDER MCKINLEY
What, you mean LIE?!

ELDER CHURCH
Well, just sort of.

ELDER SCHRADER
Are you an IDIOT?! MORMONS don't LIE! **2**

ELDERS
Yeah! / That's right! / Etc.

ELDER NEELEY
I told a lie once when I was twelve, and I had a dream that I went to hell! It was REALLY SPOOKY.

ELDER THOMAS
You, too?! I had the hell dream after I accidentally read a *Playboy*!

ELDER MCKINLEY
We've ALL had the spooky hell dream, people! I have it NIGHTLY. The issue NOW is what the heck am I supposed to tell the mission president?!

Elder Price enters, still with blood on his

shirt. He stops and just stares as the other Elders stare at him covered in blood.

ELDER CHURCH
Elder Price, what happened to YOU?

Price looks down at his blood- covered shirt for a beat, then –

ELDER PRICE
Africa...is NOTHING like *The Lion King* – I think that movie took a LOT of artistic license.

ELDER CUNNINGHAM
He's upset because we just saw a guy get shot in the face.

ELDERS
Oooh. / Ewww. / That's not good. / Etc.

ELDER PRICE
I cannot continue my mission this way! There is absolutely NOTHING I can accomplish here!

ELDER MCKINLEY
Elder Price, you cannot lose your cool on me now, we're about to get evaluated by the MISSION PRESIDENT!

ELDER PRICE
(getting an idea)
The mission president! That's it! I have to go see the mission president and get transferred!

ELDER CUNNINGHAM
Buddy! BUDDY! I know today w`as rough. But remember – tomorrow is a LATTER DAY!

Price gets in Cunningham's face.

ELDER PRICE
"LATTER DAY" DOESN'T MEAN TOMORROW!!!!
(beat)
IT MEANS THE RECKONING! THE AFTERLIFE! "LATTER DAYS" WHERE ALL GOOD PEOPLE GO TO HEAVENLY FATHER AND GET EVERYTHING THEY'VE ALWAYS WANTED!!!! I'M OUTTA HERE!

Price starts to leave.

ELDER MCKINLEY
Hey! HEY! Are you forgetting rule number twenty-three?! You cannot leave the living quarters after 9 PM!!

ELDER PRICE
To heck with the rules, I'm not wasting the most important two years of my life!

Price storms out.

ELDER CUNNINGHAM
Hey, hold up, you forgot me!

Elder Cunningham starts to go after him.

ELDER MCKINLEY
Elder Cunningham, do you ALSO want to break rule number twenty-three?!

ELDER CUNNINGHAM
Oh NO! What am I supposed to do? According to rule number twenty-three I can't leave the living quarters after curfew – but according to rule seventy-two I can never let my companion be alone! This is like a *Matrix* logic trick! Rule seventy-two – rule twenty-three – rule seventy-two – I'M SORRY GUYS! HE'S MY BEST FRIEND!

Cunningham slams the door, leaving.

– THE VILLAGE –

Price is at the bus station where he and Cunningham first arrived. Cunningham comes chasing after him.

ELDER CUNNINGHAM
ELDER PRICE! ELDER PRICE WAIT UP!! HEY COME ON!! We gotta be together at all times, remember?!

ELDER PRICE
I can't do something incredible here!

Elder Price starts walking away but Cunningham spins him around and grabs his shoulders.

ELDER CUNNINGHAM
OKAY, STOP! Breathe. THINK. This isn't what you want to do.

ELDER PRICE
Yes it IS.

ELDER CUNNINGHAM
Alright, if you want to transfer... then THAT'S WHAT WE'RE DOING!! I'm with you, buddy!!!

ELDER PRICE
I didn't say WE'RE transferring – I said I AM.

JOSH GAD: Elder Cunningham doesn't fit in. He is this complete ball of energy that nobody really knows what to do with, including himself, until somebody says to him, *We need you.* Then all of a sudden, bam, he embraces it and winds up doing something very special and significant. So to me, there's the first act Cunningham and the second act Cunningham. They are almost two different people because he really goes through this maturation process during "Man Up," and it completely changes the game for him. It gives him something he's never had before: responsibility and this leadership role.

Elder Cunningham looks like he's been slapped.

ELDER CUNNINGHAM
(hurt)
Oh... I see...

ELDER PRICE
(sighs, then –)
Look, I'm sorry, but you and I just aren't that compatible, alright?

ELDER CUNNINGHAM
Well, we only became best friends a few days ago! Maybe I could –

ELDER PRICE
I'M NOT YOUR BEST FRIEND! I was just STUCK with you by the missionary training center.

Now Cunningham looks really hurt.

ELDER PRICE
I didn't MEAN to say "STUCK"... It's just that.

ELDER CUNNINGHAM
Yeah, yeah no it's cool. I know how it goes. It's really fine. I'll be totally fine...

ELDER PRICE
You WILL be fine, we just need, you know, different things.

ELDER CUNNINGHAM
Right, different things.

ELDER PRICE
(sighs and then slowly offers –)
It was...nice meeting you.

ELDER CUNNINGHAM
(trying not to cry)
Yeah. Yeah, awesome. Take it easy.

Price walks away. Cunningham takes a few steps in different directions, not really sure what to do or where to go.

I AM HERE FOR YOU
(REPRISE)

ELDER CUNNINGHAM
EVENING STAR SHINES BRIGHTLY

GOD MAKES LIFE ANEW.
TOMORROW IS A LATTER DAY
I WAS THERE FOR YOU.

Leave Cunningham alone and quiet for a while, really let this moment land. Silence...

Finally, Nabulungi enters –

NABULUNGI
There you are!

She rushes toward Cunningham.

NABULUNGI
Thank goodness I found you!
Where is your friend?

ELDER CUNNINGHAM
I don't have any friends.

NABULUNGI
No, no! I have written Elder Price a text. Here!

She hands him a piece of paper.

NABULUNGI
It says to please come back to the village. We are ready!

ELDER CUNNINGHAM
To do what?

NABULUNGI
To LISTEN to him! I texted everyone we HAVE to give Elder Price a chance!

ELDER CUNNINGHAM
I'm sorry, he's transferring.

NABULUNGI
What is transferring?!

ELDER CUNNINGHAM
That means he'll be sent somewhere else.

NABULUNGI
No! He can't leave! We're ready to listen!

ELDER CUNNINGHAM
It's too late he's made up his mind.
She stares off in Price's direction, then turns back and sizes up Cunningham.

NABULUNGI
What about you?

ELDER CUNNINGHAM
Me? What?

NABULUNGI
He's gone. But you are still here. YOU can lead us. Teach us everything about what's in the Book of Mormon.

ELDER CUNNINGHAM
Me? No, no... I'm a FOLLOWER.

NABULUNGI
Everyone is waiting! Just come back to the village and YOU WILL HAVE YOUR LISTENERS! I SWEAR IT!!!!

She dashes away, leaving Cunningham alone to think.

Finally, he breaks out into song.

MAN UP

ELDER CUNNINGHAM
WHAT DID JESUS DO,
   WHEN THEY SENTENCED HIM TO
   DIE?
DID HE TRY TO RUN AWAY?
DID HE JUST BREAK DOWN AND
   CRY?

NO, JESUS DUG DOWN DEEP,
   KNOWING WHAT HE HAD TO DO
WHEN FACED WITH HIS OWN
   DEATH,
JESUS KNEW THAT HE HAD TO...

MAN UP.
HE HAD TO MAN UP.
SO HE CRAWLED UP ON THAT
   CROSS,
AND HE STUCK IT OUT.
HE MANNED UP.
CHRIST, HE MANNED UP.
AND TAUGHT US ALL WHAT REAL
   MANNING UP IS ABOUT.
AND NOW IT'S UP TO ME
AND IT'S TIME TO MAN UP.
JESUS HAD HIS TIME TA,
NOW ITS MINE TA MAN UP.
I'M TAKING THE REINS,
I'M CROSSING THE BEAR –
AND JUST LIKE JESUS,

I'M GROWING A PAIR!
I'VE GOTTA STAND UP,
CAN'T JUST CLAM UP,
ITS TIME TA MAN UP!

(Dance Break)

CUZ THERE'S A TIME IN YOUR LIFE
   WHEN YOU KNOW YOU'VE GOT
   TO MAN UP!
DON'T LET IT PASS YOU BY
THERE'S JUST ONE TIME TA MAN
   UP!
WATCH ME MAN UP LIKE NOBODY
   ELSE!
I'M GONNA MAN UP ALL OVER
   MYSELF!
I'VE GOT TO GET READY,
IT'S TIME TA
TIME TA.

WHAT DID JESUS DO
   WHEN THEY PUT NAILS THROUGH
   HIS HANDS?
DID HE SCREAM LIKE A GIRL OR
   DID HE TAKE IT LIKE A MAN?
WHEN SOMEONE HAD TO DIE
   TO SAVE US FROM OUR SINS
JESUS SAID "I'LL DO IT" AND HE
   TOOK IT ON THE CHIN!
HE MANNED UP!
HE MANNED UP.
HE TOOK A BULLET FOR ME AND
   YOU,
THAT'S MAN UP.
REAL MAN UP.
AND NOW IT'S MY TIME TAAAA -
   DO IT, TOO.
TIME TO BE A HERO AND SLAY
   THE MONSTER!
TIME TO BATTLE DARKNESS –
YOU'RE NOT MY FAT-HER!
I'M GONNA TIME TA, JUST WATCH
   ME GO!
IT'S TIME TA STEP UP AND STEAL
   THE SHOW!
IT'S TIME TA! IT'S MINE TA! IT'S
   TIME TA!
TIME TA TIME TA –

Nabulungi, on another part of the stage, singing to some of the Ugandans.

NABULUNGI
SAL TLAY KA SITI -

CASEY NICHOLAW: No one ever thought we were going to have backup dancers, and all of a sudden I said, *Okay, and the backup dancers come out!* Everybody was like, *What?* At first I thought it would be funny to have all backup dancing Jesuses, and we tried it once in rehearsal with beards and stuff. It was so clear the minute they came out, *no way! No way, no way, no way!* It was too much, it was creepy. It just was not right.

TREY PARKER: When we realized "Man Up" was going to be the act break, it became a quintessential moment. That's when you start taking songs you've done and weave them together, so you look like you have a reason for doing it. That's where you get to use all your music theory classes from college.

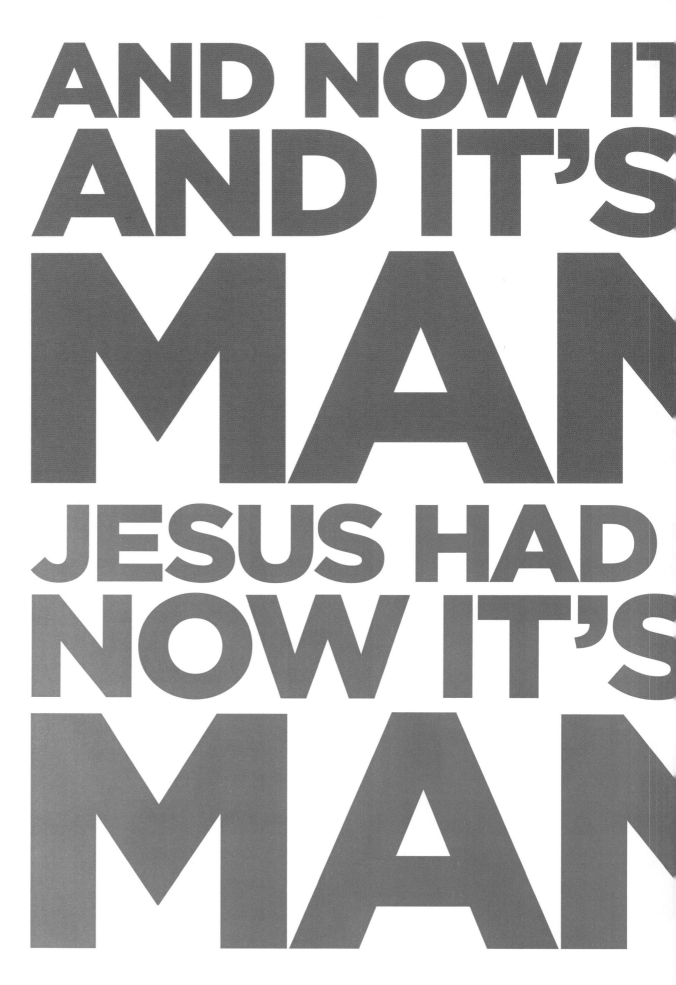

AND NOW IT
AND IT'S
MAN

JESUS HAD
NOW IT'S
MAN

'S UP TO ME

TIME TO

UP.

HIS TIME TA,

MINE TA

UP.

A PLACE OF HOPE AND JOY

ELDER CUNNINGHAM

MAN UP!

NABULUNGI

AND IF WE WANT TO GO THERE
WE JUST HAVE TO FOLLOW THAT
WHITE BOY

ELDER CUNNINGHAM

TIME TA!

Now reveal Elder Price. He looks like he's painfully hot and in need of water as he wanders around, lost.

ELDER PRICE

HEAVENLY FATHER WHY DO YOU
LET BAD THINGS HAPPEN?

UGANDANS

KA-LAY-KA CITY!

NABULUNGI

DID YOU GET MY TEXT?

ELDER PRICE

MORE TO THE POINT WHY DO YOU
LET BAD THINGS HAPPEN TO ME?

UGANDANS

KA-LAY-KAA
WE GOT YOUR TEXT!

ELDER PRICE

I'M SURE YOU DON'T THINK I'M A
FLAKE

ELDER CUNNINGHAM

MAN UP!

ELDER PRICE

BECAUSE YOU'VE CLEARLY MADE A
MISTAKE.

ELDERS

TURN IT OFF!

ELDER PRICE

I'M GOING WHERE YOU NEED ME
MOST –
ORLANDO!!!

CHORUS

ORLANDO!

UGANDANS

WE WILL LISTEN TO THAT FAT
WHITE GUY!

ELDER CUNNINGHAM

MY TIME TO TIME TA
NOW IT'S MY TIME TO TIME TA!

UGANDANS

BUT HASA DIGA EEBOWAI!

ELDER CUNNINGHAM

NO TIME TA, NOT TIME TA,
NO NOW IT'S TIME TO TIME TA!

UGANDANS

HUUH!

ELDER CUNNINGHAM

I'M IN THE LEAD FOR THE
VERY FIRST TIME!

UGANDANS

TIME TA

ELDER PRICE

I'M GOING WHERE THE SUN
ALWAYS SHINES

UGANDANS

SHINES TA
HAAAA

ELDER CUNNINGHAM

I'VE GOT TO STAND UP
GET MY FLIPPIN' CAN UP

NABULUNGI

SAL TLAY KA SITI –
SAL TLAY KA SITI –
SAL TLAY KA SITI –

UGANDANS

HAY YA YA
HAY YA YA
HAY YA YA HA

ELDER PRICE

ORLANDO!
ORLANDO!
I'M COMING
ORLANDO!

ELDER CUNNINGHAM

IT IS TIME TA –!

GOTSWANA

I HAVE MAGGOTS IN MY SCROTUM! ①

I HAVE MAGGOTS IN MY SCROTUM!

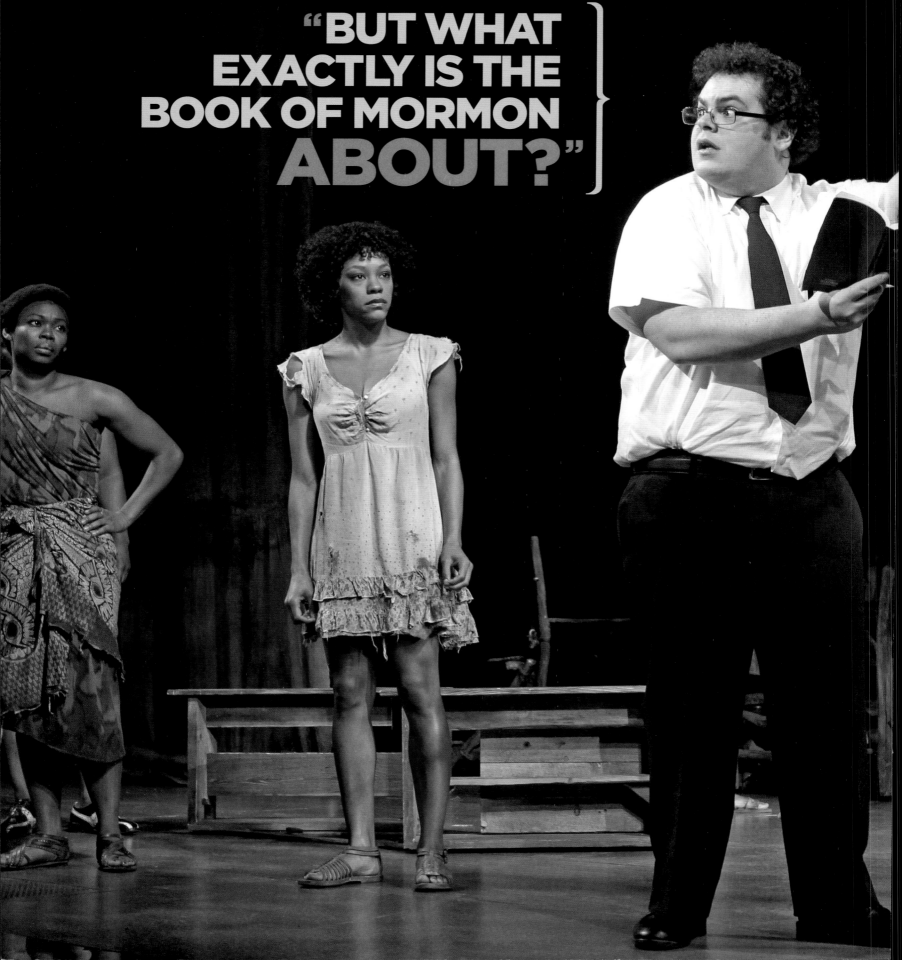

"BUT WHAT EXACTLY IS THE BOOK OF MORMON ABOUT?"

ACT 2

THE BOOK OF MORMON

- PROLOGUE -
THE HILL CUMORAH

The pageant starts once again, with the same fanfare as before. Joseph Smith is kneeling, holding the golden plates as if he has just dug them up. Near him, a scene of Christ appearing to the ancient Americans.

NARRATOR

And yea, it came to pass that the Prophet Joseph Smith discovered the Book of Mormon on golden plates. But what exactly is the Book of Mormon ABOUT? It tells of two Hebrew tribes at war in ancient America – the gentle Nephites, and the wicked Lamanites. They fought many great battles, but then, just after his crucifixion, Christ appeared!

Christ appears, as before.

JESUS

I am Jesus. I've just been crucified on the other side of the world, you guys. I only have three days before I am resurrected, but in that time, I will preach here to you in America.

NARRATOR

And LO, Christ told them many things, and a Nephite named Mormon wrote the teachings on golden plates. Plates that became the Book of Mormon! A book that is still today read by missionaries all over the world!!!

- THE VILLAGE -

Cunningham is with the Ugandans, reading from the Book of Mormon. Cunningham is trying to be a preacher, but he really doesn't have what it takes.

ELDER CUNNINGHAM
(reading with vigor)
And it came to pass that the... that the NEPHITES had gathered together a great number of men, even to exceed the number of thirty thousand! And it came to pass that they did

① BOBBY LOPEZ: We started with basically just an Act One, and we didn't really know what was happening in Act Two. When we did that first reading, people asked, *So what happens? Does Nabulungi go to Salt Lake City? Is that what's going to happen?* And we realized no, we know what happens in Act Two: Price tries to leave and kind of goes to Hell, and then Cunningham creates a new religion.

② TREY PARKER: We basically wrote the songs mostly in order. We started out writing it like an album, a collection of funny Mormon songs for a musical. You can see this in Act One. As the show goes on, the songs get more plotty; keep the plot moving through song. In Act Two, the script and the songs are interwoven. You can see us learning how to do it as we went along.

have in this same year a number of battles, in which the Nephites did beat the Lamanites and did slay many of them! **①**

Cunningham seems to finish – the Ugandans just stare at him.

UGANDAN WOMAN
So what the fuck does THAT mean?

Cunningham obviously has no idea as he scratches his head...

ELDER CUNNINGHAM
Uh... That MEANS... You know... You should... Be NICE to each other or something.
(clears throat then goes on reading –)
And lo, God was so displeased with the Lamanites that he caused a cursing to come upon them. Wherefore as they WERE WHITE and delightsome, the Lord God did cause a skin of BLACKNESS to come upon them! And thus oooh – ughhh...

Cunningham sees that the Ugandans look insulted.

ELDER CUNNINGHAM
Uh, sorry, hang on, let's skip to another part...

Cunningham turns and flips through the pages.

MAFALA
(to Nabulungi)
How is THIS supposed to make things better for us? General Butt-Fucking Naked is going to come back and if he sees us here we are all DEAD.

NABULUNGI
Baba, please, we just need to LISTEN.

MIDDALA
To WHAT?!
(standing up)
THREE HOURS we been listening to him talk about STUPID SHIT that happened on the other side of the Earth thousands of years ago! It has nothing to do with US!

SADAKA
That's right! Those "NEPHITES" probably didn't even have AIDS to deal with!

UGANDANS
(angry, leaving)
Yeah! / That's right! / Shit! / Etc.

ELDER CUNNINGHAM
UH SURE THEY DID! SURE THEY DID!! People back then had even WORSE AIDS!

Everyone quiets down and listens to him.

ELDER CUNNINGHAM
Yeah!

Cunningham pretends to look through the Book of Mormon, and then pretends to read from it –

ELDER CUNNINGHAM
(reading)
And LO! The Lord said unto the Nephites – I know you're really depressed, with all your AIDS and everything... But there is an answer in Christ!

The Ugandans look surprised. They are now paying attention to Cunningham.

NABULUNGI
You see?! This book CAN help us!

As everyone turns and chatters to Nabulungi, Cunningham goes to his own corner of the stage.

MAKING THINGS UP AGAIN ②

ELDER CUNNINGHAM
I JUST TOLD A LIE.
Wait, no I didn't lie...
I JUST USED MY IMAGINATION.
And it worked!

Cunningham's dad appears in Cunningham's imagination.

CUNNINGHAM'S DAD
YOU'RE MAKING THINGS UP AGAIN, ARNOLD.

ELDER CUNNINGHAM
Yeah, but it worked, dad!

CUNNINGHAM'S DAD
YOU'RE STRETCHING THE TRUTH AGAIN,
AND YOU KNOW IT
Joseph Smith appears on another side of the stage.

JOSEPH SMITH

DON'T BE A FIBBING FRAN,
ARNOLD

ELDER CUNNINGHAM

Joseph Smith?

JOSEPH SMITH & DAD

BECAUSE A LIE IS A LIE.

ELDER CUNNINGHAM

It's not a lie!

Now Mormon and Moroni from the previous pageant come back to life.

CHORUS

YOU'RE MAKING THINGS UP AGAIN,
ARNOLD!

ELDER CUNNINGHAM

Oh, conscience.

CHORUS

YOU'RE TAKING THE HOLY WORD
AND ADDING FICTION!
BE CAREFUL HOW YOU PROCEED,
ARNOLD.
WHEN YOU FIB, THERE'S A PRICE.

MUTUMBO

This is bullshit! The story I'VE been told is that the way to cure AIDS is by sleeping with a virgin! I'm gonna go and rape a baby!

ELDER CUNNINGHAM

WHAT!?!! OH MY – NO! You can't do that!
(scolding like a dog–)
NO!!!!

MUTUMBO

Why not?

ELDER CUNNINGHAM

Because that is DEFINITELY against God's way!

MUTUMBO

Says who!? Where in that book of yours does it say ANYTHING about having sex with a baby?! Nowhere!

Cunningham looks through his book confused.

MUTUMBO

Nowhere!
Mutumbo starts to leave.

ELDER CUNNINGHAM

Uhhh, behold –
(pretending to read)
The Lord said to the Mormon Joseph Smith, "You shall not have sex with that infant!"

Everyone stops and turns to Cunningham.

ELDER CUNNINGHAM
(pretending to read more, stammering)
LO! Joseph said, "Why not, Lord?" And thusly the Lord said, "If you lay with an infant you shall burn in the fiery pits of Mordor."

MUTUMBO

Really?

ELDER CUNNINGHAM

"A baby cannot cure your illness, Joseph Smith – I shall give unto you... A FROG..." And thus Joseph laid with the frog and his AIDS was no more!

UGANDANS

Ohhhhhh....

CHORUS

YOU'RE MAKING THINGS UP AGAIN,
ARNOLD.
YOU'RE RECKLESSLY WARPING THE
WORDS OF JESUS!

Now a light comes on two hobbit-like creatures, holding swords and on their knees with big fake hairy feet.

HOBBITS

YOU CAN'T JUST SAY WHAT YOU
WANT, ARNOLD.

ELDER CUNNINGHAM

Come on, hobbits.

HOBBITS & CHORUS

YOU'RE DIGGING YOURSELF A DEEP
HOLE.

ELDER CUNNINGHAM

I'M MAKING THINGS UP
AGAIN,
KIND OF!
BUT THIS TIME IT'S
HELPING A
DOZEN PEOPLE!
THERE'S NOTHING SO BAD
BECAUSE THIS TIME –
I'M NOT COMMITTING A SIN
JUST BY MAKING THINGS UP AGAIN,

RORY O'MALLEY: This is probably the most sensitive moment in the show. We start the song, and when the character from the African ensemble says, *"I'm gonna go and rape a baby,"* there's no laughs. You know, after laugh, laugh, laugh, there's no laughs ever at that section—they know this is horrible. This is a terrible thing that Mutumbo says. And this clown of a character that we've been watching—Elder Cunningham—is the only person who can stop this. What's amazing and surprising is that any kind of fear that you have about the audience being smart enough goes away when your script is smart enough.

YOU'RE
THING
AGA
ARN

MAKING THINGS UP AGAIN, OLD.

1 CASEY NICHOLAW: When I came on board, it was the Mormon boys that were Cunningham's conscience—as opposed to Yoda and Hobbits and Darth Vader—and we just kept growing. Then we had one person left. We wanted one more person to come out, and Rema Webb was the only singer who wasn't on stage. Trey was like, *Let's make her Uhura!* I was like, *Yes, perfect!* We went through the budget thing where they said, *We're not going to pay for a Uhura costume, it's not going to work.* We're like, *Trust us, it's totally going to work,* and we got the Uhura costume. And that costume is what pushes the number over the top.

2 ANNE GAREFINO: When we were talking about adding the Uhura character, someone said to me… *No Broadway musical with Uhura and* Star Wars *characters in it will ever win a Tony.*

RIGHT?!

CHORUS
NO!

NABULUNGI
Elder Cunningham! You have to stop him!

ELDER CUNNINGHAM
What? What is it?

NABULUNGI
Gotswana is going to cut off his daughter's clitoris!

ELDER CUNNINGHAM
HAH?!

GOTSWANA
This is all very interesting, but women HAVE to be circumcised if it's what The General wants!

ELDER CUNNINGHAM
No, no, doing that to a lady is against Christ's will!

GOTSWANA
How do you know? Christ never said nothin' about no clitoris!

ELDER CUNNINGHAM
Yes! Yes he did!
(pretending to read)
In ancient New York, three men were about to cut off a Mormon woman's clitoris! But right before they did – Jesus had Boba Fett turn them into FROGS!

GOTSWANA
Frogs?

UGANDAN WOMAN
You mean like the frogs that got fucked by Joseph Smith!

ELDER CUNNINGHAM
Yeah! Those frogs! "For a clitoris is holy amongst all things," said he!

CHORUS
YOU'RE MAKING THINGS UP AGAIN, ARNOLD.

UGANDANS
WE'RE LEARNING THE TRUTH!

CHORUS
YOU'RE TAKING THE HOLY WORD

AND ADDING FICTION!

UGANDANS
THE TRUTH ABOUT GOD.

CHORUS
BE CAREFUL HOW YOU PROCEED, ARNOLD.
WHEN YOU FIB THERE'S A PRICE.

UGANDAN
WE'RE GOING TO PARADISE.

ELDER CUNNINGHAM
Right!

ELDER CUNNINGHAM
WHO WOULD HAVE THOUGHT I
  HAD THIS MAGIC TOUCH?
WHO'D HAVE BELIEVED I COULD
  MAN UP THIS MUCH?
I'M TALKING, THEY'RE LISTENING,
  MY STORIES ARE GLISTENING
I'M GONNA SAVE THEM
  ALL WITH THIS STUFF!

UGANDANS
OOHH - LA

CHORUS
YOU'RE MAKING THINGS UP
  AGAIN, ARNOLD!

UGANDANS
ELDER CUNNINGHAM!

CHORUS
YOU'RE MAKING THINGS UP
  AGAIN, ARNOLD!

UGANDANS
HOLY PROPHET MAN!

CHORUS
YOU'RE MAKING THINGS UP
  AGAIN, ARNOLD.

UGANDANS
Our savior!

ELDER CUNNINGHAM
YOU'RE MAKING THINGS UP
  AGAIN…

YODA
Up again making things you are –

ELDER CUNNINGHAM
ARNOLD...

– THE DREAM –

The curtain opens to find Elder Price with his backpack happily bouncing through Orlando. Very happy Disney-style MUSIC plays as Price bops around like a tourist, scoping things out.

ELDER PRICE
I'm here!! I'm here!

He drops his bag and spins around like Mary Tyler Moore.

ELDER PRICE
I'MMMM HEEEERE!!!

Price walks up to the audience and explains–

EDLER PRICE
Orlando! And it's even BETTER than I could have imagined! The streets are clean, the people are happy...

Something catches his eye.

ELDER PRICE
Epcot Center! I can see the ball!

But then a quizzical look comes over him.

ELDER PRICE
The funny thing is... I don't really remember getting here...

Price now seems a little confused as the music changes to something slightly dreamy.

ELDER PRICE
Wait... This can't be Orlando... I don't even remember the plane landing.

Things start to get dark –

ELDER PRICE
What's happened to me? Where am I?

A CLAP OF THUNDER THEN A BOOMING VOICE FROM OFFSTAGE –

SATAN
Kevin Price!

ELDER PRICE
Who is that?!

SATAN
You broke the rules, Elder... Your soul belongs to ME now!

ELDER PRICE
... Mickey?

SATAN
Ha Ha HA! Think again, minion! You now dwell in eternal flame.

A CRASH OF THUNDER.

ELDER PRICE
Oh no! I remember this place...

The lights go red as Price starts to figure it out.

SPOOKY MORMON HELL DREAM 3

ELDER PRICE
LONG AGO WHEN I WAS FIVE
I SNUCK IN THE KITCHEN LATE AT
    NIGHT
AND ATE A DONUT WITH A MAPLE
    GLAZE.

Some EERIE sounds.

ELDER PRICE
MY FATHER ASKED WHO ATE THE
    SNACK
I SAID THAT IT WAS MY BROTHER
    JACK
AND JACK GOT GROUNDED FOR
    FOURTEEN DAYS.

More EERIE sounds.

3 RORY O'MALLEY: I think it's the most *South Park* moment of our show because I think the guys have a real fascination with damnation and Satan. Growing up Catholic, I certainly understand what a Spooky Mormon Hell Dream is. We have Spooky Catholic Hell Dreams while we're awake, so I love it.

4 CASEY NICHOLAW: We were like, *We've got to give Andrew a little something more.* One day in rehearsal I said to them, God, *I just read in this article that they have maple glazed donuts with bacon on them, I would absolutely kill for one of those right now!* And sure enough, Trey comes back in with a lyric that says, *I ate a donut with a maple glaze.* Next thing I'm saying is *Props, props, I need four giant donuts with maple glaze on them!* The ridiculousness of that—and the sort of wholesomeness of thinking, *That was a horrible lie and that's why I'm going to Hell!*—is brilliant.

AND NOW MY SOUL HAT

BACK

SPO

MOR

HELL D

H JUST BEEN THROWN

INTO OKY MON REAM!

❶ JASON MICHAEL SNOW: The demon crabs were originally really hard to perform. The feet were oversized, and the hands were too long and had no grips or anything. The first week in previews we were dropping hats and dropping canes, it was just a disaster. And then one by one, everyone's costume started getting little mini-hands, so that we basically have gloves that no one in the audience can see, and so we could finally grip things. But oh my God, that first week of Hell was just hats and canes dropping and people running into each other.

❷ LEWIS CLEALE: One day right before previews, they gave me a new line for "Hell Dream." I came out in my Jesus costume, with the built-in lights, and I said the line for the first time: "You're a DICK." Trey and Matt fell out of their chairs, we had to stop.

❸ RORY O'MALLEY: My mother goes to church every Sunday, and when she saw our final workshop everyone was very nervous. She was the first mom of our cast to see the show, and she loved it. Of course, my character doesn't say one bad word; maybe if I sang "Hasa Diga," we'd have a different story. But in between the final workshop and Broadway, Casey changed "Spooky Mormon Hell Dream" so that I perform a sexual act on Hitler. I was so nervous the first time my mom came to see us on Broadway, not for the show but for that moment. Being good Irish Catholics, we never spoke about the sexual act the first five times she saw it, and I thought, *She's never going to talk about it, we talk about every single moment of the show except for that.* And after the sixth time she said, *That is you with Adolph Hitler, is it not?* And I said, *Yes, Mom, yes, it is.* She said, *Okay, I thought it was.*

ELDER PRICE
I'VE LIVED WITH THE GUILT ALL OF
MY LIFE.
AND THE TERRIBLE VISION THAT I
HAD THAT NIGHT.

Price takes a falling pose and screams –

ELDER PRICE
NO PLEASE! I DON'T WANNA GO
BAAAAAAACK!!!!!

Now the stage is fully revealed as Price lands in Hell. The cast, dressed in various demonic outfits, crowds in around him. ❶

CHORUS
DOWN, DOWN THY SOUL IS
CAST!
FROM THE EARTH WHENCE FORTH
YE FELL!
THE PATH OF FIRE LEADS THEE –
TO SPOOKY MORMON HELL
DREAM!
WELCOME BACK TO
SPOOKY MORMON HELL DREAM!
YOU ARE HAVING
A SPOOKY MORMON HELL
DREAM NOW!

ELDER PRICE
AND NOW I'VE GONE AND DONE IT
AGAIN

CHORUS
RECTUS!

ELDER PRICE
I'VE COMMITTED
ANOTHER
AWFUL SIN

CHORUS
DOMINUS!

ELDER PRICE
I LEFT MY MISSION
COMPANION
ALL ALONE.

CHORUS
SPOOKYTUS!

ELDER PRICE
OH GOD, HOW COULD

I HAVE
DONE THIS TO YOU?

CHORUS
DEUS!

ELDER PRICE
HOW COULD I BREAK
RULE SEVENTY-TWO?

CHORUS
CREEPYUS!

ELDER PRICE
AND NOW MY SOUL HATH JUST
BEEN THROWN
BACK INTO SPOOKY MORMON
HELL DREAM!

CHORUS
DOWN DOWN TO SATAN'S REALM,
SEE WHERE YOU BELONG!
THERE IS NOTHING YOU CAN DO,
NO ESCAPE FROM SPOOKY
MORMON HELL DREAM!

JESUS appears.

JESUS
You blamed your brother for eating the donut and now you walk out on your mission companion?! You're a DICK! ❷

ELDER PRICE
Jesus, I'm sorry!

Price chases after Jesus but is stopped by Hell's residents.

CHORUS
JESUS HATES YOU THIS WE KNOW!
FOR JESUS JUST TOLD YOU SO!

SKELETON 1
YOU REMEMBER LUCIFER!

SKELETON 2
HE IS EVEN SPOO-KI-ER!

Satan appears.

SATAN
MINIONS OF HADES, HAVE YOU
HEARD THE NEWS?

**KEVIN WAS CAUGHT PLAYING
   HOOKY!
NOW HE'S BACK WITH ALL YOU
   CATH'LICS AND JEWS.
IT'S SUPER SPOOKY WOOKY.**

ELDER PRICE

I'M SORRY LORD IT WAS SELFISH OF ME
   TO BREAK THE RULES,
PLEASE I DON'T WANNA BE
   IN THIS SPOOKY MORMON HELL
   DREAM!

CHORUS

SPOOKY MORMON HELL DREAM!
GENGHIS KHAN,
JEFFREY DAHMER,
HITLER,
JOHNNIE COCHRAN!
THEIR SPIRITS ALL SURROUND
   YOU!
SPOOKY SPOOKY SPOOOOKY!

ADOLPH HITLER ⑤

I STARTED A WAR AND KILLED
   MILLIONS OF JEWS!

GENGHIS KHAN

I SLAUGHTERED THE CHINESE!

JEFFERY DAHMER

I STABBED A GUY AND FUCKED HIS
   CORPSE! ④

JOHNNIE COCHRAN ⑤

I GOT OJ FREED!

ELDER PRICE

YOU THINK THAT'S BAD? I BROKE
   RULE SEVENTY-TWO!

HITLER / KHAN / DAHMER /COCHRAN

HOH?!?!

ELDER PRICE

I LEFT MY COMPANION!
I'M WAY WORSE THAN YOU!
(shouting)
I HATE THIS SPOOKY MORMON
   HELL DREAM!

CHORUS

SPOOKY MORMON HELL DREAM!

ELDER PRICE
(looking up, praying)
Please, Heavenly Father! Give me one more chance! I won't break the rules again!

Members of Hell dance around Price, taunting him. Two dancing coffee cups enter.

ELDER PRICE
No more, please no more!

CHORUS

SPOOKY MORMON HELL DREAM!
SPOOKY MORMON HELL DREAM!

Demons make Price drink coffee.

CHORUS
Chug! Chug! Chug! Chug!

ELDER PRICE
Dad, Dad! I'm so glad you're here!

Price dances with demons.

ELDER PRICE

I CAN'T BELIEVE JESUS CALLED ME
   A DICK!!!!

CHORUS

WELCOME, WELCOME
TO SPOOKY MORMON HELL
   DREAM!
YOU ARE NEVER WAKING UP FROM
SPOOKY MORMON HELL DREAM!
DOWN DOWN, THY SOUL IS CAST
FROM THE EARTH WHENCE FORTH
   YE FELL.
THIS MUST BE IT YOU MUST BE
   THERE, YOU MUST BE IN
SPOOKY MORMON HELL DREAM
   NOW!

ELDER PRICE
No! Please let me wake up, I'll do anything!!! Please, Heavenly Father, I won't let you down again!

CHORUS

SPOOKY MORMON
HELL DREAM
DONE!

④ LEWIS CLEALE: Originally I started the Hell dream as Price's Dad, had a couple of lines. Then I ran off and got into Jesus, made a Jesus entrance, then run back off and get back into Dad. So in five minutes I changed my clothes, I don't know, twenty times. So we're in tech, and you know the costume changes never go quickly at the beginning. There was a day when we were rehearsing, I could not get out of Jesus in time to get into the Dad costume. So when Jeffrey Dahmer pulled me back out and does his horrible raping of me, I was still dressed as Jesus. So it was happening, I wasn't ready, and Jeffrey Dahmer he pulled me on and was about to bend Jesus over and start. They stopped us, the orchestra stopped, everybody stopped and waited for me to change. We thought, *There is a line, we've found the line that no one is willing to cross.*

⑤ MICHAEL POTTS: Originally my character was going to be Saddam Hussein. I mean, the costume was already built, I had done the fittings. Then one day they came in and said, *It's going to be Johnnie Cochran!* because they thought it was funnier, and the whole room was like, *Oh.* We weren't quite sure—is it too soon? And everyone was just really silent for a while. Then I went, *Okay, let's see what we can do with this.* It's funny, these guys don't play it safe. They do not play it safe.

SCOTT BARNHARDT: This line used to be *"Elder Cunningham, where in heavenly father's green earth have you been?"* I always thought that was one of the silliest, cutest little lines. I'm still sad that it got trimmed.

– THE VILLAGE –

After the pounding applause, Elder Price finds himself lying on the ground surrounded by the other missionaries.

ELDER MCKINLEY
I think he's coming to! Come on, Elder Price... Wake up, buddy...

ELDER PRICE
Wha– What? Where am I?

ELDER DAVIS
Looks like you fell asleep at the bus station!

ELDER CHURCH
We were SO worried!

ELDER PRICE
I'm sorry, OK?! I'm sorry I had a little meltdown last night. I'm not leaving, alright? I...realized while I was asleep that it's WRONG and I've got to stick to my work.

ELDER MCKINLEY
Ohh, you had the Hell Dream, didn't you...

Humming, Elder Cunningham enters.

ELDER CUNNINGHAM
OH, HEY GUYS!

ELDER MICHAELS
Elder Cunningham! Where have YOU been?!

ELDER CUNNINGHAM
Oh, nowhere much...
(proud of himself)
Just with TEN EAGER AFRICANS who are now interested in the church!

The Elders all rush around Cunningham.

ELDERS
WHAT?! / Are you serious?! / Oh my God?! / Etc.

ELDER CUNNINGHAM
Yup... Yup they're all completely into the teachings and willing to learn more!

Now Price rushes up to Cunningham.

ELDER PRICE
Are you serious, Elder Cunningham?! That's amazing!

ELDER CUNNINGHAM
(hurt girlfriend)
Oh. Elder Price. Hey.

ELDER PRICE
Hey...

ELDER CUNNINGHAM
So, did you find yourself a new companion?

ELDER PRICE
No. No, I'm sorry about that... But this is GREAT, Elder Cunningham! If you've got some eager followers we can really turn things around. I think we should start preparing which verses to teach them and then we can prep some exercises –

ELDER CUNNINGHAM
Uh woa – woa. You LEFT me. Remember?

ELDER DAVIS
Elder Cunningham we must always work in PAIRS. Remember?

ELDER MCKINLEY
Give Elder Cunningham a break – if it's working better this way, he can leave Elder Price out of it.

ELDERS
Yeah! / Right! / I agree! / Etc.

The Elders all crowd around Cunningham – almost pushing Price out of the way.

ELDER MCKINLEY
Now, how many of the people want to have follow-up sessions?!

ELDER CUNNINGHAM
Oh, let's see... All of them!

ELDERS
All of them! / Oh my gosh! / Wow! / You're amazing, Elder Cunningham!

Price walks off to a private section of the stage.

ELDER CHURCH
Do you think we might actually get a baptism out of this?

ELDER MCKINLEY
They always say if you can just get that FIRST BAPTISM others will follow!

ELDER CUNNINGHAM

Hold on, guys... I know I'm doing a real good job and all, but... Let's not get too carried away. I mean... A lot of these people are scared to death of that "General Butt-F-ing Naked" guy.

ELDERS

(a bit deflated)

Oh, yeah. / Oh, that guy... / The General... / Etc.

ELDER THOMAS

Well, somebody needs to tell that General Butt-F-ing Naked that people should be free to do what they want!

ELDER MCKINLEY

Nobody is going to change how a crazy warlord thinks! That would take something INCREDIBLE.

A DING goes off. A light shines on Price's face.

ELDER PRICE

(realizing)

    SOMETHING... INCREDIBLE...

    SOMETHING INCREDIBLE...

ELDER MCKINLEY

(ignoring Price)

Well, look, let's just be happy that Elder Cunningham has people interested.

ELDERS

That's true! / Yeah! / At least we have that! / Etc.

Price suddenly bursts in front of them – filled with new energy.

ELDER PRICE

It's alright, guys! I've got everything under control!! I know what the Lord wants from me now! This village is gonna be SAVED!

ELDERS

So anyways... / Great! / Come on... / Etc.

The Elders walk off, leaving Price on stage alone and confused.

I BELIEVE ❷

ELDER PRICE

    EVER SINCE I WAS A CHILD

      I TRIED TO BE THE BEST...

    SO WHAT HAPPENED?

    MY FAMILY AND FRIENDS ALL SAID I

      WAS BLESSED....

    SO WHAT HAPPENED?

The song picks up.

ELDER PRICE

    IT WAS SUPPOSED TO BE ALL SO

      EXCITING

    TO BE TEACHING OF CHRIST 'CROSS

      THE SEA.

    BUT I ALLOWED MY FAITH TO BE

      SHAKEN –

    OH WHAT'S THE MATTER WITH ME?

    I'VE ALWAYS LONGED TO HELP

      THE NEEDY.

    TO DO THE THINGS I'VE NEVER

      DARED.

    THIS WAS THE TIME FOR ME

      TO STEP UP.

    SO THEN WHY WAS I SO SCARED?

    A WARLORD THAT SHOOTS PEOPLE

      IN THE FACE.

    WHAT'S SO SCARY ABOUT THAT?

    I MUST TRUST THAT MY LORD

      IS MIGHTIER –

    AND ALWAYS HAS MY BACK.

    NOW I MUST BE COMPLETELY

      DEVOUT.

    I CAN'T HAVE EVEN ONE SHRED

      OF DOUBT!

    I BELIEVE – ❸

    THAT THE LORD GOD CREATED

      THE UNIVERSE.

    I BELIEVE –

    THAT HE SENT HIS ONLY SON TO DIE

      FOR MY SINS.

    AND I BELIEVE –

    THAT ANCIENT JEWS BUILT BOATS

      AND SAILED TO AMERICA.

    I AM A MORMON, AND A MORMON

      JUST BELIEVES.

❷ **BOBBY LOPEZ:** During one of the workshops, Scott Rudin had been strongly urging us to write a song for Elder Price to help explain his motivation in Act Two. We were resisting writing it, but Scott made an impassioned case that unless we wrote something we'd have squandered the whole workshop. So we unwillingly started brainstorming. I suggested only half seriously that if this was to be Elder Price giving himself a pep talk on his way to confront the warlord, maybe we should look at the song "I Have Confidence" from *The Sound of Music*. Trey didn't know it, so we watched it on YouTube and he said, *Let's just do that.* We ended up pretty much in hysterics.

❸ **CASEY NICHOLAW:** It was always our intention to do this with an enormous slideshow behind it; slides of Mormon portraits, Mormon moments, and Mormon life. This would build to Elder Price being lifted to the sky on a platform, like a Super Bowl halftime number. We did it in the workshop without the projections, only because we didn't have them yet, and we thought it worked beautifully. We decided it was just as powerful, if not more, with the song—and Elder Price—being the star of the number.

1 STEPHEN OREMUS: When Trey, Bobby, and Matt wrote "I Believe," it felt like a real turning point for Elder Price as well as the entire show. They wanted it to be epic and anthemic, and so we used the full cast and arranged a big gospel choir to back him up. Which they do, providing the audience with a number that blows the roof off the theater.

2 BOBBY LOPEZ: At first I resisted having the song extend and transition into the warlord scene. The original warlord scene was absolutely hilarious. Price pulled out this diagram on a placemat, which we had bought in Palmyra, showing the extremely complicated "Mormon path to salvation."

YOU CANNOT JUST BELIEVE PART-
WAY.
YOU HAVE TO BELIEVE IN IT ALL.
MY PROBLEM WAS DOUBTING THE
LORD'S WILL,
INSTEAD OF STANDING TALL.
I CAN'T ALLOW MYSELF TO HAVE
ANY DOUBT.
IT'S TIME TO SET MY WORRIES FREE.
TIME TO SHOW THE WORLD WHAT
ELDER PRICE IS ABOUT
AND SHARE THE POWER INSIDE OF
ME!
I BELIEVE–

CHORUS

AHHH... **1**

ELDER PRICE

THAT GOD HAS A PLAN FOR ALL OF
US.
I BELIEVE –

CHORUS

I BELIEVE AAHHH....

ELDER PRICE

THAT PLAN INVOLVES
ME GETTING MY OWN PLANET.
AND I BELIEVE

CHORUS

BELIEVE OHO...

ELDER PRICE

THAT THE CURRENT PRESIDENT OF
THE CHURCH, THOMAS MONSON,
SPEAKS DIRECTLY TO GOD.
I AM A MORMON AND, DANG IT,
A MORMON JUST BELIEVES.

CHORUS

A MORMON JUST BELIEVES.

ELDER PRICE

I KNOW THAT I MUST GO AND DO –
THE THINGS MY GOD COMMANDS.

CHORUS

THINGS MY GOD COMMANDS

ELDER PRICE

I REALIZE NOW WHY HE SENT ME
HERE!

CHORUS

AHHH! AHHH!

ELDER PRICE

IF YOU ASK THE LORD IN FAITH
HE WILL ALWAYS ANSWER YOU
JUST BELIEVE

CHORUS

JUST BELIEVE

ELDER PRICE

IN HIM AND HAVE NO FEAR!

– THE GENERAL'S CAMP –

The General does what he can to seem impressive. He sits on a mound of guns and ammo.

GENERAL'S GUARD
(entering)
General! We have an intruder! He just walked right into camp!

Elder Price bursts into camp. **2**

ELDER PRICE

I BELIEVE!!!!

CHORUS

AAHHH

ELDER PRICE

THAT SATAN HAS A HOLD OF YOU.

CHORUS

SATAN HAS A HOLD

Everyone looks at each other, confused.

ELDER PRICE

I BELIEVE!

CHORUS

I BELIEVE!

ELDER PRICE

THAT THE LORD GOD HAS SENT ME
HERE!

CHORUS

GOD HAS SENT ME HERE

ELDER PRICE

AND I BELIEVE!

CHORUS

BELIEVE

ELDER PRICE

THAT IN 1978 GOD CHANGED HIS
  MIND ABOUT BLACK PEOPLE!!!

CHORUS

BLACK PEOPLE!!!

ELDER PRICE & CHORUS

YOU'LL BE A MORMON!
A MORMON WHO JUST BELIEVES.

THE GENERAL

The fuck is this?

ELDER PRICE

AND NOW I CAN FEEL THE
  EXCITEMENT. ✸
THIS IS THE MOMENT I WAS BORN
  TO DO.
AND I FEEL SO INCREDIBLE –
TO BE SHARING MY FAITH WITH
  YOU.
THE SCRIPTURES SAY IF YOU ASK
  IN FAITH,
IF YOU ASK GOD HIMSELF YOU'LL
  KNOW.
BUT YOU MUST ASK HIM WITHOUT
  ANY DOUBT,
AND LET YOUR SPIRIT GROW!

CHORUS

LET YOUR SPIRIT GROW!

*Price takes the General's hand and pulls
the confused warlord up from his seat as if
asking him to join him in prayer.* ④

ELDER PRICE

I BELIEVE!

CHORUS

AAHHH

ELDER PRICE

THAT GOD LIVES ON A PLANET
  CALLED KOLOB!
I BELIEVE!

CHORUS

I BELIEVE

ELDER PRICE

THAT JESUS HAS

ELDER PRICE & CHORUS

HIS OWN PLANET AS WELL.

CHORUS

BELIEVE...

ELDER PRICE

AND I BELIEVE
THAT THE GARDEN OF EDEN WAS
  IN JACKSON COUNTY, MISSOURI.

CHORUS

OOOO....

ELDER PRICE

IF YOU BELIEVE, THE LORD WILL
  REVEAL IT.
AND YOU'LL KNOW IT'S ALL TRUE –
YOU'LL JUST FEEL IT.
YOU'LL BE A MORMON!!!!
AND BY GOSH –

ELDER PRICE & CHORUS

A MORMON JUST BELIEVESSSSS!!!!

ELDER PRICE

OH, I BELIEVE!

CHORUS

A MORMON JUST...

ELDER PRICE

I BELIEVE!

CHORUS

BELIEVES!

*After the applause, POW!! The General hits
the book out of Price's hand.*

THE GENERAL

JUMAMOSI!!!

*The guards pounce on Price. Price looks
very scared.*

ELDER PRICE

NO! WAIT! God has spoken to me, sir!

*The guards advance on Price and slap him
around.*

ELDER PRICE

BY THE POWER OF GOD ALMIGHTY
TOUCH ME NOT!!! The power of Christ
compels you!!!!

③ ANDREW RANNELLS: Trey
likes to say there's not a single joke
in the song, it's all facts about the
Mormon religion. But it's so well-
crafted and the tune is so great. It's
like you really do see the earnestness
of these missionaries. Why else would
these nineteen-year-old guys leave
home and volunteer for two years
just to try to convert people to their
religion? It's because they really believe
it, and the most passionate thing in
their lives is to go spread this around.
Structurally, this is the heart of the
show. It sort of boils it all down to
one number.

④ BRIAN TYREE HENRY This
was an improv in rehearsal. I went to
Andrew and was like, *If you trust me
I'll trust you.* He is bursting into my
camp, I'm sitting on all these boxes
of guns, why wouldn't I shoot him? I
have to be in on the joke. So he just
literally pulls me into the song, I go
with it, and we really work off each
other. It's always fun to do. How can
I make the audience laugh, doing as
little as possible? When he finally hits
that last note, that's when I have to
give in.

Price contorts his body almost as if he expects lightning to come shooting out his hands –

ELDER PRICE
NO! NO WAIT PLEASE!!! WHAT ARE YOU – NO!!!!!

Very serious Les Misérables "Look Down"-style music starts to play as the scene gets even more violent. The Gereral begins to remove his clothes. Price screams at the top of his lungs as he appears to be very close to being killed.

ELDER PRICE
AHGHGHHGHG HGHGHGHGGH!!!!!

The curtain closes.

- THE VILLAGE -

Cunningham is preaching and pretending to read from the Book of Mormon.

ELDER CUNNINGHAM
And so, yeah, so then Christ said to the Nephites, "be strong!" You know?! "Just because Lamanites got big Death Star weapons and stuff doesn't mean they should run your lives! There's more of you than there are of them, you know? You should always... stand up for yourselves," Christ said!

MIDDALA
Just like the way the Hobbits all stood up to Brigham Young's killers!

ELDER CUNNINGHAM
Yes! Very good, Middala! So the Nephites fought off the wicked Lamanites and for punishment the Lord God turned the Lamanites YELLOW!

KALIMBA
Ooh! Like the Chinese!

ELDER CUNNINGHAM
Right! Right! Okay, we better stop there for today. Hopefully we'll see everyone tomorrow?

UGANDANS
Okay! / Bye! / Thank you!

UGANDAN WOMAN
(to another Ugandanwhile walking out)
The Book is right. We must not fight amongst each other! The Chinese are the real problem!

MAFALA
I LOVE all these Mormon stories! They are so fucking weird.

SADAKA
Elder Cunningham... I just want to say thank Heavenly Father you are here.

Mafala and the Ugandans leave, but Nabulungi stays with Cunningham.

NABULUNGI
I've never seen the people here so happy. Even Baba... You are amazing.

ELDER CUNNINGHAM
Aw, I really haven't done that much...

NABULUNGI
But you have. I texted my friend the story you told us about Joseph Smith's battle with diarrhea. He said all the people in his village read it! You are a great man.

ELDER CUNNINGHAM
(overwhelmed)
I... I kind of AM, huh?

NABULUNGI
Do you think we're good enough to join the Mormons? We are all trying very hard! We are ready to do whatever tasks you require of us!

ELDER CUNNINGHAM
You don't understand, there's nothing they have to DO to become a Mormon. We let anybody who wants to join up! As long as they're willing to commit to the church, then we can baptize them!

NABULUNGI
Well then – would you like to... Baptize me?

ELDER CUNNINGHAM
Sure, of course! That would be great!

NABULUNGI
Okay, let's do it!

Cunningham immediately looks nervous.

ELDER CUNNINGHAM
Wha– you mean right now?

NABULUNGI
Why not?

ELDER CUNNINGHAM
Well, I...
Cunningham walks away nervously and rubs his palms.

ELDER CUNNINGHAM
To be honest I've...never done it before.

NABULUNGI
That's okay – neither have I.

She smiles at him. He starts to get really nervous.

ELDER CUNNINGHAM
Oh yeah! Guess that's true!

She crosses back over to him.

NABULUNGI
Do you know HOW to baptize someone new into the church?

ELDER CUNNINGHAM
Of course! It's something we study over and over at the –
(forgetting what it's called–)
– Missionary Control Center.

NABULUNGI
Then please, Elder Cunningham, I want to be baptized. I swear to dedicate my life to the church.

ELDER CUNNINGHAM
Ha... Okay, uh, I'm gonna need a little time to get ready.

NABULUNGI
Okay, I'll get ready, too.

They go to opposite ends of the stage. Cunningham sets his Book of Mormon down and starts to wash his hands. Nabulungi pulls her hair back to get ready to get wet.

BAPTIZE ME

ELDER CUNNINGHAM

I'M ABOUT TO DO IT FOR THE
FIRST TIME
AND I'M GONNA DO IT WITH A
GIRL!
A SPECIAL GIRL –

WHO MAKES MY HEART KIND OF
FLUTTER
MAKES MY EYES KIND OF BLUR –
I CAN'T BELIEVE I'M ABOUT TO
BAPTIZE HER!

NABULUNGI

HE WILL BAPTIZE ME!
HE'LL HOLD ME IN HIS ARMS
AND HE WILL BAPTIZE ME.
RIGHT IN FRONT OF EVERYONE
AND IT WILL SET ME FREE –
WHEN HE LOOKS INTO MY EYES –
AND HE SEES JUST HOW MUCH
I LOVE BEING BAPTIZED...

ELDER CUNNINGHAM

I'M GONNA BAPTIZE HER.

NABULUNGI

BAPTIZE ME

ELDER CUNNINGHAM

BATHE HER IN GOD'S GLORY
AND I WILL BAPTIZE HER

NABULUNGI

I'M READY

ELDER CUNNINGHAM

WITH EVERYTHING I GOT.
AND I'LL MAKE HER BEG FOR
MORE,

NABULUNGI

OOH

ELDER CUNNINGHAM

AS I WASH HER FREE FROM SIN.
AND IT'LL BE SO GOOD SHE'LL
WANT ME TO

ELDER CUNNINGHAM & NABULUNGI

BAPTIZE HER/ME AGAIN.

② JOSH GAD: One time I forgot the lyrics, but that was actually brilliant because I just ad-libbed the lines. The song is supposed to start, *"I'm about to do it for the first time and I'm going to do it with a girl."* And I go, *I'm falling in love like I've never been before*, like it wasn't even from the same show. But somehow I rhymed the entire four verses, which was a remarkable feat. So the audience had no clue, they were, like, *That's kind of shitty writing, but at least he's selling it.*

CLARK JOHNSEN: The thing that moves me most is the baptism section. I baptized upwards of seventy people into the church as a missionary, so I just remember this experience. You're holding the person, and you immerse them in the water, and then they come out of the water; just to see the water coming over their faces, and they've chosen to believe that this is a rebirth, that their sins are washed away, it's the most beautiful idea ever. You've got these people, and you've taught this to them and they believe it. They come out of the water, and they really feel like they're a brand-new person. When we started performances, I said to the guy I baptize, *You're going to have to bear with me, because I might feel a little bit moved a couple of times, because the feeling is true.* To me it's true, because I lived it.

Finally they come together, almost like they're going to kiss, but then Cunningham suddenly loses his nerve and backs away.

ELDER CUNNINGHAM
Uh – I'm gonna need another minute – excuse me.

He walks away and Nabulungi stares off at him.

NABULUNGI
NEVER KNOWN A BOY SO GENTLE.
ONE LIKE HIM IS HARD TO FIND –
A SPECIAL KIND
IT MAKES MY HEART KIND OF
    FLUTTER
LIKE A MOTH IN THE COCOON.
I HOPE HE GETS TO BAPTIZING ME
    SOON.

Cunningham comes back after having collected himself.

ELDER CUNNINGHAM
I'M GONNA BAPTIZE YOU.
I'M THROUGH WITH ALL MY
    STALLING.

NABULUNGI
YOU'RE GONNA BAPTIZE ME.
I'M READY TO LET YOU DO IT.

BOTH
AND IT WILL SET US FREE.
IT'S TIME TO BE IMMERSED.
AND I'M SO HAPPY YOU'RE ABOUT
    TO BE MY FIRST.

ELDER CUNNINGHAM
Okay, you ready?

NABULUNGI
I'm ready. So how do we do it?

ELDER CUNNINGHAM
Well, I hold you like this –

NABULUNGI
Yeah?

ELDER CUNNINGHAM
And I lower you down –

NABULUNGI
Yeah?

ELDER CUNNINGHAM
And then –

He drops her and she gets soaking wet. Suddenly Cunningham bursts out –

ELDER CUNNINGHAM
I JUST BAPTIZED HER!
SHE GOT DOUSED BY HEAVENLY
    FATHER!
I JUST BAPTIZED HER GOOD!

NABULUNGI
YOU BAPTIZED ME!

ELDER CUNNINGHAM
I PERFORMED LIKE A CHAMP!

NABULUNGI
I'M WET WITH SALVATION!

BOTH
WE JUST WENT ALL THE WAY.
PRAISE BE TO GOD I'LL NEVER
    FORGET THIS DAY...

ELDER CUNNINGHAM
I BAPTIZED YOU!

NABULUNGI
YOU BAPTIZED ME!

ELDER CUNNINGHAM

I GOTCHA GOOD!

NABULUNGI

BAPTIZE ME

ELDER CUNNINGHAM

YOU WANT IT MORE, BABY?

NABULUNGI

BAPTIZE ME!

The scene ends with the two looking at each other tenderly.

NABULUNGI

I'll text you later.

– DIRTY RIVER NEAR THE VILLAGE –

A new, more church-like and happy vamp of "Baptize Me" plays as we see all the Mormon Elders, except for Price and Cunningham, wearing white and getting ready to baptize the Ugandan people.

As the baptisms continue in the background, Elder McKinley steps forward into a light and dictates as if writing a letter.

ELDER MCKINLEY

Dear Mission President, it is my HONOR to inform you that the elders of Uganda District 9 have brought TWENTY NEW MEMBERS into the church...

Now a new person, the MISSION PRESIDENT, steps forward into a light reading the note.

MISSION PRESIDENT

...They are all fully committed to the Church of Jesus Christ of Latter-Day Saints, and our numbers continue to grow!
(no longer reading)
This is outstanding! These boys have converted more Africans than any district in the COUNTRY!

The mission president again steps forward this time as if reading from a letter HE wrote.

MISSION PRESIDENT

Elders of District 9! You have truly honored the church by your success! Congratulations on becoming ONE with the people of Africa!

McKinley steps forward.

I AM AFRICA ❷

ELDER MCKINLEY

I AM AFRICA...
I AM AFRICA.
WITH THE STRENGTH OF
    THE CHEETAH,
MY NATIVE VOICE SHALL SING

ELDERS

WE ARE AFRICA!
WE ARE THE HEARTBEAT OF AF-RI-CA!

ELDER SCHRADER

WITH THE RHINO

ELDER THOMAS

THE MEERKAT

ELDER CHURCH

THE NOBLE LION KING

ELDERS

WE ARE AFRICA!
WE ARE THE WINDS OF THE
    SERENGETI,
WE ARE THE SWEAT OF THE
    JUNGLE MAN
WE ARE THE TEARS OF NELSON
    MANDELA –
WE ARE THE LOST BOYS OF
    THE SUDAN.

Now Cunningham steps out through the line of Elders, with Nabulungi.

ELDER CUNNINGHAM

I AM AFRICA!
JUST LIKE BONO! I AM AFRICA!
I FLEW IN HERE AND BECAME
    ONE WITH THIS LAND!

ELDERS

HA NA HEYA! AZ BA NEYBA!

ELDER CUNNINGHAM

I'M NOT A FOLLOWER ANYMORE
    NO! NOW, I AM FRICKIN' AFRICA!
WITH MY ZULU SPEAR, I RUN

❷ **TREY PARKER:** We realized in previews that we had this golden stretch, from "I Believe" to "I Am Africa." We have the audience and the plot keeps moving. The better the musical numbers are, the harder it is to get the audience to pay attention to the dialogue. We realized you had better musicalize the dialogue or get through it as fast as you can.

WITH MY ZULU

BAREFOOT THRO

I A

AFR

U SPEAR I RUN
OUGH THE SAND!

AM!
ICA!

BOBBY LOPEZ: There used to be a scene in the last act in the doctor's office, where you saw that Elder Price had gotten the book shoved up his ass, and the doctor is saying, *Something incredible. You've done something incredible. I can't believe you got it all the way up there.* We loved that scene so much, and we just didn't want to move it. And Casey said, *It stops the flow, we wanna go straight through, is there any way we can get that scene into "I Am Africa"?* It just went against every grain of what we wanted to do. It was the very last thing we did before we moved to the theater from the rehearsal room, and it was the best decision we ever made. Casey gets the credit.

BAREFOOT THROUGH THE SAND!
I AM AFRICA!

ELDERS

AHH,
HA NA HEY A ZABA NEYBA.
HA NA HEY A ZABA NEY. AHH!
AH AH AH AH AH AHA AH-T

As the song continues – we go to another part of the stage where Elder Price is on a crappy hospital bed.

An X-RAY comes up for all the audience to see. It is of Price's lower body, and we can clearly see that the Book of Mormon has been violently shoved up his ass.

Then finally, the Doctor sings –

GOTSWANA
(singing softly)

SOMETHING INCREDIBLE...
YOU DID SOMETHING
  INCREDIBLE...
I HAVE NEVER SEEN A RECTAL
  BLOCKAGE OF THIS KIND.
I'VE SEEN PATIENTS IN THE PAST,
WITH RODENTS OR BOTTLES IN
  THEIR ASS,
BUT THIS IS SOMETHING
  INCREDIBLE,
AND IT BLOWS MY FUCKING MIND.

Back to the "I Am Africa" song with the Mormon boys.

ELDERS

WE ARE THE SNOWS OF
  KILIMANJARO
WE ARE GORILLAS IN THE MIST
WE ARE THE GALLEYS OF THE

AMISTAD
WE ARE FELA'S DEFIANT FIST!
WE ARE AFRICA!

Now Cunningham and Nabulungi step forward into their own light.

ELDER CUNNINGHAM

It's just AMAZING, Neosporin! The mission president wants to meet ME personally! He's going to give me a MEDAL!

NABULUNGI

Oh, Elder! That is INCREDIBLE!

Cunningham and Nabulungi run off.

ELDERS

WE ARE AFRICA,
THE ZEBRA AND GIRAFFE-RICA.

Now a part of the stage where The General stands with one guard.

THE GENERAL

Are you telling me EVERYONE in the village is now joining some religious CULT?! They must be trying to power up their clitorises to oppose me. I WILL KILL THEM ALL!!!

ELDERS

WE ARE AFRICA
WE ARE AFRICA, WE ARE THE ONE,
  THE ONLY AFRICA
THE ONE AND ONLY AFRICA
AND THE LIFE WE LIVE
  IS PRIMITIVE AND PROUD

ELDER MCKINLEY, ELDER CHURCH & ELDER ZELDER

LET US SMILE AND LAUGH-RICA

ELDERS

WE ARE AFRICA
WE ARE DEEPEST DARKEST AFRICA
SO DEEP AND DARK IN AFRICA
WE ARE FIELDS AND FERTILE
  FORESTS WELL-ENDOWED!
WE ARE AFRICA.

ELDER MCKINLEY

WE ARE THE SUNRISE ON THE
  SAVANNAH

ELDER ZELDER

A MONKEY WITH A BANANA

ELDER CHURCH

A TRIBAL WOMAN WHO DOESN'T
WEAR A BRA

ELDERS

AHHH AFRICANS ARE AFRICAN,
BUT WE ARE AFRICA!

– A KAFE IN KITGULI –

Price is sitting on a stool at the bar of some shitty counter. There are coffee cups lined up in front of him. Price is just finishing the last sip of coffee like it's scotch – his leg is trembling.

ELDER PRICE

Hit me up... Another one. COME ON!

The bartender finally pours him another cup and Price slams it.

Cunningham walks up just in time to see Price start chugging his twelfth cup of coffee.

ELDER CUNNINGHAM

Elder Price? You alright?

ELDER PRICE

Well, well... If it isn't the SUPER MORMON. Spreading "the word"?! Making more – BRAINWASHED zombies?!

ELDER CUNNINGHAM

Elder Price, what's happened to you?

ELDER PRICE

I WOKE UP, that's what happened!

ELDER CUNNINGHAM

Of course you woke up, you drank TWELVE CUPS OF COFFEE.

ELDER PRICE

(gets up)

How is it, huh?! You tell me how it is that YOU converted ALL those people into Mormons!

ELDER CUNNINGHAM

I don't know. Once I baptized Nagasaki the others just fell into place.

Price looks extra hurt.

ELDER PRICE

YOU get everything you pray for. YOU do all the things I was supposed to do. Doesn't that seem a LITTLE telling to you?!

ELDER CUNNINGHAM

Telling of what?!

ELDER PRICE

That the universe doesn't work the way we were told!

Price steps downstage to have his monologue.

ELDER PRICE

When I was nine years old... My family took a trip to Orlando, Florida. It was the most wonderful, most magical place I had ever seen. I said to myself, "THIS is where I want to spend eternity!" My parents told me that if I made God proud, and did what the church told me, in Latter Days I could have whatever I wanted. So I WORKED and I WORKED. And even when I studied Mormon stories and thought, "That doesn't make ANY SENSE," I KEPT WORKING because I was told ONE DAY – I would get my reward!! PLANET ORLANDO. But what do I have now? I can't even get a ticket home...

ELDER CUNNINGHAM

Alright, uh, look... The mission president is coming, and if I'm without my companion, well, you know that looks very bad. So if you could just –

ELDER PRICE

Oh THAT'S why you came!

ELDER CUNNINGHAM

No! I CAME because I care and –

ELDER PRICE

(loudest thing yet)

BULL POOP!

This is like a slap in the face to both boys.

ELDER PRICE

(brings it down)

That's bull poop, Elder. And you know it.

ELDER CUNNINGHAM

I know we aren't the best companions, but if we can PLEASE just ACT like we're still together in front of the mission president, you can get your ticket home, I can get my medal and we never have to see each other again.

ELDER PRICE

FINE. But don't TALK to me and DON'T touch me.

2 STEPHEN OREMUS: We had this whole song here, "They Lie." It was Price's breakdown musicalized, a scathing song that attacked the dogma: *They told me all these Mormon stories, they told me I would get my own planet.* It's all there, now, in the speech in the Kafe.

ELDER CUNNINGHAM
FINE.

ELDER PRICE
FINE.

Cunningham walks away. Price takes a moment and stares off to the sky and sings.

ORLANDO

ELDER PRICE
ORLANDO...
ORLANDO...
I LOVED YOU ORLANDO.
YOUR BRIGHT LIGHTS
YOUR BIG DREAMS
YOUR PROMISES YOU COULDN'T
  KEEP.
ORLANDO, ORLANDO,
WITHOUT YOU, ORLANDO
I'M JUST A GUY
WHO WILL DIE
AND NEVER GO BACK TO
  YOU.

– OUTSIDE THE MORMON MISSIONARIES' LIVING QUARTERS –

A FORMAL VERSION OF "I AM AFRICA" PLAYS as the Elders are all lined up to receive their awards. The mission president parades in with his assistants.

MISSION PRESIDENT
Boys, you have all done the most amazing work on your missions! You are the GLEAMING EXAMPLES of Latter-Day Saints!

MORMON MEN
Praise Christ!

ELDERS
Alright! / We did it! / Thank you! / Etc.

MISSION PRESIDENT
And YOU two – Elder Price and Elder Cunningham. You are the most successful missionaries in all of Africa!

ELDER CUNNINGHAM
Thank you, sir –
(sarcastic)
my companion was so VERY HELPFUL and THERE for me!

MORMON MEN
Praise Christ!

Nabulungi bursts into the center of the room with the villagers.

NABULUNGI
Excuse me! Excuse me – Mr. Mormon President! My people wish to give you a special welcome!

ELDER CUNNINGHAM
Nabulungi, what are you doing?

NABULUNGI
We have learned so much from Elder Cunningham, and as our gift to you, we wish to present the story of Joseph Smit and the first Mormons!

The Mormon leaders CLAP.

ELDER CUNNINGHAM
UH NO!!! NO! I THINK THAT'S A BAD IDEA! Let's NOT DO THIS!

ELDER MCKINLEY
No, no, no, Elder! This is JUST THE KIND OF THING the Mormon leaders NEED to be seeing!

MISSION PRESIDENT
Yes, let's see what these noble Africans have learned!

ELDERS
Alright! / Cool! / Awesome! / Etc.

JOSEPH SMITH
AMERICAN MOSES

NABULUNGI
AND NOW, we wish to honor you with – the story of JOSEPH SMIT – THE AMERICAN MOSES!!!!

MISSION PRESIDENT
OH! THIS IS VERY GOOD!!!

UGANDANS
MORMON!

NABULUNGI
I'm going to take you back in time.

UGANDANS
MORMON!

NABULUNGI
To the United States, 1823.

UGANDANS
MORMON!

NABULUNGI
A small and poor village called Oopstate New York!

UGANDANS
OOPSTATE.

NABULUNGI
There was disease and famine.

UGANDANS
SO SICK.

NABULUNGI
But also in this village lived a simple farmer who would change everything. His name...was Joseph Smit.

UGANDANS
YA YA YA YA YA YA YA YA YA YA YA!
JOSEPH SMIT
AMERICAN MOSES.
PRAISE BE TO JOSEPH,
AMERICAN PROPHET MAN.

JOSEPH SMITH (MUTUMBO)
Ay, my name is Joseph Smit. I'm going to fuck this baby. ❷

MISSION PRESIDENT
WHAT?!?!

UGANDANS
NO, NO, JOSEPH!
DON'T FUCK DA BABY!
JOSEPH SMIT
DON'T FUCK DA BABY!

NABULUNGI
Suddenly the clouds parted! And Joseph Smit was visited by GOD!

GOD (MAFALA)
JOSEPH SMIT!
DO NOT FUCK A BABY.
I'LL GET RID OF YOUR AIDS
IF YOU FUCK DIS FROG.

UGANDANS
YA YA YA YA YA YA YA YA YA YA YA!

NABULUNGI
Joseph Smit fucked the frog God gave to him and his AIDS went away! And then, a great wizard named Moroni appeared from the Starship Enterprise!

❷ **JOHN ERIC PARKER:** They gave us this song and they said, *You're playing Joseph Smith.* And my first line is: *My name is Joseph Smit, I'm going to fuck this baby.* No, I'm not! Are you kidding me? I am so not going to do that! But I waited to see how the authors tied it up, and they did so I was okay.

NIKKI M. JAMES: This number is really the first time we "break the fourth wall." The actual audience becomes the real audience for those few moments. As the narrator of the Joseph Smith story, there are moments when I actually make eye contact with audience members. I had no idea what to expect from those first audiences. Were they going to enjoy it? Hate it? Get up and leave? During our first week of previews, I was nervous about this number. I would fake my looks by glancing just above people's heads. I have since gotten much more comfortable. Honestly, it is fun to see people's shocked faces; to see them slap their knees, or cover their mouths, or turn to their neighbors in delight or horror.

MORONI (MIDDALA)
Joseph Smit. Your village is shit. You shall lead your villagers to a new village. TAKE THESE FUCKING GOLDEN PLATES!

UGANDANS
OH-WAY!

NABULUNGI
And on the plates were written the directions to a new land – SALT-TALAAAAY- KA SITI!

UGANDANS
SAL-TALAAAAA KA SITI!

NABULUNGI
Joseph tried to convince ALL the villagers to follow him and his golden plates!

JOSEPH SMITH
Liberation! Equality! No more slavery for Oopstate Mormon people!
I GOT THE GOLDEN PLATES.

UGANDANS
GOLD PLATES

JOSEPH SMITH
GONNA LEAD THE PEOPLE

UGANDANS
WE HEAD WEST

JOSEPH SMITH
WE GOTTA STICK TOGEDDAH

UGANDANS
MORMONS!

JOSEPH SMITH
WE GOTTA HELP EACH UDDAH

UGANDANS
WE'RE MORMONS!

JOSEPH SMITH
AND SO WE CLIMB THE MOUNTAIN

UGANDANS
WE HEAD WEST!

JOSEPH SMITH
AND WE CROSS THE RIVER

UGANDANS
WE HEAD WEST!

JOSEPH SMITH
AND WE FIGHT THE OPPRESSION

UGANDANS
MORMONS!

JOSEPH SMITH
BY BEING NICE TO EV'RY ONE

UGANDANS
WE'RE MORMONS!

BRIGHAM YOUNG (GOTSWANA)
Not so fast, Mormons! You shall not pass MY mountain!

UGANDANS
Down from the mountain, look who comes! The American warlord, Brigham Young!

BRIGHAM YOUNG
Yes, I am Brigham Young! I cut off my daughter's clitoris! That made God angry so he turned my nose into a clit for punishment!

UGANDANS
BRIGHAM YOUNG!
HIS NOSE WAS A CLITORIS.
WHAT WILL YOU DO, JOSEPH?
WILL YOU FIGHT THE CLITORIS
MAN?

JOSEPH SMITH
Not fight him... Help him.

UGANDANS
Ohhh!

NABULUNGI
Joseph Smit took his magical fuck frog and rubbed it upon Brigham Young's clit face. And behold, Brigham was CURED!

UGANDANS

JOSEPH SMIT – MAGICAL AIDS
FROG
BRIGHAM YOUNG – FROG ON HIS
CLIT FACE

NABULUNGI

Brigham Young was so grateful, he decided to JOIN the Mormons on their journey!

JOSEPH SMITH

Compassion!

BRIGHAM YOUNG

Courtesy!

JOSEPH SMITH

Let's be really fucking polite to everyone!

I GOT THE GOLDEN PLATES!

UGANDANS

GOLD PLATES

JOSEPH SMITH

GONNA LEAD THE PEOPLE

UGANDANS

WE HEAD WEST!

BRIGHAM YOUNG

WE GOTTA STICK TOGEDDAH

UGANDANS

MORMONS!

NABULUNGI

Now comes the part of our story that gets a little bit sad.

UGANDANS

Ohhhh...

NABULUNGI

After traveling for so long, the Mormons ran out of fresh water. And became sick...with DYSENTERY!

UGANDANS

MORMON GO TO DA WATAH,
WATAH GO TO DA CUP.
CUP GO TO DA STOMACH,
SHIT COME OUT DA BUTT.
SHIT GO IN DA WATAH,
WATAH GO IN DA CUP.
SHIT GO DOWN DA STOMACH,
SHIT COME OUT DA BUTT.

JOSEPH SMITH

Oh fuck!

NABULUNGI

Oh no! The prophet Joseph Smit is now getting sick!

UGANDANS

SHIT GO IN DA WATAH,
WATAH GO IN DA CUP.
CUP GO TO DA THIRSTY,
SHIT GO TO DA STOMACH,
BLOOD COME OUT DA BUTT.
BLOOD GO IN DA WATAH,
WATAH GO IN DA CUP.
CUP GO TO DA THROAT.
SHIT BLOOD IN DA STOMACH,
SHIT BLOOD IN DA MOUTH.
SHIT BLOOD ON DA INSIDES,
WATAH COME OUT DA BUTT!

JOSEPH SMITH

Augh! Brigham Young! You take the golden plates and lead the Mormons to the promised land!

BRIGHAM YOUNG

Desperation! Mortality! Loss of Faith! Ahhhh –

GOT DE GOLDEN PLATES

UGANDANS

GOLD PLATES

BRIGHAM YOUNG

GONNA LEAD DE PEOPLE

UGANDANS

WE HEAD WEST!

BRIGHAM YOUNG

WE GOTTA STICK TOGEDDAH

UGANDANS

MORMONS!

NABULUNGI

Even though their prophet had died, the Mormons stuck together and helped each other...

BRIGHAM YOUNG

WE GOTTA HELP EACH
UDDAH

UGANDANS
WE'RE MORMONS.
WE HEAD WEST.

NABULUNGI
...And were really nice to everyone they came across.

UGANDANS
WE HEAD WEST!
MORMONS!

NABULUNGI
And then one day, the Mormons finally FOUND Sal Tlay Ka Siti!

UGANDANS
SAL TLAY KA SITI!!!!

NABULUNGI
And there, the Mormons danced with Ewoks! And were greeted by Jesus!

JESUS (GHALI)
Welcome, Mormons! Now let's all have as MANY BABIES AS WE CAN! To make BIG MORMON FAMILIES!!!!

UGANDANS
FUCK YOUR WOMAN
FUCK YOUR MAN,
IT IS ALL PART OF GOD'S PLAN,
MORMONS FUCK ALL THAT THEY
 CAN
HERE IN SAL TLAY KA SITI LAND!
THANK YOU, THANK YOU GOD!
 (NOW WE ARE FUCKING)
THANK YOU, THANK YOU GOD!
 (GOD WANTS US FUCKING)
THANK YOU, THANK YOU GOD!
 (GET BACK TO FUCKING)
THANK YOU, THANK YOU GOD!
JOSEPH SMIT FUCK FROG,
BRIGHAM YOUNG CLIT FACE,
SHIT COME OUT DE BUTT,
JESUS SAYS FUCK FUCK
 MORMONS!!!!!!

The song ends and all the white people just look horrified and in shock. **1**

MISSION PRESIDENT
ELDERS... I'd like to have a word with you all... NOW!!!!

The mission president and the committee

storm out of the room. The Elders all follow. Then finally, after they are gone:

MUTUMBO
I THINK THEY LIKED IT!!!

UGANDANS
Yeah! / Alright! / We did it! / Etc.
The furious mission president and LDS leaders are alone with the Elders.

ELDER MCKINLEY
We are sorry, mission president! We had no idea –

MISSION PRESIDENT
YOU KEEP YOUR MOUTH SHUT! YOU'RE IN ENOUGH TROUBLE AS IT IS!

ELDER CUNNINGHAM
Sir, I was just trying to help the villagers! They all really wanted to learn.

Nabulungi walks in with a large manuscript.

NABULUNGI
Elder?! Elder, I wanted to give you this! It's the entire play written in text!

She looks at all the long faces.

NABULUNGI
What's going on?

Silence.

MISSION PRESIDENT
What's going on is that you have all brought ridicule down onto the Latter-Day Saints!

NABULUNGI
But...we are ALL Latter-Day Saints now, right?

MISSION PRESIDENT
YOU AND YOUR PEOPLE ARE ABOUT AS FAR FROM BEING LATTER-DAY SAINTS AS IT GETS!
(turns to the missionaries)
YOU ALL ARE!

NABULUNGI
Elder Cunningham, TELL THEM! We are ready to go to Sal Tlay Ka Siti! My things are packed!

ELDER CUNNINGHAM
Nabulungi, I'm so sorry – I never meant that you were ACTUALLY going to Salt Lake –

NABULUNGI
—But you said WE could find paradise by listening to you!

ELDER CUNNINGHAM

When we say that we mean paradise within YOURSELF – you know it's like a – a Jesus thing.

NABULUNGI

(extremely hurt)

Oh... I see... So when you baptized me...it meant nothing?

ELDER CUNNINGHAM

It meant EVERYTHING!

NABULUNGI

Everyone disobeyed The General because I told them to listen to you! Where are uncircumcised women supposed to go now?!

Cunningham stammers as he looks to the Elders for help.

ELDER CUNNINGHAM

Wul, no...We're gonna stay here and help
(to other Elders)
Right?

NABULUNGI

I KNOW what you people are now. You travel from your sparkling, lovely paradise in Ootah to tell ridiculous stories to people less fortunate. To make fun of them.

ELDER CUNNINGHAM

It isn't like that!

NABULUNGI

You have crushed my soul... I hope you all had a good laugh.

MISSION PRESIDENT

ELDERS! You may as well PACK YOUR THINGS. This district is SHUT DOWN. You'll be given tickets home and you can EXPLAIN to your parents you have ALL FAILED as missionaries!

Sad and pounding Les Misérables *"Look Down" music starts to play.*

Nabulungi runs out.

**HASA DIGA EEBOWAI
(SAD REPRISE)**

Nabulungi is left alone on the stage holding her Book of Mormon...silence and stillness...

NABULUNGI

I WAS SUCH A FOOL TO HAVE
  FOLLOWED THIS ADVICE.
THERE IS NO TRIP TO PARADISE.
HOW COULD I LET MY HOPE GET
  SO HIGH...?

She looks up to the sky and pauses just a beat before singing –

NABULUNGI

HASA DIGA ... EEBOWAI.

Now she belts it out.

NABULUNGI

HASA DIGA EEBOWAI!
YOU GAVE ME A DREAM BUT IT WAS
  ALL A LIE.
I THINK YOU LIKE TO SEE ME CRY.
  HASA DIGA...

She can't finish, so she runs off, crying. Cunningham and Price enter.

ELDER CUNNINGHAM

(about to cry)

Boy... I really did it this time, huh? I mean... I've always been a screw up but THIS –

ELDER PRICE

Joseph Smith dying of dysentery? Moroni from the Starship Enterprise? That play...was the most MIRACULOUS thing I've ever seen!

ELDER CUNNINGHAM

Huh?

Price crosses to Cunningham.

ELDER PRICE

I mean, it was a bunch of made-up stuff but it POINTED to something bigger, and–

MUSIC STING. Elder Price suddenly seems to get it –

ELDER PRICE

Wait a minute... You little SNEAK! You've been trying to teach me something all along, haven't you?!

ELDER CUNNINGHAM

(confused)

What?

ELDER PRICE

I thought I could fly in here and change

ANDREW RANNELLS: When Nabulungi yells at Cunningham, that's a super-effective moment: if everyone is on board, then you hear people crying in the audience. It's very unexpected, because they certainly didn't expect to weep at *The Book of Mormon*, but she just breaks your heart in that moment. That's a nice surprise, I think, because audiences don't expect there's going to be any heart in the show at all, and there's a lot of heart in it.

NIKKI M. JAMES: There's this moment where Nabulungi realizes that the things she believed to be true are not actually true, and what that means. It's devastating. I sing this sad "Hasa Diga," and it's the moment when this girl grows up. During previews the creatives were struggling with how do we get Andrew and Josh back together? How do we end this Nabulungi thing? So one night they cut the sad "Hasa Diga"; I just exited after "you have crushed my soul." And it crushed my soul. I felt cheated—not as an actor, but like they cheated Nabulungi. She needs that moment, and the audience needs it too. It lasted one performance. We were all sitting in notes and Casey said, *So, it doesn't work. Sad "Hasa Diga" is going back in.* That's one of those things that's cool about our team. They were trying to solve a problem, they made a choice, and they weren't embarrassed to say that it was a mistake and put it back in.

everything. But I made it all about ME. While I was losing faith, you went and did—

SOMETHING INCREDIBLE

ELDER PRICE

> SOMETHING INCREDIBLE.
> YOU DID SOMETHING
> INCREDIBLE...
> FOR A PEOPLE WHO HAD
>   NOWHERE ELSE TO GO ...
> I THOUGHT THEY WERE
>   UNREACHABLE –
> BUT THEN THEY WERE HAPPY AND
>   HOPEFUL AND WEARING
>   COSTUMES
> IT WAS ALMOST LIKE...
>   ORLANDO...

Sorry it took me so long to realize what you were trying to teach me, Elder.

ELDER CUNNINGHAM
(not really understanding)
Oh, that's okay.

Cunningham gives another look to show that he has no idea what Price is talking about.

ELDER CUNNINGHAM
But what about that poor girl?! I– I made her believe in a bunch of made-up crap!

ELDER PRICE
It doesn't matter if the stories are true or not. That isn't the point...

ELDER CUNNINGHAM
No, it doesn't MATTER now cuz she's gonna get her clit cut off and it's all my fault!

ELDER PRICE
No, come on, Elder! You can't give up now! We have to try and FIX THIS!

Price leads Cunningham offstage.

– THE VILLAGE –
Back in the Ugandan village, the people all wait as Nabulungi enters.

MAFALA
So what did the Mormon president think of our play?

MUTUMBO
Did Elder Cunningham like it?

The General enters, with one of his guards. ①

THE GENERAL
JUMAMOSI!

The Ugandans huddle together in fear.

UGANDANS
(random screaming and fear)

THE GENERAL
There have been RUMORS that the people in this village are uniting to oppose me.

MUTUMBO
Yes, we have been shown another way!

But Nabulungi steps in front of him.

NABULUNGI
No... NO! We do not oppose you... We will do what you say.

MUTUMBO
Nabulungi, what's wrong? Our prophet has taught us to stick together and FIGHT oppression!

NABULUNGI
Forget about Elder Cunningham. You aren't

going to see him ever again.

MIDDALA
What?! Why not?

NABULUNGI
Because Elder Cunningham...he was eaten by lions, alright?

UGANDANS
Lions? What?

GOTSWANA
Our prophet was eaten by lions???

THE GENERAL
ENOUGH! There is ONE LAW you will obey here, and it is MINE!

MIDDALA
We believe in something ELSE!

NABULUNGI
STOP IT, ALL OF YOU! I told you, our prophet is gone! There is no promised land. There is no salvation.

SADAKA
NO! You must not talk like that Nabulungi. Remember the teachings of the first Mormons. When Joseph Smit died they did not give up on their hope.

NABULUNGI
But it's not TRUE. We aren't going to Sal Tlay Ka Siti.

KIMBAY
Nabulungi, Sal Tlay Ka Siti isn't an actual PLACE... It's an IDEA. A metaphor. ❷

MAFALA
You need to remember that prophets ALWAYS speak in metaphors.

UGANDAN WOMAN
Yeah, you don't think a man ACTUALLY fucked a frog, do you? That's fucking stupid. ❸

NABULUNGI
And you all believe this?

UGANDANS
Yes!

Elder Price and Cunningham enter the village.

ELDER CUNNINGHAM
Excuse me, everyone –

UGANDANS
(GASP)

MIDDALA
He is risen!

KALIMBA
It is a miracle!

MAFALA
Our prophet returns even from the dead! ❹
(to The General)
THERE, YOU SEE?!

UGANDAN WOMAN
He must have fucked a frog!

THE GENERAL
Who has risen from the dead?!

ELDER PRICE
HE HAS, you IDIOT! So you might as well PUT THAT GUN DOWN BECAUSE IT WILL NOT WORK AGAINST THE UNDEAD. And if you do not get OUT of this village he WILL command the angel Moroni, ON the Death Star, to unleash the Kraken! Which will then... Uh...

ELDER CUNNINGHAM
Which will then – fire Joseph Smith torpedoes FROM its mouth of Christ and turn YOU into a LESBIAN!

ELDER PRICE
Oh – don't think he can't do it.

The General runs off. ❺

UGANDANS
Alright! / Yeah! / We did it! / Etc.

❹ **JUSTIN BOHON:** There is a revelation after Elder Cunningham comes back from the dead. The audience is like, *Oh, they're not these unintelligent creatures out in Africa,* they get it. It doesn't matter what *it* is, it's what works for today, and that's the most important thing

❺ **CLARK JOHNSEN:** Elder Price is sort of the conscience of the audience. They're seeing him realizing the ridiculousness of these Mormon stories, and then that ridiculousness is heightened by the fact that his companion makes up stories that are even more ridiculous than the ones of Joseph Smith. By the end, though, Elder Price realizes that these stories have united a group of people against the warlord. Now the warlord's afraid of us. We're powerful because we're now united. We're united by stories that are totally made up and totally dumb, but we're united. And what's more important than that?

1 ANNE GAREFINO: At Josh Gad's 453rd and final performance, he choked up the entire cast and crew—and provoked twenty seconds-worth of cheers from the audience—with his last ad lib, "*Oh, Nikki M. James, I am so sorry.*"

2 CASEY NICHOLAW: At first we had all of the boys with rolling suitcases, but then there was no graceful way to get them offstage so we cut them except for Rory's. He had picked out a bright pink-flowered rehearsal prop suitcase. It was so funny and got a laugh, so we kept that even though it wasn't meant to be used onstage.

ELDER CUNNINGHAM
Oh Nala, I am so sorry. But please, if you just give me a chance – ❶

Nabulungi puts her hand over Cunningham's mouth.

NABULUNGI
Elder, it's okay... I understand now what you have been trying to teach me all along.

ELDER CUNNINGHAM
(still confused)
Oh, okay. Great.

Cunningham and Nabulungi hug.

The other Elders all walk in, rolling carry-on bags. ❷

ELDER PRICE
Woa – woa Elders where are you going?

ELDER MCKINLEY
What do you mean "Where are we going?" We've been shut down!

ELDER NEELEY
Yeah, we have to go home!

ELDER PRICE
Who says we have to?

ELDER ZELDER
What?

Price gets in the middle of everyone.

ELDER PRICE
Look, we all wanted to go on a mission so we could spend two years of our lives helping people out. So let's DO it!

ELDER NEELEY
But the mission president said we're all as far from Latter-Day Saints as it gets!

ELDER PRICE
No... You know what guys? FUCK HIM.

Everyone looks a little shocked.

ELDER PRICE
We are STILL Latter-Day Saints. ALL of us. Even if we change some things, or break the rules, or have complete doubt that God exists... We can still work together to make THIS our paradise planet. ❸

ELDER CUNNINGHAM
You wanna stay here with me?

ELDER PRICE
I'd do anything for you. I'm your best friend.

Cunningham smiles and dives into Price with a big hug.
A chime, and then Price steps forward to sing:

ELDER PRICE
DON'T WORRY LITTLE BUDDY.
KNOW THIS MUCH IS TRUE.
TOMORROW IS A LATTER DAY

ELDER PRICE & ELDER CUNNINGHAM
AND I AM HERE FOR YOU.

TOMORROW IS A LATTER DAY ❹

ELDER MCKINLEY
TOMORROW IS A LATTER DAY...

ELDERS
TOMORROW IS A LATTER DAY!
TOMORROW IS A LATTER DAY!

(Intro dance break)

ELDER PRICE
I AM A LATTER-DAY SAINT!
I HELP ALL THOSE I CAN!

ELDER CUNNINGHAM
AND SEE MY FRIENDS THROUGH
TIMES OF JOY AND SORROW.

ELDER PRICE
WHO CARES WHAT HAPPENS
WHEN WE'RE DEAD?
WE SHOULDN'T THINK THAT FAR
AHEAD.

ELDER PRICE & ELDER CUNNINGHAM
THE ONLY LATTER DAY THAT
MATTERS IS TOMORROW!

ELDERS
THE SKIES ARE CLEARING AND
THE SUN'S COMING OUT.
IT'S A LATTER DAY TOMORROW!

UGANDANS
HAYYA YA!

ELDERS

PUT YOUR WORRIES AND YOUR
SORROWS
AND YOUR CARES AWAY
AND FOCUS ON THE LATTER DAY!

ENTIRE COMPANY

TOMORROW IS A LATTER DAY!
WOO!

NABULUNGI

I AM A LATTER-DAY SAINT
ALONG WITH ALL MY TOWN.
WE ALWAYS STICK TOGETHER
COME WHAT MAY!

ENTIRE COMPANY

SHOODOOWOW!
BA DA BA!
BA DA BA!
WANNA THANK YOU LORD!

ELDER MCKINLEY

WE LOVE TO DANCE AND SHOUT
AND LET ALL OUR FEELINGS OUT!

MORMONS

AND WORK TO MAKE A BETTER
LATTER

ENTIRE COMPANY

DAY!

UGANDANS

HANNA HEYA HA HANNA HEYA

ENTIRE COMPANY

WE'RE GONNA BE HERE FOR EACH
OTHER EVERY STEP OF THE WAY
AND MAKE A LATTER DAY
TOMORROW!

UGANDANS

HANNA HEY!
AMERICANS ALREADY FOUND A
CURE FOR AIDS
BUT THEY'RE SAVING IT FOR A
LATTER DAY!

ENTIRE COMPANY

YEAH!
TOMORROW IS A LATTER DAY!

ELDER PRICE

I BELIEVE!
I BELIEVE!
I BELIEVE!

ENTIRE COMPANY

TOMORROW IS A LATTER DAY!
LOVE AND JOY AND ALL THE
THINGS THAT MATTER DAY!
TOMORROW IS A BIGGER BADDER
LATTER DAY!

ELDER PRICE & ELDER CUNNINGHAM

I BELIEVE
I BELIEVE
I BELIEVE

ENTIRE COMPANY

TOMORROW, TOMORROW IS A
LATTER DAY,
A HAPPY ENDING ON A PLATTER
DAY
TOMORROW'S A DOPER, PHATTER
LATTER DAY
WHY ARE MORMONS HAPPY?
IT'S BECAUSE WE KNOW
IT'S A LATTER DAY TOMORROW.
SO IF YOU'RE SAD,
PUT YOUR HANDS TOGETHER AND
PRAY
THAT TOMORROW'S GONNA BE A
LATTER DAY!
IT PROBABLY WILL BE A LATTER
DAY!
TOMORROW IS A LATTER DAY!

ELDER CUNNINGHAM

SO WHAT WILL TOMORROW BRING?

ELDER PRICE

WHAT DOES THE FUTURE HOLD?

NABULUNGI / PRICE / CUNNINGHAM

I CAN ALMOST SEE IT NOW...

③ BRIAN SEARS: You can always get an idea of what kind of audience we have when Elder Price says *maybe God doesn't even exist.* We can pretty much tell if there's a lot of true believers in the house, because they won't laugh at it. But if we have some people that are a little less spiritual or don't really know what they believe, it gets uproarious laughter. It's either one or the other, either dead silence or it kills them.

④ BOBBY LOPEZ: This song was a tricky one. We always knew what the *message* of the show would be, all the stuff about the truth of the scripture not being the point. But people don't go to a Broadway show to be told a message—they want to go on an emotional journey and be entertained. So really, the trick of writing this show, and what took us five years, was to craft an engaging, entertaining, funny story that led the audience to this message rather than hit them over the head with it. We had a few hit-you-over-the-head versions of this song. The first one was a pretty song called "Metaphorical Miracle," which began with the awesome line *I believe in metaphors, metaphors happen every day.* When we finally came up with "Tomorrow Is a Latter Day," we knew we had the right title. To me it felt like the title to a funny/deep Beatles-ish song. Matt liked it because on one level it seemed to be saying something stupid and obvious, like "water's wet." Basically, "Tomorrow will be later than today."

TOMORR
LAT
DA

ROW IS A

TER

AY!

One of the Ugandans suddenly appears wearing a white shirt and black tie as the song transforms –

HELLO
(REPRISE)

MUTUMBO

HELLO! MY NAME IS ELDER
    MUTUMBO!
AND I WOULD LIKE TO SHARE
    WITH YOU
THE MOST AMAZING BOOK!

KIMBAY

HELLO!

GOTSWANA

HELLO!

KIMBAY

MY NAME IS SISTER KIMBAY!
IT'S A BOOK ABOUT A PEOPLE WHO
    WERE POOR AND SAD LIKE YOU!

NABULUNGI

A SACRED TEXT –

MAFALA

HELLO!

NABULUNGI

– OF PIONEERS AND FROGS

MAFALA

FUCKED FROGS!

NABULUNGI

AND HOW YOU CAN FIND
    SALVATION IF YOU JUST BELIEVE.

UGANDAN WOMAN

HI HO!

KIMBAY AND MIDDALA

DING DONG!

KALIMBA

HELLO!

UGANDAN WOMAN

BOBA FETT!

KALIMBA

YOU HAVE A LOVELY MUD HUT.
AND IF YOU JUST PUT DOWN THE
    GUN I'LL SHOW YOU –
OH OKAY I'LL LEAVE.

SADAKA

HELLO!

GHALI

HELLO! MY NAME IS ELDER GHALI.
YOU WILL LOVE ALL OF THE
    HAPPINESS THIS BOOK CAN
    BRING.

THE GENERAL

HELLO.

MIDDALA

HELLO!

THE GENERAL

MY NAME IS ELDER BUTT-FUCKING
    NAKED. ❶
DID YOU KNOW THAT THE
    CLITORIS IS A HOLY SACRED
    THING?

UGANDANS

FIND PARADISE!

KIMBAY

WITH JESUS CHRIST!

UGANDANS

AND NO MORE WAR!

THE GENERAL

HELLO!

MIDDALA

NICE DOOR!

UGANDANS

YOU'VE READ THE BOOK OF
    MORMON
DID YOU KNOW THERE'S MORE?

NABULUNGI

PART FOUR!

UGANDANS

WE SWEAR –

THE GENERAL

WE REALLY CARE.

UGANDANS

THIS IS NOT A SCAM.

THE GENERAL

NO, MA'AM.

UGANDANS

HAVE YOU HEARD THE STORY
OF OUR PROPHET ARNOLD
    CUNNINGHAM?
ARNOLD CUNNINGHAM?
    HELLO!
ARNOLD CUNNING...

ELDER CUNNINGHAM

(entering, followed by all the Mormons)
HELL-O!!!!!

ENTIRE COMPANY

HELLO! OUR CHURCH IS GROWING
    STRONG!
AND IF YOU LET US IN WE'LL SHOW YOU
    HOW YOU CAN BELONG!
JOIN OUR FAMILY.
AND SET YOUR SPIRIT FREE.
WE CAN FULLY GUARANTEE YOU
    THAT
THIS BOOK WILL CHANGE YOUR LIFE.
THIS BOOK WILL CHANGE YOUR LIFE.
THIS BOOK WILL CHANGE YOUR LIFE.
THIS BOOK WILL CHANGE YOUR LIFE.
THE BOOK OF ARNOLD.
HELLO!

The entire company joyously raises high the
BOOK OF ARNOLD.

FINALE

ENTIRE COMPANY

(clapping)
WE ARE LATTER-DAY SAINTS,
WE TAKE LIFE ONE DAY AT A TIME.
WHEN THE CHIPS ARE DOWN,
WE KNOW JUST WHAT TO SAY.

SOLOIST

KNOW JUST WHAT TO SAY!

ENTIRE COMPANY

THE PAST MAY BE IN TATTERS BUT
    TODAY IS ALL THAT MATTERS.

SOLOISTS

HANA HEYA!

ENTIRE COMPANY

BECAUSE TODAY IS YESTERDAY'S
    LATTER DAY!

SOLOISTS

HOO HOO HOO OHO OHO

ENTIRE COMPANY

THANK YOU GOD!
    MA HA NEI BU,
    EEBOWAI!
TOMORROW IS A LATTER DAY!

GOTSWANA

I STILL HAVE MAGGOTS IN MY
    SCROTUM!

❷ TREY PARKER: For a long time, the show ended with "Tomorrow Is a Latter Day." We had tried a bunch of songs here, big happy joyous revival songs. Then the idea came to do "Hello" again. We had a little recording studio where we could record demos. We just went in and turned on a mic and started throwing down lyrics. We wrote the African "Hello" basically using a tape recorder. We immediately realized the Africans would have a lot of funny things to say. As soon as we added "Hello" to it, it instantly added more plot. "Tomorrow Is a Latter Day," alone, seemed sort of a standard ending, like *we'll be okay tomorrow.* Adding "Hello" let's us flash forward, like in a movie.

"THERE'S A A REAL EMOTIONAL SORT OF PRESENCE THAT HAPPENS TO ALL OF US."

ANDREW RANNELLS

"SO HIE THEE HENCE, NONBELIEVERS (AND BELIEVERS TOO), TO 'THE BOOK OF MORMON', AND FEAST UPON ITS SWEETNESS."

THE NEW YORK TIMES BEN BRANTLEY

PART 4
THE EXULTATION

Trey Parker and Matt Stone
in Conversation with Jon Stewart

Aired March 10, 2011

STEWART

My guests tonight, the creators of *South Park*, have now ventured into the theater world with their new Broadway musical, *The Book of Mormon*. Please welcome back to the program Trey Parker and Matt Stone!

Cheers. Applause.

STEWART

Nice to see you again. Sit! I'm gonna hold up the Playbill—this is the first time I've gotten to do this on the show. You're the first guys with the Playbill, *The Book of Mormon*. Now I went and I saw this. You guys probably didn't see me there, I was in the audience.

Laughs.

STEWART

And I have to tell you something. Now, you've always set a bar here at Comedy Central that we've all kind of aimed at. But this thing is so good, it makes me f**king angry.

Laughs.

STEWART

It's—I have to—I—I can't tell you how impressed I was with what—I feel like it's—I don't know how—it's like your doctoral thesis. You have somehow

managed to satirize religion while simultaneously almost celebrating it in this sweet yet really hard-edge musical... I don't know what to say, honestly.

STONE

Wow.

PARKER

Thank you very much, Jon.

Trey gets up to leave.

STONE

Just keep talking.

STEWART

Okay, that's good. That's beautiful. How do you is this? You're used to doing things on such a short lead—what has this experience been like?

PARKER

It's been crazy because we've actually been working on this for seven years. So it does kind of feel like everything's been kind of pushing towards this because we've been trying to force musicals into everything we do. When Paramount wanted us to do a *South Park* movie, we were like, *Let's make it a musical!* And they were like, *No, that's a bad idea.* And then we made *Team America*, and we're like, *Let's put a bunch of music into it!* And they're like, *No, no, don't do that.* So, we, I've been wanting to make musicals since I was a kid, so for both of us, it just sort of feels like the big thing we've been leading towards.

STONE

And we've been doing stuff with Mormons for a long time.

Laughs.

STONE

Inexplicably, yes. So we've just put Mormons and musicals together and this is our thing.

STEWART

What has been the response? Because looking at it, it struck me that there was a fear like, *Oh, these guys are gonna come in and they're gonna just slime it,* but that's not what it is.

STONE

Yeah, that was never our intention when we met our co-author Bobby Lopez.

STEWART

Mormon!

Laughs.

STEWART

LOPEZ!

STONE

Yes, a real Mormon last name.... When we met him, it was this really weird moment when he asked us like we were his, like, elder statesman, that we were people he looked up to: *What should I do next, you guys?* And we said, *Well, what do you want to do?* And he says, *Something about Mormons!*

Laughs.

PARKER

And we're like, *We love that stuff!*

STONE

Is there a camera on us? Because we're the only people who are freaked out and fascinated by Mormons. You know, like, we love Mormons! We love that whole mythology. And it was in that moment, we decided to do it. It was just too weird to meet someone else who was that into Mormons and musicals.

Laughs.

STEWART

It is kind of hard. Did you need one more connection? Mormons,

musicals... and do you like pizza?

PARKER

Good enough!

STEWART

But it does, to a large extent... it isn't really about being a Mormon. That just seems like the vessel or the vehicle for whatever the metaphor is. That's what is so great about it.

PARKER

That's what always fascinated us about the Mormon religion is it's this religion that is so young and so American. You can go up to upstate New York and see the little log cabin that Joseph Smith grew up in and the hill that he found the golden plates on... supposedly...

Laughs.

PARKER

And, um, you know, growing up in Colorado, we were always close to Utah. We went to Temple Square a bunch.... So it's just this example we have of a religion that's still really young and is still, you know, growing and changing.

STEWART

What I like about it too is that it didn't feel like you were expressing any certainty about things; you were expressing, it felt like, an expression of confusion.

STONE

Yeah, embrace the mystery.

STEWART

Yes!

PARKER

We're extremely confused.

Laughs.

STEWART

Now you get away with something... there is a song in this, and I don't want to give away any of the spoilers because it will take away from some of the enjoyment. There is a song in this that will be, I think, celebrated when the aliens come thousands of years from now—it may exist as our only memory of earth. And I gotta say, I'm happy to go down with that. If it is the record of our time here on earth, I will be absolutely satisfied with that. It is made, to me, it is a crowning achievement of what you guys do, translated to the Broadway stage.

> # "'THE BOOK OF MORMON' IS SO F**KING GOOD IT MAKES ME ANGRY."
> **THE DAILY SHOW** JON STEWART

PARKER AND STONE

Aw, thanks, man.

STEWART

Have you been able to get a perspective on it from people that have been on Broadway? What's been the response from that community?

PARKER

People seem to be very first surprised and then happy that it's a very traditional musical. We really studied our musicals, and we wanted to give something that obviously has a modern twist on everything. Actually, we can also tell when Mormons are in the crowd! We've already had a lot of them.

STEWART

What, do you just see this?

Jon sways his arms in the air from side to side.

Laughs.

PARKER

We'll have references to like Abinadi the Prophet, and they'll be like [smugly], Oh Abinadi, they got him in there?

Laughs.

STEWART

Has there been a good response from the Mormon community who have seen it?

STONE

Well, for the most part. There were a couple, I've met a couple Mormons that came to the show and they really liked it. The Mormons we hear in the crowd, they like it! I don't know if it's just because someone's paying attention to them at all and that's why they like... but really, not to be flippant, the musical is kind of a celebration of Mormonism by some guys who aren't Mormons.

Laughs.

STONE

It's like, *Why would you commit seven years of your life to doing that?*

STEWART

Most folks love being celebrated by people who are not of the, you know...

PARKER

Every time we make fun of a group on *South Park*, they love it, people love it!

Laughs.

STEWART

Yes, I remember the security. Was there any thought—and again, you guys have done such an amazing job and I hate to throw in notes at you and I know you gotta close this thing—but any thought of throwing people off of rafters on webs?

PARKER

It's been done.

STEWART

It just seems like concussions are the way to go on Broadway now.

STONE

It sells tickets!

STEWART

I can't tell you how impressed I am with this whole thing. I wish you nothing but success. I think this is gonna be huge and a huge smash success, and I'm so, just, happy for you guys. It's just great.

PARKER AND STONE

Oh, thanks. Thanks. That's awesome. That's great.

STEWART

The Book of Mormon. It's playing at the Eugene O'Neill Theatre here in New York City. That guy over there wanted to go, but it's on standby, so he can't. And I'm not asking you guys to get him tickets.... You know what, f**k that guy! But this is how it's gonna be for a long, long time. *The Book of Mormon*, Trey Parker and Matt Stone!

Applause. ◆

"MUSICAL COMEDY HEAVEN"

TIME OUT
NEW YORK

"This is to all the doubters and deniers out there, the ones who say that heaven on Broadway does not exist, that it's only some myth our ancestors dreamed up. I am here to report that a newborn, old-fashioned, pleasure-giving musical has arrived at the Eugene O'Neill Theatre, the kind our grandparents told us left them walking on air if not on water. So hie thee hence, nonbelievers (and believers too), to *The Book of Mormon*, and feast upon its sweetness. *The Book of Mormon* achieves something like a miracle. Trust me when I tell you that its heart is as pure as that of a Rodgers and Hammerstein show. These men take pleasure in the transcendent, cathartic goofiness of song-and-dance numbers. Witty, ridiculous, impeccably executed, and genuinely stirring. All the folks involved in Mormon prove themselves worthy, dues-paying members of the church of Broadway. A celebration of the privilege, for just a couple of hours, of living inside that improbable paradise called a musical comedy."

NEW YORK TIMES BEN BRANTLEY

"★★★★★ A heavenly musical. Oh boy, it's a real winner. The show is blissfully original, irreverent, outspoken and hilarious. And all that's tucked inside a good—no, great—old-fashioned musical. It's a show where you catch yourself laughing one minute, mouth agape the next, eventually wiping away tears and, finally, cheering. Polished and exuberant and surging with surprises, and amazingly fun with enormous wit and imagination. This musical spills over with confidence in the material and cast. There is such infectious energy you want to join in onstage. Being among the converted is what it's all about. A fantastic musical in every way. Sheer joy."

NEW YORK DAILY NEWS JOE DZIEMIANOWICZ

"*The Book of Mormon* manages to offend, provoke laughter, trigger eye-rolling, satirize conventions and warm hearts, all at the same time. An inventive, subversive, roof-raising show. You might expect Parker, Stone and Lopez to utterly disrespect traditional musical conventions, but you'd be wrong. What they've done is faithfully maintain the structure and rhythm of a classic musical—think Rodgers and Hammerstein's *The King and I*—even while filling it with utter zaniness. Ultimately, believe it or not, this is a pro-religion musical, or at least a story about the uplifting power of stories. Far from being nihilistic, the moral seems to endorse any belief system—no matter how crazy it sounds—if it helps us do good. Amen to that. Consider us converted."

AP MARK KENNEDY

"Anyone who saw *South Park: Bigger, Longer & Uncut* shouldn't be surprised to learn that Trey Parker and Matt Stone appear genuinely to love musicals even as they subvert them. What's perhaps less expected is that while *The Book of Mormon* packs plenty of blissful profanity, sacrilege and politically incorrect mischief, the defining quality of this hugely entertaining show is its sweetness. One of the freshest original musicals in recent memory. It has tuneful songs, clever lyrics, winning characters, explosive laughs and disarmingly intimate moments. The show manages to have a comic field day with Mormonism while simultaneously acknowledging—maybe even respecting—the right of everyone to follow any faith they choose. Or invent. Number after number hits a bull's-eye. In terms of construction and song placement, *Mormon* masters a classic formula. What makes the musical irresistible, however, is its panache in making naughty mockery of a whole string of untouchable subjects, without an ounce of spite."

HOLLYWOOD REPORTER DAVID ROONEY

"**B**ehold *The Book of Mormon*. An exhilarating Broadway musical at once revolutionary and classic, hilarious and humane, funny and obscene, uncompromising in production standards and unafraid of just about anything. A spectacular, rather perfect Broadway musical not only grounded in a serious love and understanding of the traditions that make a Broadway musical great but also filled with love for the very flawed, mortal characters who populate this romp. This is what 21st-century Broadway can be. If Broadway has the balls. Lord knows, *The Book of Mormon* does. I'm sold; I believe in *The Book of Mormon*."

ENTERTAINMENT WEEKLY LISA SCHWARZBAUM

"**I**f any show could make the case that you can have fun with absolutely anything in the oft-painful run of human experience, then that show is *The Book of Mormon*, a shrewd, remarkably well-crafted and wholly hilarious new Broadway musical. By the end of a night more emotional than many will expect, the show is arguing the importance of finding a spiritual center, if not exactly embracing the doctrinal details of that most American of religions. And *The Book of Mormon* even makes a case that it takes those suffering real pain to understand the real role of religion in our lives."

CHICAGO TRIBUNE
CHRIS JONES

"**A** hilarious musical. *The Book of Mormon* is gleefully funny. It seldom goes more than 10 seconds without a big laugh. And it's not just about the jokes. They're embedded in a satisfying story, supported by witty, character-relevant songs. Most important for its overall success, the show's creators understand that even a satirical musical needs to have characters you can care about. *Mormon* is that rare creature that isn't based on a book or a play or a movie—it came totally out of its creators' heads. And what they thought up is one of the most purely enjoyable musicals in years."

BERGEN RECORD ROBERT FELDBERG

"**D**o you believe in theater, friend? Or has your faith been strained to the breaking point? If so, I say unto thee, go forth to the tabernacle otherwise known as the Eugene

O'Neill Theatre! It's an often uproarious, spiritually up-tempo satire not just of Mormonism, and not just religion in general, but of (no kidding) Occidental civilization itself, in all its well-intentioned, self-mythologizing, autoerotically entitled glory. *Mormon* chipperly shitcans all pieties... Except the sacred, mystic conventions of musical theater. What's so uniquely winning about *The Book of Mormon* is its scruffy humanism, its eagerness to redeem its characters—even its smaller ones. When Lieutenant Uhura, Frodo, Yoda, Jesus, Satan, Joseph Smith, Darth Vader, and the Angel Moroni all converge to sanctify a show, that's what I call a quorum. After *Mormon*, I like to imagine, the Broadway musical might be free to be a Broadway musical again."

NEW YORK MAGAZINE SCOTT BROWN

"'THE BOOK OF MORMON' ACHIEVES SOMETHING LIKE A MIRACLE."

THE NEW YORK TIMES BEN BRANTLEY

"**B**oisterously outrageous. It's hard to imagine anyone topping the ding-dong hilarity set off by *The Book of Mormon*. It has all the fearlessness one would expect. Sacred cows, let's just say, are there for the riotous milking. But for all its irreverence, *The Book of Mormon* has the old-fashioned musical comedy heart of adults who spent much of their adolescence lip-syncing to original cast albums in their finished basements. Nothing is off limits. The farcical stampede is unstoppable. It's not easy to shock a modern-day audience, but *The Book of Mormon* succeeds with alarming regularity. *The Book of Mormon* has the propulsive verve of a runaway hit."

LOS ANGELES TIMES CHARLES MCNULTY

"★★★★★ Musical-comedy heaven. If theater is your religion and the Broadway musical your sect, you've been woefully faith-challenged of late. *The Book of Mormon* is a sick mystic revelation, the most exuberantly entertaining Broadway musical in years. In fact, the uses and abuses of faith, the strange persistence of these ancient (or in the case of Mormonism, not so ancient) bedtime stories, is a central theme. Religion, the creators firmly point out, is showbiz, and the satire

bites into both the absurdities of Joseph Smith and his angel Moroni, and the intoxicating frivolity of musicals. A show that examines, with impressive insight, cultural transmission, adaptation, and assimilation.It's about our ineradicable hunger for narrative and mystery. A viciously hilarious treat."

TIME OUT NEW YORK DAVID COTE

"**M**att and Trey: Where have you been all my life? Along with Robert Lopez, Stone and Parker have devised *The Book of Mormon*, a pricelessly entertaining act of musical comedy subversion. The mighty O'Neill himself would have to have given it up for this extraordinarily well-crafted musical assault on all things holy. The marvel of *The Book of Mormon* is that even as it profanes some serious articles of faith, its spirit is anything but mean.

particularly crazed moment, 10 more follow. By the time *The Book of Mormon* ends in an orgy of over-the-top cheer, you just can't wait to get on that ride all over again."

NEW YORK POST ELIZABETH VINCENTELLI

"**W**ildly original, jubilant and expert. Everything you should expect from a show by the heat-seeking rascals of *South Park*. What you may not expect, however, is the sweetness. An outcasts' love letter to musical theater. And for all the ridicule bludgeoned on the faithful, the musical seems smitten with the basic desire—however twisted and self-deluded—to do good."

NEWSDAY LINDA WINER

"HISTORY IS MADE. THEY HAD ME AT 'HELLO.'"

ROLLING STONE PETER TRAVERS

One of the most joyously acidic bundles Broadway has unwrapped in years. The sin it takes such fond aim at—blind faith—is one that this musical suggests observes no religious bounds. No matter how brazenly the writers question the precepts of Mormonism—and boy, do they ever make mincemeat of the religion's genesis—their respect for the traditions of the American musical borders on devotional."

WASHINGTON POST PETER MARKS

"★★★★ A fiendishly well-crafted, hilariously smart— or maybe smartly hilarious—song-and-dance extravaganza. The show's a hoot. The show's a hit. A full-blooded tuner that rejuvenates musicals while displaying a genuine love for the form. An avalanche of filthy gags, butt jokes and wickedly catchy show tunes. Each time you think they can't possibly top a

"**A** raucously funny new show. Every song enhances the hilarity, expert staging heightens every gag, and the cast of fresh faces is blissfully good. A show that never quits. For all its sacrilegious jabs, the show is earnestly about the power of faith. The Ugandan natives believe, and ultimately embrace religion, while the heroes realize that doctrine is all metaphor—'a bunch of made-up stuff, but it points to something bigger.' And that describes *The Book of Mormon*, an original made-up-for-Broadway production that approaches musical comedy Rapture."

VARIETY STEVEN SUSKIN

"**T**he most surprising thing about *Mormon* may be its inherent sweetness. There is an exuberance in the show's spirit that makes it feel both fresh and unabashedly traditional. Makes us laugh and cheer."

USA TODAY ELYSA GARDNER

"★★★★ History is made. They had me at 'Hello'. It should keep audiences in shock and awe for years. The funniest show on Broadway by far, it's on its march into legend. But Parker and Stone also show an un-ironic compassion for the fallible humans caught in the web of religious hypocrisy. *The Book of Mormon* is as good as it gets. Come on, Mormons, go into your dance."

ROLLING STONE PETER TRAVERS

"Parker and Stone's *The Book of Mormon* may offend thousands, if not more. And bless their iconoclastic hearts for it! It grabs the audience by the lapels and won't let go. Parker and Stone are actually morality-minded believers. The pair, who would seem to have made a career of contending that nothing's sacred, eventually suggest that something definitely is. They send a message that while organized religion—based on trumped up dogma, as it too often is—may be a stultifying and questionable experience for many, there is decidedly something behind truly religious behavior. It's based, they suggest, on conciliatory aspects that draw people together rather than force them apart."

HUFFINGTON POST DAVID FINKLE

"Rarely has a show come along as consummately crafted as *The Book of Mormon*. Adhering to all the Broadway conventions, creators Trey Parker and Matt Stone, along with Robert Lopez, deliver a work that is brilliantly original, hysterically funny and tunefully irresistible. The plot, which is dense with twists and turns, unfolds with great clarity and is splendidly paced. The extended songs are not only melodic, they cleverly advance the narrative which by show's end completes a perfect and highly satisfying arc. All the while, the show achieves the near impossible. While it ingeniously spoofs the hypocrisy within the Mormon scriptures, it manages to leave you with a renewed sense of spiritual faith. *The Book of Mormon* is an inspired collaboration made in theater heaven."

NY1 ROMA TORRE

"A screamingly funny yet sharply insightful full-length take on religion. There are also pointed but loving tributes to musical comedy conventions, shockingly vulgar humor, and that rarity on Broadway these days: topical and effective satire. The authors are focusing their blisteringly boisterous lens on cultural stereotypes and the extremes of fundamentalist faith to demonstrate their absurdity. Ultimately, they acknowledge that the altruistic element within the Church of Jesus Christ of Latter-Day Saints and other religions is worth preserving. That they manage to do this without compromising their gleefully vicious vision is nothing short of miraculous."

BACKSTAGE DAVID SHEWARD

"It's something just spectacular. New, exciting, chance-taking, funny, inappropriate, filthy, beautifully staged, a great brilliant romp of a musical. It's hysterical. It's hysterical. It's hard to believe that a play this funny and this outrageous can have a kind of tenderness about it. One of the funniest, most original things I've seen on Broadway. This is fresh, it's original, it's invigorating. We're laughing at ourselves and the ridiculousness of so many things that we are taught to believe in. I couldn't even go to sleep last night 'cause I kept thinking of this stuff. This is a winner."

WOR

JOAN HAMBURG

"The shocking thing about *The Book of Mormon* is that after all the production numbers that make searing fun of Mormonism, African culture, AIDS, terror, mainline religion and every Western creation myth—after all of that, the show ends up an unbridled celebration of faith. *The Book of Mormon* is a triumph—that's not too strong a word: For all its outrageous mockery, the show encourages you to appreciate whatever creation story gives you comfort and allows you to appropriate mystery."

PHILADELPHIA INQUIRER HOWARD SHAPIRO

"*The Book of Mormon* is the funniest comedy I've seen on Broadway in years. Outrageously profane, yet it has the sweetest heart; it's completely bonkers, but supremely clever. I loved this show."

DAILY MAIL BAZ BAMIGBOYE

★★★★★ *The Book of Mormon* is the work of the brilliant duo, Trey Parker and Matt Stone. Although fearlessly offensive, the two are always deeply moral, even occasionally sentimental, and this show is no exception. *Mormon* is terrific and smart as hell."

THE GUARDIAN HADLEY FREEMAN

"Broadway's most obscene and—yes—reverent musical yet. What is it about those Latter-day Saints that's so funny? Just about everything. It's a coming-of-age story dripping in dirty jokes, with irreverent, offensive showstoppers. The standing ovations are rapturous."

NEWSWEEK JACOB BERNSTEIN

"Such a buoyant, old-fashioned Broadway song-and-dance show that, once past the four-letter words, you just might mistake this for a revival of *Oklahoma!*. *The Book of Mormon* just might have opened up new territory."

TIME RICHARD ZOGLIN

"What could be a hotter ticket than the improbable triumph of *The Book of Mormon*, the musical-comedy moon shot of the season? Its creators, Matt Stone and Trey Parker, are the most unlikely Rodgers and Hammerstein team ever to bowl a thundering strike. I've never heard such roof-shaking laughter in a Broadway theater."

VANITY FAIR JAMES WOLCOTT

"Trey Parker and Matt Stone apply their Midas touch to a cheerfully rude, lewd, and well-polished romp. How they amazingly accomplish this triggers the subversive gags of a show that skewers so many sacred cows so fast, you can barely keep track. *The Book of Mormon* lands its jabs with wide-eyed gusto and an inherent sweetness."

SEATTLE TIMES MISHA BERSON

"A faith-based extravaganza of jaw-dropping obscenity, hair-raising blasphemy, and irresistible good cheer that may just be the funniest musical of all time. More like a revival meeting than a night at the theater, with an ecstatic audience laughing, screaming, stomping, and all but speaking in tongues. Parker and Stone may just be the saviors of the American musical. Don't be surprised if you find yourself kind of moved, too. *The Book of Mormon*'s dirty little secret is its big heart."

VOGUE ADAM GREEN

"*The Book of Mormon* is the best thing Trey Parker and Matt Stone have ever done—musically, theatrically, comically. They are the Hogarths and Swifts of our time—because by trashing the world with anarchic humor and biting commentary, they are obviously also intent on saving it. And loving it regardless."

THE ATLANTIC ANDREW SULLIVAN

"*The Book of Mormon* is straight-up brilliant, by far the best new musical of the twenty-first century. Savagely funny and smart with serious ideas, moving moments, and irresistible uplift."

NPR KURT ANDERSEN

"After years of cloaking good storytelling in irreverence, Trey Parker and Matt Stone have found a new level of success in bringing that formula to the stage in their divine comedy, *The Book of Mormon*. It is *that* funny. And outrageous. And profane. It is also a razor-sharp satire. But mostly, it is a heartfelt testament to anyone who has undergone a crisis in faith, and come out stronger for it. This is a Broadway hit of Biblical proportions."

DENVER POST JOHN MOORE

"Wildly inventive and endlessly funny. Trey Parker, Matt Stone, and Robert Lopez have written a skewering book with irreverent lyrics, and wrapped them in a huge, joyful, uncynical embrace of big, bold Broadway music and choreography. Shockingly hilarious with one riotous song after another. A great Broadway show"

INDIEWIRE CARYN JAMES

"The Book of Mormon demonstrates what is possible when young artists call the shots on Broadway. Trey Parker, Matt Stone, and Bobby Lopez can poke fun at anything and everything and get away with it. The best surprise about *Mormon* is that there's an uplifting message about life and faith that would make Rodgers and Hammerstein blush."

CLEVELAND PLAIN DEALER TONY BROWN

"Hallelujah! The Book of Mormon is vulgar, hilarious, and sweetly touching. Matt Stone, Trey Parker, and Bobby Lopez serve up an irreverent, observant, yet empathetic look at those recognizably clean-cut guys who wear short-sleeved white shirts, black ties, and big smiles."

MIAMI HERALD CHRISTINE DOLEN

"The happiest play ever, and full of feeling. *The Book of Mormon* made the audience insane with joy in this way I don't think I've ever seen in a theater. In row H they were gasping and squealing and covering their mouths with their hands. It made me feel hopeful for the very idea of putting on a show, and it made musicals seem like a wonderful, magical invention. One of my favorite things I've ever seen. I couldn't stop thinking about it and humming the songs and telling everyone I know to get tickets immediately and wanting to see it again, which I never do. I mean seriously: laughs, great numbers, frogs and clitorises—what else does a theater-going audience want?"

THIS AMERICAN LIFE IRA GLASS

"**T**here is a dirty secret hidden within *The Book of Mormon*. Indeed, the infamously irreverent Trey Parker and Matt Stone offer foul language, obscene jokes and plenty to offend, especially should you be a Latter-Day Saint. But their fantastic show isn't just fun, funny and immensely enjoyable; it's also surprisingly—and here's the dirty word—wholesome. An old-fashioned, toe-tapping, optimistic Big Broadway Musical, a buddy story about a mismatched pair of young Mormon missionaries sent to Uganda to convert the benighted natives. It argues for the social value of religion—no matter how implausible and arguably invented the stories upon which a religion is based—while teaching (if winkingly) the old showbiz lesson that the golden boy can be flawed, and the young misfit, if only he believes in himself, can come back a star. The whole enterprise is also a comfortably traditional show, in the best sense. Messrs. Parker, Lopez and Stone's tuneful score is memorable and hummable, show music that tells stories, deepens characters and gets laughs. So this is the lesson of *The Book of Mormon*: the elusive trick to succeeding on Broadway today is to write a smart, funny, sweet show, insert tuneful songs and a talented cast and give it a great staging. Subversive, ain't it?"

NEW YORK OBSERVER JESSE OXFELD

LEFT TO RIGHT: TREY PARKER, MATT STONE, CASEY NICHOLAW, ROBERT LOPEZ, SCOTT RUDIN, STEPHEN OREMUS, LARRY HOCHMAN, ANNE GAREFINO

Awards

WINNER OF **NINE 2011 TONY AWARDS**®
(with fourteen nominations)

Best Musical

Best Book of a Musical
Trey Parker, Robert Lopez, Matt Stone

Best Original Score
Trey Parker, Robert Lopez, Matt Stone

Best Direction of a Musical
Casey Nicholaw, Trey Parker

Best Orchestrations
Larry Hochman, Stephen Oremus

Best Featured Actress in a Musical
Nikki M. James

Best Scenic Design of a Musical
Scott Pask

Best Lighting Design of a Musical
Brian MacDevitt

Best Sound Design of a Musical
Brian Ronan

WINNER OF THE **2011 NY DRAMA CRITICS CIRCLE AWARD**

Best Musical
Trey Parker, Robert Lopez, Matt Stone

WINNER OF **FIVE 2011 DRAMA DESK AWARDS**
(with twelve nominations)

Outstanding Musical

Outstanding Music
Trey Parker, Robert Lopez, Matt Stone

Outstanding Lyrics
Trey Parker, Robert Lopez, Matt Stone

Outstanding Direction of a Musical
Casey Nicholaw, Trey Parker

Outstanding Orchestrations
Larry Hochman, Stephen Oremus

WINNER OF **FOUR 2011 OUTER CRITICS CIRCLE AWARDS**
(with six nominations)

Outstanding New Broadway Musical

Outstanding New Score
Trey Parker, Robert Lopez, Matt Stone

Outstanding Actor in a Musical
Josh Gad

Outstanding Direction of a Musical
Casey Nicholaw, Trey Parker

WINNER OF THE **2011 DRAMA LEAGUE AWARD**
(with three nominations)

Distinguished Production of a Musical

WINNER OF THE **2011 GRAMMY**® **AWARD**

Best Musical Theater Album

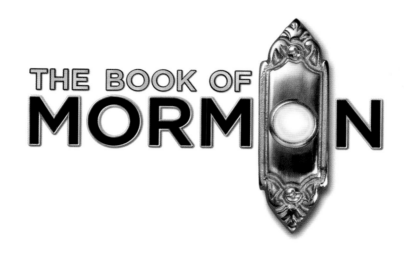

THE BOOK OF MORMON

BOOK, MUSIC AND LYRICS BY

TREY PARKER, ROBERT LOPEZ AND MATT STONE

WITH

JOSH GAD   ANDREW RANNELLS

NIKKI M. JAMES   RORY O'MALLEY   MICHAEL POTTS

LEWIS CLEALE   BRIAN TYREE HENRY   SCOTT BARNHARDT   JUSTIN BOHON
GRAHAM BOWEN   TA'REA CAMPBELL   DARLESIA CEARCY   KEVIN DUDA
JARED GERTNER   ASMERET GHEBREMICHAEL   TYSON JENNETTE
CLARK JOHNSEN   JOHN ERIC PARKER   BENJAMIN SCHRADER
MICHAEL JAMES SCOTT   BRIAN SEARS   JASON MICHAEL SNOW   NICK SPANGLER
LAWRENCE STALLINGS   REMA WEBB   MAIA NKENGE WILSON   TOMMAR WILSON

COSTUME DESIGN	LIGHTING DESIGN	SOUND DESIGN
ANN ROTH	**BRIAN MacDEVITT**	**BRIAN RONAN**

HAIR DESIGN	CASTING	PRODUCTION STAGE MANAGER
JOSH MARQUETTE	**CARRIE GARDNER**	**KAREN MOORE**

ORCHESTRATIONS	DANCE MUSIC ARRANGEMENTS	MUSIC COORDINATOR
LARRY HOCHMAN & STEPHEN OREMUS	**GLEN KELLY**	**MICHAEL KELLER**

ASSOCIATE PRODUCER	PRESS REPRESENTATIVE	PRODUCTION MANAGEMENT	GENERAL MANAGEMENT
ELI BUSH	**BONEAU/ BRYAN-BROWN**	**AURORA PRODUCTIONS**	**STP/DAVID TURNER**

MUSIC DIRECTION AND VOCAL ARRANGEMENTS

STEPHEN OREMUS

CHOREOGRAPHED BY

CASEY NICHOLAW

DIRECTED BY

CASEY NICHOLAW AND TREY PARKER

Dramatis Personae

This *Book of Mormon* book features comments
from the following, in alphabetical order:

Scott Barnhardt .... cast

Justin Bohon .... cast

Darlesia Cearcy .... cast

Lewis Cleale .... cast "Joseph Smith" et al

Kevin Duda .... cast

Josh Gad .... cast "Elder Cunningham"

Anne Garefino .... producer

Asmeret Ghebremichael .... cast

Brian Tyree Henry .... cast "General"

Larry Hochman .... co-orchestrator

Nikki M. James .... cast "Nabulungi"

Clark Johnsen .... cast

Glen Kelly .... dance music arranger

Robert Lopez .... author

Brian MacDevitt .... lighting designer

Karen Moore .... production stage manager

Casey Nicholaw .... co-director, choreographer

Rory O'Malley .... cast "Elder McKinley"

Stephen Oremus .... musical director, vocal arranger, co-orchestrator

John Eric Parker .... cast

Trey Parker .... author, co-director

Scott Pask .... scenic designer

Michael Potts .... cast "Mafala Hatimbi"

Andrew Rannells .... cast "Elder Price"

Brian Ronan .... sound design

Ann Roth .... costume designer

Scott Rudin .... producer

Benjamin Schrader .... cast

Michael James Scott .... cast "Doctor"

Brian Sears .... cast

Jason Michael Snow .... cast

Lawrence Stallings .... cast

Matt Stone .... author

Rema Webb .... cast "Mrs. Brown" et al

Maia Nkenge Wilson .... cast

Tommar Wilson .... cast

Acknowledgments

The publisher wishes to thank the entire *Book of Mormon* family for their enthusiastic participation and support. Trey Parker, Matt Stone, Bobby Lopez, and Casey Nicholaw graciously recounted their many adventures while creating the show. Andrew Rannells, Josh Gad, Nikki M. James, Rory O'Malley, and Michael Potts made themselves available for extended interviews, eager to share their *Mormon* stories and what the show has meant to them. The rest of the original Broadway cast provided recollections and insights, as did members of the creative team responsible for bringing the show to life on the stage.

Behind-the-scenes help and support for this book was generously provided by press agents Jim Byk and Chris Boneau of Boneau/Bryan-Brown; production stage manager Karen Moore and her fellow stage managers, Rachel McCutchen and Michael Zaleski; Stuart Thompson, David Turner, and Adam Miller of Stuart Thompson Productions; producers Anne Garefino and Scott Rudin; and especially Steven Cardwell of Scott Rudin Productions, who coordinated the entire process.

Special thanks to drama critic Steven Suskin for writing the text and distilling dozens of interviews into hundreds of pertinent comments and annotations; Joan Marcus, whose expert photography provides the reader with a comprehensive testament of the many riches visible to the in-theater audience; Linda Sunshine, the book's editorial consultant and coordinator in Los Angeles; the HarperCollins production staff, especially Dori Carlson, Lorie Pagnozzi, Karen Lumley, Mary Beth Constant, and Bethany Larson; the overall editor for the project, Esther Margolis, Founder and Executive Editor of Newmarket Press, now an imprint within It Books/HarperCollins Publishers; and the expert design team at BLT Communications in Hollywood, California, whose unique talent and devotion to the show resulted in the captivating pages that you hold in your hands.